your day, your way

other books by sharon naylor

100 Reasons to Keep Him/100 Reasons to Dump Him
1001 Ways to Have a Dazzling Second Wedding
How to Have a Fabulous Wedding for $10,000 or Less
How to Plan an Elegant Wedding in 6 Months or Less
The Complete Outdoor Wedding Planner
The Mother-of-the-Bride Book
The New Honeymoon Planner
The Ultimate Bridal Shower Idea Book

your day, your way

the essential handbook for the 21st-century bride

michelle roth ∽ henry roth ∽ sharon naylor

THREE RIVERS PRESS

NEW YORK

Published by Three Rivers Press, New York, New York.
Member of the Crown Publishing Group, a division of Random House, Inc.
www.randomhouse.com

THREE RIVERS PRESS and the Tugboat design are registered trademarks of Random House, Inc.

Printed in the United States of America

Design by Vanessa Perez
Illustrations by Michelle Roth and Kate Vasseur

Library of Congress Cataloging-in-Publication Data
Roth, Michelle.
    Your day, your way : the essential handbook for the 21st-century bride / Michelle Roth,
    Henry Roth, Sharon Naylor. — 1st ed.
        p.   cm.
        Includes index.
        1. Weddings—Planning. 2. Wedding etiquette. 3. Wedding costume. I. Roth, Henry.
    II. Naylor, Sharon. III. Title.
    HQ745.R68   2003
    395.2'2—dc2   2003007176
ISBN 0-7615-2539-4
10 9 8 7 6 5 4 3 2 1

First Edition

In memory of our wonderful grandparents, Franka and Samuel Baral Fania and Chaim Weinreich, and my incredible husband, Peter Roth.

—MICHELLE ROTH

❧

To the most wonderful parents, Aneta and Joseph Weinreich, and the greatest sisters, Lilian Weinreich and Michelle Roth.

—HENRY ROTH

❧

To my parents, Joanne and Andrew Blahitka; my family and friends near and far; and to my grandmother Rose Foglio Montenaro Potuto who would have loved to see it all.

—SHARON NAYLOR

contents

acknowledgments

We must start off by thanking the incredible team who brought this book to life: Denise Sternad, our acquisitions editor and guiding force; literary agent Meredith Bernstein; Michelle McCormack, our project editor; Vanessa Perez, interior and cover designer; and Ruth Younger, our copyeditor.

Also, Joseph and Aneta Weinreich in Sydney, Australia, for their wealth of information, support, and book guidance; Lilian Weinreich, who provided excellent feedback and background information; and Peter Roth, for loving and supporting our Michelle twenty-four hours a day.

Next, we thank the many wedding couples who shared their stories and wedding day photos with us: Shaunie and Shaquille O'Neal, Jodi Della Femina and John Kim, Amber Parsell Lynch and George Lynch III, Carrie Marcus Youngberg and David Allen Youngberg, Karri-Leigh Paolella and Joseph John Mastrangelo, Danielle Dobin and Christopher Smith, Michelle Marks and Erez Tal, and Tiffany Hosey Brown and Avery Brown. Thanks also to the additional brides who shared their stories through Sharon's website and in Michelle Roth's flagship salon and at trunk shows across America.

Our book would never have the depth and richness of information without the generosity and expertise of the following (in order of appearance in the book): Mara Leighton of Fred Leighton Designs, Lauren Winer and Melvyn Kirtley from Tiffany, Todd and Krista Meikle from www.wedstudio.com, Ellen Weldon from Ellen Weldon Designs, Linda Zec-Prajka from An Invitation to Buy—Nationwide, Michael and Lisa George from Michael George Flowers, David Coake from *Florists' Review*, Ed Stone from the Bernards Inn, Robert DeMaria from the Hotel InterContinental, Sylvia Weinstock from Sylvia Weinstock Cakes, Ron Ben-Israel and Tad Weliczko from Ron Ben-Israel Cakes, the staff of Bridgewaters in New York City, Wendy Dodds and Monica Morgan from Indigo Moon, Lois Pearce from Beautiful Occasions, Annie Block, Corinne Soikin Strauss from Hampton Weddings, Daniele Doctorow from Music in the Air, Edward Tricomi from the Warren Tricomi Salon, author Barbara Heller, makeup artist Laura Geller, Radu from Radu Physical Culture, Beth Reed Ramirez from www.brideagain.com, Sarah Stitham from Charmed Places, Andrea Rotundo Hospidor from www.getawayweddings.com, and all of the other wedding luminaries who shared their best ideas with us.

Thank you to all the staff at Michelle Roth, who provided us with their insights with tremendous professionalism and dedication.

We thank you all for being a part of our book, and we wish you a 21st century filled with the best of everything.

introduction

Congratulations on your engagement!

We created *Your Day, Your Way: The Essential Handbook for the 21st-Century Bride* with you in mind. You may or may not be a celebrity, a famous diva, or even a model, but you are a bride, and to us *you* are The Celebrity. Being a bride is an equalizer that inevitably makes any woman beautiful.

As a 21st-century bride, you have won tremendous autonomy when it comes to making wedding plans. You're free to plan the wedding *you* want, something brides of years and decades past never got to do! The trappings (or traps) of Old World etiquette are flying out the window as we speak. Today's couples are throwing the crusty old rules to the winds and embracing today's freedom to plan ceremonies, receptions, even wedding day wardrobes according to their *own* rules, to what speaks *to* and *about* them—even when their ideas contradict centuries-old customs. Want to wear white to your second wedding? Absolutely! Want to include your own poetry in your ceremony readings? Fabulous!

Want to have your closest guy friend stand up for you along with your bridesmaids? We applaud you! After all . . .

it's your day, so it's your way!

Through this book, we champion your wedding planning freedom, making sparks fly as we cut away the have to's, must's, and should's that strangled brides of years past and encourage you to be bold in your wedding planning choices, to make decisions that please *your* heart, to embrace your 21st-century groom's wishes for the day, and to create an unforgettable celebration that announces your unique partnership and style.

We're here to take you through this new stratosphere of wedding privilege, as you glide into this new bridal era with confidence and calm. We'll provide a bit of encouragement as you plan your dream wedding in a world that sometimes seems hasn't quite gotten the message. *(You're not wearing a backless dress! You can't have the minister say that! What will people think?!)* We know you'll get this kind of input—perhaps shockingly more from family members who seem to think it's *their* day so it should be *their* way, as prescribed by the rules of yesterday. We understand. For that reason, we have created a professional team to help you through the issues that arise during wedding planning. You now have bridal gown designers Michelle Roth and Henry Roth, who hail from three generations of bridal experience, along with Sharon Naylor, the bestselling author of a dozen "must have" bridal how-to books, on your side to gently lead you through that minefield called Weddings.

Will you wobble on your lovely pumps along the way? Of course. Not just once or twice, but many times! The ups and downs of wedding planning emotions are an inevitable part of the process.

You're about to undertake a magnificent journey, entering areas in which you have little to no experience. (Even those of you who have been married before are entering uncharted territory since to-day's weddings are *so* different than they were just a few years ago!) Add the weight of this new role to your job stresses, social and spiritual activities, and the lightning-fast speed of the world you live in, and you're bound to experience a broad spectrum of emotions. You'll display fluctuating moods through your smiles of extreme happiness, excitement, and love to your tears of extreme frustration and disappointment. Welcome to the wedding rollercoaster, with its highs and lows, its spiral turns, and upside-down thrills and chills!

We liken the beginning of the wedding planning experience to getting a promotion or starting a new job. Your heart beats faster at the prospect of new responsibilities and the feeling of pride! At the same time, your adrenaline races with fear that you might mess something up! So much expectation! So much pressure! Practically since birth, you've waited for "your day," the most important day of your life! The spotlight is on you, and it's *up* to you to make it perfect while everyone watches and weighs your decisions. Hundreds of details mount, the clock keeps ticking, the cash flow flowing. Who, from time to time, wouldn't crack under pressure like that?!

Yet you must continue your everyday role while you prepare for your starring role, supported by a colorful cast of characters—perhaps a doting mother, meddling mother-in-law, cranky bridesmaid, spirited vendor, bratty flower girl, and judgmental cousin. Your ability to cope during these heightened emotions will dictate the mood and spirit of your wedding day. How you deflect the negatives and accentuate all the glorious positives will determine the success of your day—for you and for all your guests—and allow you to *enjoy* the entire process from start to finish! We've seen too many brides struggle through the process, weary after just a few weeks, grimacing instead of glowing, slumping instead of shining, crying into their veils that they're ready to forgo their fantasy wedding and have a simple wedding with 20 guests! The stress from their own and others' expectations—unrealistic expectations for perfection—nearly do them in!

With *Your Day, Your Way* as your guide to new rules of 21st-century weddings, you can embark upon the adventurous journey with tremendous excitement and the knowledge that you are free to plan your own celebration, your own ceremony, and your own circle of loved ones with whom to share it all. We're thrilled for you, and happy you chose us to accompany you on your adventure of a lifetime.

Most likely you have been brought up with the idea that everything should be perfect, that the day is all about *you*. The reality is that true perfection is impossible. Aim instead for *close* to perfect, so that life's changes to your best-made plans do not overwhelm you with disappointment. Allow "perfect" to take its *own* form, to let *both of you* enjoy your shared day.

Of course, there will be tears—more of joy than frustration, we hope! However, when all seems overwhelming, remember why you said "I will" in the first place. Remember the true meaning of your day, which illuminates the hidden coves and dark shadows of your plans, and love, with a helping hand from *Your Day, Your Way*, will conquer all. We wish you all the best throughout your exciting journey.

getting set for the adventure of a lifetime

After the Thrill of "I Will"

creating your
matrimonial master plan

Whether you fully expected the proposal or were taken by a wonderful and well-planned surprise . . . , whether yours has been a whirlwind romance or a prolonged "Time is up, buddy. This girl has better things to do!" . . . , or whether *"Will you marry me?"* came from his mouth or yours, your experience is likely the same: Your heart skips a beat when you hear the words *"Yes! I will!"* You will?! Then, you feel relief as you realize your lifelong dream has come true: *I am getting married.*

wedding lobbyists at the threshold

Once you hear the proposal from him (or he hears it from you), some couples honor the centuries-old custom of making an appointment for the groom (or both bride and groom) to speak to the father (and/or mother) of the bride. For those who choose to include that rite of passage, do so graciously and with respect. There is beauty in the tradition of your fiancé asking for your hand in marriage, and only you will know how to balance this ritual with the realities of your 21st-century wedding. You know what is expected, so do it with confidence.

This juncture of the wedding process—sharing the news with those closest to you—speaks volumes. Whether the groom approaches your father before he asks you, or you ask him and you *both* speak with your father, the way you handle the situation sets up the autonomy you will have over the rest of your wedding.

A lot of unnecessary drama and tension can unfold as various "wedding lobbyists" try to take control of your day. As much as possible, recognize up front the amount of tradition and level of involvement you can expect from all sides of the family, from your father right down to your in-laws. We *know* it's your wedding, but smooth negotiating with family members is going to be a skill you will need for the rest of your lives. Use the wedding-planning experience as your training ground. Learn to compromise on the small stuff and stay firm on the principles right from the get-go.

look at me, up in the sky!

Once you have stepped over the "sticky proposal threshold," you most likely will enter an interesting new state commonly called "cloud nine." Cloud nine is totally removed from reality, but what a world it is! You pop champagne corks, you clink glasses, families and friends toast to your happiness, you get *great* flowers, and you hug your nearest and dearest. This, you might feel, is the best time of your life.

Yet, while your cloud drifts in a holding pattern somewhere above planet Earth, as you wave to the world below, showering its inhabitants with something love does to you, you feel something strange—

a bit of tightening in your stomach, quickening in your pulse, and thoughts flying in every direction from anxiety to elation then starting all over again with anxiety.

Relax! You're not getting cold feet, and it's unlikely you made a mistake saying "Yes." What you're feeling is perfectly normal. You are processing, absorbing the tremendous meaning of the great transition you're experiencing. You realize the importance of your commitment, the magnitude of what it means to join hands with your partner and set out on your uncharted course through life. Looking into the crystal ball of your future will be both exciting and terrifying, and it all starts now. If your heart is pounding with both joy and trepidation, *you're on the right track.* We would, in fact, worry if you *didn't* experience some degree of mixed emotions.

You are entering what we call the "snowglobe state." You're at the center of the beautiful image inside a glass bubble and, with one good shakeup, find yourself amid a swirling storm of thoughts like so many twinkling, glittery snowflakes. And much like a snowglobe set down to rest, your thoughts eventually slow their pace and settle down like flakes of snow, leaving you with a clear, beautiful image to enjoy.

from sharon

Take time to enjoy your engagement bliss! Let that beautiful engagement ring find its comfortable place on your finger before you launch into the planning stage for the wedding itself. Too many brides break land-speed records launching into the dizzying world of wedding details and worries, before they've even absorbed the wonderfully warm feeling of being engaged. Revel in your love and in the promises of your life to come before you take on the monumental issues of your wedding day.

And that's why we implore you to *WAIT* rather than immediately move into the planning stage of your wedding. When your adrenaline is working overtime is not the moment to plan the details and make decisions about a wedding. It is the moment to rejoice and celebrate, to sink into the bliss of this wonderful time in your life. Enjoy being the bride-to-be before you must become a wedding facilitator as well!

once the stardust settles

Once you've let some time pass, collected yourself and your thoughts, and descended to a more workable cloud *seven,* take a pencil in hand and sketch out your wedding day plans. This is where your dream starts to take shape, where you magically transform ideas into reality. On paper, your thoughts take form and shape. You will become "The Queen of Lists," shielded from insanity by your bridal binder.

Cloud seven is time to get a head start before the Wedding Lobbyists deluge you with questions. (By the way, caller ID can be a bride's best friend!) Now, sit down with your groom to share your wish lists of what, how, and where you see your wedding taking place.

Do you want a formal wedding or an informal one? A wedding set during a magnificent sunset over the ocean with 300 guests in attendance, or a more intimate ceremony in your parents' backyard? Do you want to marry this summer or next? Or in the fall during more temperate weather? These are questions you two must answer on your own. Too many opinions at this point can set the stage for tears, and for your losing control of your wedding planning. Take it from us: The *best* strategy is to decide together, as *partners,* what the basic shape of your wedding will be. The others will find out soon enough, and will undoubtedly have their own pencils poised to draw shades and shapes on your wedding sketches and add items to your lists. People from all sides may pressure you into revealing your

from michelle

There can be no better time spent than first pre-planning the fundamentals with the one you love. Begin working as a team by making sure you're on the same page with regard to wedding plans.

from sharon

Today's groom can be extremely involved in the wedding plans from the very beginning of the process. The new 21st-century Man of the Hour is a far cry from grooms of previous decades, who did virtually nothing after popping the question but show up at the church on time on the wedding day! Grooms often participate in planning as the full partner of the bride, investing in creating a day that speaks of both partners in this marriage.

plans. They practically jump up and down asking where and when your wedding will be. Hold off answering until you know yourself.

here comes the supporting cast!

Very, very few couples plan a wedding without *any* input from families and friends (and even those couples generally receive plenty of advice after they elope!). As many brides tell us, joining forces with family members and prospective in-laws is a blessing and a curse. It's wonderful and necessary to share such an important time with them, but their input can bring on many a migraine. The chapters ahead discuss

don't show until you know...

Before you bring in an excited mother or a paying parent, take your first step as a couple by setting out these fundamental goals:

- *Season.* Determine the season in which the wedding will take place—spring, summer, winter, or fall?

- *Date.* Discuss the approximate wedding date, perhaps even the weekend you wish for.

- *Ambience.* Talk about the feeling of the wedding. Indoor or outdoor? Ball gown with full train or wispy sundress? Six-course sit-down meal or informal afternoon tea party or champagne and gourmet desserts only?

- *Style.* Since all aspects of your wedding must come from your vision of style, flesh out your collective picture.

- *Number of guests.* Decide approximately how many you'll invite to the engagement party (if you will have one) and to the wedding.

- *Venue.* Come up with ideas for the kind of location that will comfortably suit your guest list, fit within your budget, *and* satisfy your dreams.

- *Budget.* Come up with a general idea of the wedding budget (as in low, average, high, stratospheric) *and* settle on whether and how much you'll be willing and able to contribute to the wedding fund. (Look to chapter 3 for more on the B-word: Budget.)

- *Result.* Brainstorm what you want the end result to look like by creating lists, worksheets, and sketches of your ideas.

in depth the diplomacy and the politics of dealing with supporting cast members during the months of planning, but we want to cover the basics here. After all, the first step you take with your family sets an almost unbreakable precedent.

Here you set forth the heart and soul of your plans, establishing clear boundaries on who will be involved and just how involved they will be. The tradition of the bride's family taking on most of the planning and financial responsibility is now only one option among a number of 21st-century variations. Parents—or mixtures of parents, step-parents, in-laws-to-be, guardians, and foster or adoptive parents—may take roles from "main player" to "bit part" to no role at all. What makes this century's wedding so unique, and at the same time wondrously intricate, is that brides and grooms are surrounded by a blend of loved ones three or four layers deep. This enables couples to spread the joy around but also takes them into uncharted territory. You've seen the old traditional charts of what the bride's family pays for and what the groom's family pays for, but what happens when one couple shares four or five sets of parents? The rules must be broken and remolded so often these days that now it's up to the bride and groom to share the wealth of planning their wedding. It's all up to you.

Here Are Your Assignments

Once you have your list of main players in hand, it's time to let everyone know the basics of the wedding you have in mind. You'll need to keep everyone informed from this moment on, so it's a great idea to set up an initial informational meeting, either in a relaxed atmosphere at home, at a prearranged time by phone (especially if parents live far away), or through the Internet (even Grandma can get into this one if she's online!). This initial meeting sets the mood and tone for months of planning to come and a lifelong interaction between different parts of your family. You couldn't start off in a better way. It's also an excellent idea to write down and print out several copies of your master matrimonial plan to send out or pass out at your meeting. This way all involved are literally on the same page.

Accept and share with everyone the good news that not all your thoughts are set in concrete at this time. Allow for compromise on what you consider "insignificant" areas (perhaps the music during the ceremony or dessert choices in addition to cake). Make sure you and your groom understand what each of you considers non-negotiable. This way, you can back each other up when the inevitable comments begin, such as *"Oh, but you must have the wedding in the church where your father and I were married!"* or *"We have to invite all your second cousins!"* Be assertive (but not aggressive) in stating what are your *wishes* as opposed to your *ideas.* You'll read more on this in chapter 2.

Of course, the more financial responsibility you take with your own wedding, the greater say you will have in the decisions. Whether or not you're footing the bill, try not to offend. You may be confronted with values that clash with yours, as parents on either side want financial control as a matter of pride, social upbringing, or tradition. You're likely to get deeper insight into the "fabric" of your own parents' lives and certainly into your fiancé's parents throughout the process. You will need to keep a positive attitude and an open mind when you forge your own household, so you may as well start now!

> ### get in the same groove
>
> You and your groom need to be in tune with each other during wedding planning. Consider this experience as a magnificent opportunity for lessons in harmony and unity between you. Who knew your relationship would be tested over napkin color choices? But it will be.

setting out on your adventure

We can't send you into the world of wedding planning, without providing you with ten key themes to keep at the forefront of your mind. Without these reminders, you're more likely to get caught up in the dizzying whirlwind of planning the big event in addition to keeping a hectic schedule filled with career, social and spiritual activities, family responsibilities, Us time, and Me time.

from henry

Typically, the modern-day bride is a working woman. Brides, realize this: You have just taken on another full-time job and all the pressures that come with it. You therefore need to break down your wedding planning into bite-sized categories, rather than allow yourself to be overwhelmed by the total process. The success of your wedding depends on your keeping a level head. As long as you and all your major players know what they are doing and why, you are halfway there.

These reminders will help you experience the true joy of planning a wedding and avoid getting swallowed up by the inevitable stresses, ups and downs, and out-of-control directions weddings can take—especially in today's fast-paced world, where decisions can change as quickly as they're made.

Be like that resting snowglobe as often as possible, by sitting quietly and letting your thoughts settle. If you're always in a chaotic rush, you may pick up such mass and speed that, like a snowball rolling downhill, you'll flatten everything in your path.

So, hear us now on these tenets:

Ten Tenets for Successful Wedding Planning

1. *Work with what you have.* Now is not the moment to question your family dynamics for attacking and trying to change your reality. (That should be left for another time, perhaps a session with your favorite shrink.)

2. *Create a positive mindset.* Planning a wedding is an adventure and a challenge. Expect that there will be disappointments along with the highs. Life is not perfect, so why would the process of planning a wedding be different?

3. *Remember why you said "Yes" in the first place!* Keep in mind that you're not simply planning a party; you're celebrating one of the greatest blessings on earth: You and your true love plan to spend your lifetime together enjoying one another.

4. *Have fun as you plan your wedding.* If you try too hard or press too much against the hands of time, you will miss the humor and joy in this process.

5. *Realize that flaws and compromise are part of your course.* So when a less-than-perfect detail inevitably arises, fling your arms around it and reset your expectations to make it work.

6. *Take advantage of the opportunity for family interaction.* Weddings are unique. Draw from the intensity of family interaction and involvement, and the high emotions the wedding-planning process brings.

7. *Expect and allow for nervousness.* Everyone is nervous during weddings, and that is natural. People react differently under pressure, so allow for even extreme differences.

8. *Remain respectful.* Bitching is so passé! Yes, some things will *really* bother you. However, complaining and gossiping will only lead to more frustration and tears . . . guaranteed.

9. *Don't overextend.* Keep your perspective. Remember that you and your fiancé are trying to create magnificent memories of your lifetime, not planning the next space mission to Mars.

10. *Do your day with meaning.* Whatever you do on your wedding day, do it with meaning. Weddings can be spectacularly visual, but without deep meaning, they may leave you and your guests cold. Warmth is very 21st century.

Now that you have your main concepts for your wedding in place, have assembled your main supporters, and have the right mindset to keep the meaning in perspective, you and your groom are ready to step forward into the adventure of a lifetime!

chapter 2

Navigating the Minefield of Family and Bridal Party Politics

Planning a wedding is stressful—not just because you must attend to an enormous volume of details and mini-details, and the day is perhaps the most important one in your life, but also because such a large number of *people* are involved in creating this big day. Once the bliss of the marriage proposal starts to fade, you hear the voices of mothers, sisters, fathers, and bridal party members coming at you from every direction in your wedding universe. Hearing everyone's opinion (and often intense reactions to each other's opinions!) can leave you dazed, confused, and teary-eyed. Is it normal for brides to burst into tears at the drop of a hat? Absolutely! You are definitely not alone.

We think this minefield of family and friends is perhaps the last remaining universal truth of wedding planning. Nearly every bride we've seen has crumbled, if only for an unguarded moment, beneath the weight of unwelcome input, family pressures, and interpersonal dramas.

the top 10 hot spots of family conflict

1. Number of guests who should be invited
2. Where the wedding and reception should be located
3. What the budget should be and who should pay for what
4. What the mothers and bridesmaids wear, and who will star in the show
5. How elaborate the wedding should be
6. How to blend tradition and interfaith weddings
7. What the role of step-/estranged/divorced parents should be
8. Who will be main players and what their roles should be in your wedding
9. How to handle table seating and friends and family members who aren't speaking
10. Which wedding dress to select

Did we say top 10? We meant top 11: mother troubles. You might also deal with the mother-in-law blues, if she feels left out of the planning and envious of your mother's higher "rank" in the planning scheme.

The reason brides are so ill-prepared for the stress wedding planning can bring is this: They do not factor in all that is *not* "sugar and spice." As a girl playing dress-up bride, and during all the years you imagined your dream wedding, your fantasies undoubtedly did not include your mother shrieking about your in-laws' poor taste or your sister sulking because you've beaten her down the aisle. Unpleasant moments, you might say, were not part of your plan.

While we can't promise that we can fully protect you from family politicking, *Your Day, Your Way* is written to help you battle emotional rollercoaster reactions by preparing a plan for sanity.

Remember one thing: Weddings are right up there with milestone events such as births of children and holidays when it comes to bringing all family members together. Will life always be like the planning of your wedding? So intense? So dramatic? So readily pulling the worst behavior out of normally civilized and serene family members (and perhaps you as well)? We doubt it!

So put into perspective this initiation by fire and brimstone, this adventure that seems to drop you in the middle of a Greek epic tale. You're starting a valiant journey, and must face many battles ahead. And in the end, as the hero you will prevail against immense struggles and emerge a wiser, stronger person with greater character. You're likely to discover strengths and an arsenal of "weapons" you didn't know you had. You won't encounter actual monsters (though from time to time Mom or Mom-in-law may take on frightening Medusa-like proportions), but you may battle personal demons along the way. We say that wielding your sword is great not only for your inner strength but will make your arms look wonderful in a gorgeous sleeveless gown!

preparing to detonate the minefield

First, define who you're dealing with and identify which of *their* character traits are likely to pose a problem *or* perhaps be a blessing to you. You know your siblings and parents well, so you're certainly aware of what they're like under pressure. You know how to communicate with them, and how to handle their moods. You may also know your future in-laws well, and the groom certainly does. Together, you can pre-think how to handle each individual personality, and share your foresight on what mixing all the characters together under one roof will be like.

And then there are your chosen bridal attendants, your maids and your men and the little children who will lead them down the aisle. They too play supporting roles in your colorful cast of characters. Who among them is reliable? Who is opinionated? Who is pushy and manipulative? Who might pout and groan throughout the affair? And who is your "go-to" girl, your "go-to" guy—the ones you know you can count on to spread their angel wings and calm any gathering? Again, ponder your attendants' interpersonal styles and center yourself on the dynamics of that particular mix.

First Things First: You and the Groom

Between you and your intended, you should each have "first say" before you make your joint decision. But respect the level of involvement that your fiancé wants to take. Some grooms truly want to defer the main decision-making to their bride, as they feel they lack the experience and knowledge to contribute significantly in the realm of weddings. It can be fine for a bride to take on the leading role, leaving the groom responsible for as little as the ring, the groom's and groomsmen's suits, flowers (on occasion), moral support for you, and, of course, showing up on time for the wedding!

Once you know where your groom stands, once he's made clear that he intends to be your full partner and not another supporting cast member, you can determine what your expectations of *him* should rightly be. Not clearly expressing expectations between you is a promise of disaster. Each of you should state your intentions outright, be sure they're heard fully, and unequivocally accept each other's aims.

Know the Players

Once you've established your goals as a couple, determine who the fundamental players are and involve them from day one. This is the secret to all weddings that are enjoyable to plan and experience rather than contentious. Establish right away who will enjoy which level of involvement, and state your intentions clearly to each major participant. Don't constantly broaden your circle, bringing in others to assume what was previously a main player's job. No one likes to be "replaced" or "fired." Keep in mind that a mother or sister may so value her appointed tasks that she may interpret your bringing in partners for her as an unspoken sign that she can't handle the job. Diplomacy is essential, since each assignment harbors so much underlying emotion.

Disarm with Your Good Attitude

It's all in your attitude, which starts from minute one. You set the stage, you lay the foundation through your demeanor the moment you assemble your players and announce in a sweet but assertive way, "Here's how it's going to be." As we mentioned earlier, your first initial meeting with the players is all important. Here they learn what's expected of them, and—more important—what they can expect in working with you. To begin your shared journey well, we suggest you and your intended keep the following tips in mind:

- *Start off with a positive, fun approach.* A wedding is supposed to be enjoyable, after all, and a positive tone and attitude will help you start off on the right foot.

from sharon

Brides are sometimes shocked at how attached main players get to their appointed roles. Because even the smallest tasks get enlarged in the responsible player's mind and emotions, the bride may wind up dumbfounded that choosing place card holders was earth-shatteringly crucial to her mother-in-law. Remember, everything gets magnified in the world of weddings, and people can be intensely possessive of their tasks.

- *Don't just talk at your group.* Listen, talk, and discuss *with* them. Invite input from others, using diplomacy and good listening skills.

- *Involve with resolve.* Allow opinionated family members to make their points, too, gently reminding them of the ultimate goal.

- *Concede the small issues, and stand firm on your main principles.* Assertiveness is a key ingredient to starting your wedding process off right. That is why you really need to know what the basic feel of your wedding is going to be before you can protect its style.

Steady Goes It

We have no doubt that pulses will quicken at this meeting, tensions may flare just a bit—especially when parents hold the purse strings for the big day and flex their financial power by pressuring you while waving their checkbook over your head. This, too, can be an enduring legacy in the wedding world, the controlling parental battle cry of "We're paying for this wedding, so we say what goes!" (We hope you can hear our collective sigh of empathy for you if this is your situation.)

Indeed, this can be a great obstacle to peaceful family planning, as we know that some parents feel that they have total influence by virtue of their Platinum cards. We've seen it from time to time, and we can help you with this bit of advice: Stay calm. Your remaining calm in the face of this kind of power play *returns the power to you.* If you fight, cry, demand, pout, or otherwise show your defiance when the money card is played, then (you might be surprised to realize) you're doing the *exact wrong thing!* You're acting childish, throwing a tantrum, exhibiting a kind of adolescent rebellion against your parents' need to control your plans, and *that* is exactly the message your parents would use to defend their own misbehavior: They are the adults, and you are the "child" they can control. If you remain calm and treat them as you would any client you experience in your workday, if you think strategically instead of emotionally, you're likely to set a precedent that shows you cannot be controlled with money.

It may take several doses of self-control and deep breathing before they get the message, but they will catch on. By holding steady, you have increased your odds of defusing the money-is-power card.

> ### we'll let you have that one
>
> It's the wise bride who establishes ahead of time on which points she's willing to compromise. So have your list of concessions handy, so that at this first meeting you can show where you're willing to concede and where you'll take your stand. An added benefit is this: You're proving to your group that you're not going to be rigid and difficult. You are willing to allow them *some* of their wishes. Flexibility is a key strength at this point.

Market Your Style Plans

Again, we'll use a bit of corporate know-how. You are, after all, the CEO of your wedding. And a good CEO knows how to keep her business and her "employees" working together smoothly for the ultimate good of the project. So consider how you will market your wedding vision and plans to your team so that you are all working toward the same goal. Your initial, organized presentation will assist in breaking the ice and setting the standards for the months ahead.

Blend Style and Tradition

Conservative traditions have a place in even the most modern of weddings. Blending contemporary style with traditional values can add depth and meaning for your wedding, and there is no better mixture for a wedding than the gold that is the past with the platinum present. Plus, when it comes to dealing with family and friends whose own strongly held values cling to the traditional above all else, your willingness to incorporate family and societal customs accomplishes two very important things:

1. You're showing common ground and common values with the others
2. You're avoiding a bitter values showdown between you and your loved ones

That's half the deadly minefield dug up and thrown away right there!

from sharon

In this new and fabulously freeing time of wedding autonomy, where Your Way *is the main rulebook, don't forget that your mother, your soon-to-be mother-in-law, and all of the usual Unsolicited Input Mavens may* not *have adapted to the way things work now. They may have grown up with the strict and crusty old etiquette rules wired into their central nervous systems and DNA. You'll need to actually explain the new rules of the 21st-century wedding to them, so they might become open-minded to the freedoms you're exercising and still find a comfortable way to express their wishes. So many of the usual family-oriented wedding nightmares can be avoided with a simple but very diplomatic explanation of how things are right now, and how things* will *be* from this point on.

You Can't Please All the People All the Time

Some cliches hold true no matter how much life and the world change with dizzying speed. Can you please everybody? Certainly not. Any bride who *tries* to appease everyone is not holding herself to any great value. We call such people doormats, and we know you're too smart to staple a welcome mat to your back! The best you can hope for is to please *some* of the people *some* of the time, and then let them concern themselves with pleasing you. We don't, however, suggest diva behavior unless you want your wedding planning process to be argumentative, anxious, and perhaps fully destructive to some of your closest relationships. It's all about give and take. Be true to yourself, your groom, and the people you care for the most.

from henry

Don't look for reasons to be upset; look for reasons to rejoice. Take time to smell the roses and let yourself be a princess this once in your life.

You're the Last Person I Suspected . . .

Imagine this: You've been spine-tinglingly nervous about how your mother would be during the gown-shopping stages. You thought she would tilt her head, raise an eyebrow, and declare your chosen gown "too trashy." You thought she would nix anything with a pricetag over $3,000 and say, "You've always been irresponsible with money" while you twirl before the mirror in your dream ballgown. You stayed awake nights imagining horrible disasters and your mother's patented digs. And then . . . when you go to the gown salon, your mother is a dream! She loves your style, your taste, the gowns you're selecting; and she believes, as you do, that even $25,000 would be a bargain for a dress that makes you look like a heavenly vision. *Instead* it's the groom's sister who's acting like a tyrant—complaining about the color you've chosen for the maids' gowns, whining about the price, and bringing everyone down to her level. Surprise! Sometimes the people you least expect it from can cause the most perilous undercurrent.

Don't be surprised if someone from whom you expect nothing but cooperation can cause your biggest headaches, seeming to take pleasure in stealing a bit of your glow. How do you handle *that?* Simple. Just be ready with your finely tuned assertive flair to take her aside and ask her to adjust her attitude. Ask her to voice her concerns. Is she having problems with money right now? Fine, you're willing to find a more affordable dress. She may look shocked. As well she should, because she knows that *you* know it's not about the price or color of the dress. It's about her feeling very small in your presence— very jealous of your happiness.

Little did you know that the minute an engagement ring found a home on your finger, you became not just a bride-to-be, but an amateur psychologist! Herein lies the key to navigating the minefield of family and friend politics during the wedding plans: *You need to look beyond the words of the complaint to see where that person's fear lies.* Once you get that concept, you're in the right place to identify the problem, work with the person, and create a solution together. Your job is multifaceted, just like that engagement ring on your finger.

we're all one big happy family

Keep this in mind now, and remind yourself again and again down the road: The people with whom you're planning this wedding, who may seem like adversaries now, are going to be with you forever. This is your *family.* Even your friends are part of your extended family, and the depth of your relationship with each of them will last far beyond the wedding day.

We cannot emphasize enough that dealing with others during the planning process goes far beyond who gets her way with the flowers or who is unhappy about the seating chart. That is exactly why this process is so emotionally charged! You are, at this moment, establishing relationships with these people! You're not *just* planning a wedding;

you're showing your prospective in-laws what kind of daughter-in-law you will be. You're revealing your true character in how you handle adversity, and—most important—you're revealing much about yourself by how you handle others' wishes. And at the same time, they are revealing themselves. It all adds up to your saying this: "Here I am! Here is the woman who's joining your family!" You can't expect them to open their arms and hearts to you if you're constantly angry and lashing out against anyone who defies your will. We need to be blunt about this: Some of the landmines are your own.

Our solution? Don't forget that this is about joining hearts with your fiancé, *and* with his family. And the same goes for your groom with your family. Navigating the family minefield may seem a tremendous burden, but it's actually a valuable part of the process. The wedding cake doesn't last. The flowers don't last. The band can't play forever. When all is said and done, the relationships you form with your new family through an admittedly difficult and emotional journey enrich your life and pave the way to your future together. You've heard this statement before: "When you marry someone, you're not just marrying him. You're marrying his whole family." It's true.

So when dealing with the other players in this wedding, remember that even the wedding readings about faith, hope, and love apply

from michelle

Your family is the cornerstone of your life and the direction it takes. Your in-laws-to-be now become an extension of your family. Respect the differences (you can learn much from them) and focus on the positives. Treat them always as you would want to be treated yourself, and leave behind old differences with your family or his. This is a perfect opportunity to write the next chapter as you want it to be. After all, the canvas of your married life starts out blank and pure white.

from henry

Just as you are "in love" with your groom, you need to be seriously "in like" with your in-laws to be! I don't care what people tell me the in-laws-to-be have done to them. Complaining about your prospective family is inappropriate and sets the wrong tone. Now is the time to set up a footprint of respect, love, and communication—for life. The days of the "battling bride or groom" are over.

the 10 golden keys

Keep in mind these keys to assertive, harmonious group planning. Share them with your loved ones, too, if they need a black-and-white reminder. In fact, put this on your refrigerator right now!:

1. We want to plan this wedding *with* you, not through you.

2. We play no favorites. We love all our family members, and we don't take sides.

3. We know our wedding will hold more meaning and value to us if we can include some of your ideas in it. So we welcome your suggestions, but we reserve the right to make our own decisions.

4. You're allowed to have a bad day, and I'm allowed to have a bad day. Even if we argue about something on the to-do list, we'll apologize and understand one another.

5. We're not very concerned with "What will other people think?" so don't even start with that or your guilt will consume you. Unless it's the opinion of someone you hold very dear to you, maintain your decision.

6. The groom and I are partners who tell each other everything. Don't even think about getting *us* to manipulate each other by assigning one to convince the other to do it your way. That's not going to happen.

7. We're nervous, but we're glad to have something this wonderful to be nervous about. We admit we might not always think clearly in our heightened emotional state, and we understand that you won't always think clearly either.

8. We reserve the right to change our minds about certain plans for the wedding. We're flexible with your ideas as well as our own, but that's only because we're trying to get it right.

9. We have a history with all our respective loved ones, and we plan to make a future with all of you collectively. That's why we've invited you into our inner circle.

10. We plan to play fair and are counting on you to play fair as well. If things get too intense, we promise not to be disrespectful to you and of course hope you'll pay us the same courtesy.

to more than just the relationship between you and your intended. They apply, now and forever, to both sides of your extended family as well. Start now with this principle in mind, and you have a great chance at a loving future with the new side of your family. Defy the principle, and you can create an everlasting wedge between you and any family members that we have seen become a stumbling block for "happily ever after" by growing and festering until it ultimately damages a marriage beyond repair.

chapter 3

Wedding Budgets
That Don't Break the Bank

The number one contention during the planning of any wedding—and generally later in life—is the issue of money. This is not, and never will be, an easy topic to discuss. It can create a lot of stomach churning and anxiety. However, facing the issue head-on and realistically is your key to budgeting harmoniously. Don't forget that high emotions and "raw nerve endings" provoke and magnify *many* areas of contention between families during the wedding-planning period, and the topic of money is not immune to the stress spotlight. The money issue, however, can become the king of all conflicts and is often the source of much wedding-planning tension, especially for those who are not prepared for the expenses that lie ahead.

Money is, after all, typically the limiting factor to what your wedding plans can be. It is your biggest reality check. Obviously, money is generally what brings your greatest bridal dreams into reality. Considering that the average wedding budget can run anywhere from

$25,000 to $40,000 (and that's a *national* average; some brides spend half that much on their gowns alone!), you are facing considerable expenses. If you allow it to, the enormity of the amount can take your breath away and quickly shatter your dreams. Don't let financial matters clip your bridal wings. Your imagination can still take flight; you just need to be savvy. We will show you exactly how to do this by describing the many options open to you.

If only it weren't all so expensive! But it is. And the point is that no matter what your budget, the wedding you plan is worth memories of a lifetime; and is a hundred, if not a thousand, times more than whatever you spend. You will hear that over and over again from wedding planning experts and others. Keep the money issue in perspective.

No matter how you, your family, or his family react to the "B-word" (budget), and no matter how tense it makes you, remember that you will undoubtedly *never* have to go through such excruciating number games with so many people ever again. Never again are you likely to sit before a budget chart and agonize over the cost of linen napkins, cream-colored roses, and mini-quiches, to struggle over such people-for-food trades such as *"Should we not invite our clients so that we can have an extra two stations at the cocktail party?"* Never again are you likely to find yourself in *this* unique position. So be patient and calm. This will only hurt for a short time.

Besides, this financial minefield is good training ground for a couple's life challenges ahead. Think of it this way: The costs of balancing your wedding budget will be canceled out by all the insight you will gain in smart negotiating and planning strategy. Consider this a blessing in disguise!

from michelle

Because you'll always have to balance your budget in the future, you should greet discussions about money positively. Frankly, I think exploring your budget boundaries is not only healthy, but is also a magnificent reality check. Talking budget now is good practice for your future life together, as money matters will surely be a frequent discussion topic. If your wedding is more humble, so be it. Your budget has nothing to do with the level of your love or joy.

making dollars and sense

Before you begin crunching numbers and doing comparison-shopping, you *must* take a moment to consider the basic framework and inner workings of your wedding budget. We've broken down our "Cash Code" into the following main concepts:

- *Know your boundaries.* The financial framework defines how you will create the wedding, and also sets the *tone* for the entire planning process. If you are on a limited budget, you will take on a very different mindset than the bride who has carte blanche and a big blank check at her disposal. Working your numbers to make more out of less provides you with a unique challenge, requires a different mindset, and sets a distinctive tone for the planning of your day.

- *Get the best for the least.* On a more restricted budget, *all* of your wedding planning players are also adopting the mindset of stretching and molding your dollars to attain more wedding elements for less. Everyone must be mindful of expenses, and everyone must share the same goals of finding ways to get the best for less. This can lead to some of the most creative weddings ever planned.

- *Practice skillful preplanning.* The wisest of today's brides and grooms do not just go out and start charging items and services for their big day without first sitting down to pre-picture their plans and pre-think their financial methods (see pages 30 to 41 for more on this topic). You don't build a house without blueprints, one brick at a time, hoping that the finished house will look fine and sit evenly on its foundation. "Blueprints" are crucial for building a wedding as well. A well-thought-out plan at the outset is the best way to keep a handle on your expenses and avoid letting the issue of money ruin your wedding experience.

- *Focus on theme-ing, not dreaming.* Plan your budget around the mood and feeling you want to create. The new rules of the 21st-century have given you license to express your individuality, and this will affect your vision for your ceremony, reception, gown, music, and décor—all of which play a part in determining your budget. If you dream large and ornate, then your budget will reflect that vision.

- *Negotiate and compromise.* When you have several players helping to plan the wedding—even if you and your fiancé cover all the expenses—you will need to negotiate and compromise when making decisions, from the big ones to some of the tiniest. It's vital that you "discuss, compromise, resolve, and agree." If you are not well practiced in being assertive about your desires and negotiating with those whose desires conflict with yours, consider this a crucial crash course that will make you stronger in all aspects of your future.

- *Settle all financial details.* Cross your t's and dot your i's. You would be surprised how many pre–wedding day flare-ups happen due to "open sores" left from non-finalized financial details. So be thorough from the start, and save your sanity by having a plan in place to settle those little extra money details that arise throughout the process.

- *Commit to paper.* Once you have come to a final resolution regarding the size and scope of your budget, the wedding will fall into a more defined framework. Set your budget and responsibilities in writing, holding yourself to the rules you made for yourselves. *However . . .*

- *Factor in a percentage leeway.* Allow yourselves some level of flexibility. Use your money discipline within a range of reason. Within the final overall budget, factor in 5 to 10 percent variance. Just as restrictive diets don't work well for weight loss, restrictive budgets don't work well for planning a wedding. You *must* give yourselves permission to make "trades" within your wedding plans, perhaps shifting some of your expected budget for invitations to, say, the selections of wines for your reception. You'll find that granting yourselves the freedom to sculpt your budget as you wish—*while staying within a reasonable range*—will remove much of the potential wedding stress. You no longer have to deal with so much "We can't do that," or "We can't change our minds." Without a level of flexibility, you will feel frustration and resentment.

- *Clue your coordinator in on budget limitations.* If you are planning your wedding with a professional event coordinator, let him or her know your budget limitations and flexibility level so you will be presented with plans and options that are within your capability. There's no need to tempt yourselves with ideas that are beyond your scope. Plus, a good coordinator can show you how to fit more into your budget without the price shavings showing to others!

from henry

Why should reality of the bridal budget be hidden during wedding planning? Embrace the opportunity to balance budgets and delegate responsibility. The experience offers deeper insight into your fiancé and the family dynamics. Don't confuse your feelings for your intended with the money issue. Don't allow money to interfere with the spirit and joy of your wedding day, however grand or humble it may be. No amount of money can pay for your happiness. Paying for grandeur does not buy a genuine celebration. Money alone cannot buy you a harmonious future together.

Now, with perhaps a sigh of relief and a better perception of the importance of your budget, the undeniable emotion of it, and the power you hold over it, let's get into further detail on how you will set the foundation for your wedding with a financial plan. Stay in charge of your power over the money issue so that money does not become a growling monster that wrests your wedding plans from you. Read on to learn how to work out your plans.

dividing your plans into categories

First things first. You *must* sit down with your groom to record your initial plans for budget in every financial category that will be used to plan your wedding. We mean *everything* from the largest expense (the reception) to the smallest (the mints set out on the bar, the candles decorating the restrooms). *Please note:* Make *two* copies of this chart (see table 1 for an example of the Wedding Budget Worksheet). The first will be for your initial "guesstimates," or for a range such as $$$$$ (meaning that you're willing to spend top dollar on an item) to $ (meaning either that this particular item won't cost much or that you don't highly value it and could eliminate it completely). Our favorite is the FREE category, such as complimentary items you will enjoy writing for or the borrowing of a friend's classic car rather than renting a limousine for your getaway.

You can then use the second copy of this chart to record your actual working numbers as you're making your plans and discovering the *true* costs of wedding cakes, tuxedos, and videographer services. Here, then, is our starter list for your main wedding budget categories. Please fill in any extras you may need at the bottom.

Before you go on, take a moment to answer these questions, further defining your most important budget priorities:

Defining Budget Priorities

What are the five most important elements of our day, the ones to which we're willing to devote the most significant portion of the budget?

1. _____

2. _____

3. _____

4. _____

5. _____

Table 1. Wedding Budget Worksheet

Item/Service	Who's Paying	Budgeted	Actual
Engagement announcement			
Engagement party			
Ceremony site			
Ceremony decor			
Officiant's fee			
Marriage license			
Blood tests			
Pre-wedding counseling/classes			
Reception site			
Rentals for reception site			
Preparation of reception site (landscaping, cleaning, and such)			
Additional permits for parking and other			
Wedding gown			
Wedding gown fittings			
Accessories and shoes			
Bride's manicure, pedicure, hairstyling, and makeup			
Bridesmaids' dresses (if applicable)			
Bridesmaids' hairstyling and makeup (if applicable)			
Groom's clothing			
Groom's accessories			
Wedding coordinator			
Rehearsal dinner (if applicable)			
Invitations			
Postage			
Programs			
Thank-you notes			

continues

Table 1. Wedding Budget Worksheet *(continued)*

Item/Service	Who's Paying	Budgeted	Actual
Caterer costs			
Liquor			
Cake			
Flowers			
Reception decor			
Reception entertainment			
Photography			
Videography			
Wedding cameras			
Limousines or classic cars			
Other guest transportation			
Favors			
Gifts (for bridal party, parents, each other, guests' hotel room baskets)			
Toss-its (items such as bubbles or birdseed for guests to toss at you after the ceremony)			
Honeymoon			
Travel expenses and lodging for couple			
Travel expenses and lodging for guests			
Travel expenses and lodging for bridal party			
Daycare for children of guests			
Tips			
Other:			
Other:			
Other:			
Other:			
Other:			
TOTALS			

how much should you tip?

The following list of suggested tips is for your consideration only. Different vendors may apply a different scale for tipping, and what is appropriate may vary with location as well. (For example, in some foreign cultures, tipping is looked down upon!) Here are suggested tip amounts for vendors supplying services for weddings held in the U.S.:

- *Site manager:* 15 to 20 percent of entire bill for the reception
- *Valets:* $1 per car
- *Waiters:* $20 to $30 each, depending upon quality of service
- *Bartenders:* 15 percent of liquor bill
- *Coat check:* $1 per coat
- *Limousine drivers:* 15 to 20 percent of transportation bill
- *Delivery workers:* $10 each if just dropping items off, $20 each if dropping off and setting up to great extent

- *Tent assemblers and rental agency assemblers:* $20 each
- *Entertainers:* $25 to $30 each
- *Beauticians and barbers:* 15 to 20 percent of beauty salon bill
- *Cleanup crew:* $20 each
- *Baby-sitters:* $30 to $40 each, plus a gift; more if the baby-sitter is putting in extra hours or caring for several children
- *Event planner:* 10 to 20 percent of your bill, *depending on the terms of contract*
- *Security (if applicable):* $20 to $30 each
- *Officiants:* $75 to $100 tip is usually expected as a "donation"
- *Ceremony site staff:* $20 to $30 per person
- *Organists and ceremony musicians:* $20 to $50, depending on length of service

What are the five least *important elements of our day, the things we can do without if our budget means we have to eliminate something?*

1. _____

2. _____

3. _____

4. _____

5. _____

What elements can we expect to get for FREE? (Examples: the use of a relative's beach house for a wonderful wedding setting, the use of a friend's classic car or our own decorated convertible, desserts that helpful relatives can contribute to the cake table.)

1. _____

2. _____

3. _____

4. _____

5. _____

determining who will pay for what

Ah, here is where it gets interesting. *Who* is paying for *what?* We hope you've already sat down with your parents and the groom's parents (if they're contributing financially to the big day), and you and your groom have sat down to figure out who will add money to your wedding fund. Now it's time to decide who will take on which specific expenses. In chapter 2, you read about discussing who will join your inner circle of planners and what their individual responsibilities will be. Now, you must get specific.

Notice the column "Who's Paying" on the budget chart we provided (see pages 31–32). Obviously, you'll write the name of the person who volunteered to pick up the price tag for that particular item. We'll stop for a second to point out one big departure from wedding days of olde: Wedding planners of the 21st century no longer adhere strictly to those old rules that assigned most wedding expenses to the bride's family, and only a few to the groom's family. Now, because more couples are paying larger percentages of their own wedding costs, and because the financial positions of the groom's and bride's families vary (plus the groom's family is often excited to contribute to this lavish production), the budget categories are less defined and perhaps up for grabs.

Sometimes the groom's family will pay for a full half of the wedding, and some even pay the majority of costs for the event. Even grandparents, legal guardians, and birth parents who recently reunited with an adopted son or daughter are getting into the game. Another restrictive rule has been tossed out the window of the swiftly moving 21st-century wedding-planning process. The liberalization of wedding etiquette has opened the doors for many potential new players, enabling anyone to play a part.

> ### a word about taxes
>
> Many of your individual wedding expenses will be subjected to taxes, according to your state's rules and applicable percentages. Some states, for instance, do not levy sales taxes, while some tack on a notable fee for select types of purchases or services. When figuring your budget, always take into consideration this extra expense.

As wonderful as this is, you must tread lightly if you decide to follow this new trend. After all, your *parents and the groom's parents* may not fully understand or agree with the current practice of wedding bill—splitting. Your Old World father might be insulted to hear you've accepted your future in-laws' lovely offer to pay for the wedding cake. *"You don't think I can afford it?"* Egos are scarred, tensions flare, even tantrums take place, and all of a sudden your parents and his are engaged in "Us vs. Them" warfare. (We are amazed that the issue of splitting wedding expenses can turn stable parents into raving lunatics!) How does this happen?

Now is the time to back up and take stock of your parents' thoughts. A bit of preemptive communication is vital here. You and your groom (or you alone, depending on sensitivities) should sit down with your parents to discuss your wishes to allow others to help pay for what has always been traditionally the bride's family's financial domain. Ask for their true feelings about allowing others to help plan and pay for some of the wedding, and try to understand those feelings. Explain that things have changed in the world of weddings, and that sharing expenses among family members is now considered completely acceptable. Broach the topic first by showing respect for your parents' wishes; and then clearly explain how things are done now. You're in an excellent position to proceed diplomatically from here.

carving the turkey

Splitting expenses equally between families of the bride and groom is common today, and we believe this growing trend has no end. If this seems the direction both families would like to go, call everyone together (even via telephone if you're at a distance from one another) to assign those charted expenses. Many brides we've known have created a "tier system" that defers to the bride's family, meaning that they allow the bride's parents to choose first which top wedding elements they most want to fund. Then the groom's family gets to choose. Some couples take their own categories off the top, reserving the items and services they'd most like to provide themselves.

We don't expect you to put wedding expenses in a top hat so participants can draw assignments for financial responsibility, or to deal out the tasks like you're trading baseball cards (although some like-minded families who thrive on making good "trades!" find this method successful). Select a method that works well for your group's individual style and personalities, sensitivities and generosities, and divide the wedding expenses until everyone is satisfied with their "hand." Following these tips will make this process easier for you:

> ## surprise: they're fine with it!
>
> In many cases, the bride's traditionalist parents are *relieved* to share expenses, and they don't mind sharing the role of official wedding hosts . . . as long as their name goes first on the invitations. Fine! Give them the ranking they wish, and continue on, knowing you've handled what could have become an explosive situation with grace, tact, and the appropriate amount of respect.

Eight Tips for Dividing Finances

1. *Work off the same page.* Prepare a photocopied sheet that you could hand out to all at the family gathering indicating the categories of responsibilities from Dresses to Dinner Napkins.
2. *Make no assumptions.* Don't presume or expect what each family member will take on. Leave plenty of room for their maneuvering without embarrassment.

3. *Don't talk numbers.* This is not the time or place, in a shared audience, for discussing specific dollar figures. Speaking about money and income level still remains taboo in mixed company, so deal only with the categories.

4. *Scope it out.* Be prepared to explain the *scope* of your plans for each category when asked. For instance, your mother-in-law might not be aware that your wishes in the flowers category means a sea of white roses and gardenias, flowered trellises, dramatic arrangements on marble pillars, and nosegays on the back of all 200+ ceremony seats. Be clear *now,* so everyone knows what to expect.

5. *Final call.* Let everyone know their selections are commitments and they should take only what they can realistically handle.

6. *Updates are essential.* Let each party know what you estimate you will spend and communicate your plans with them individually throughout the process. This shows your respect for their financial positions and proves that you are far from greedy. In addition, continue communicating after making these initial assignments so you can keep a keen eye on the planning progress and prevent anything important from slipping through the cracks.

7. *Another way forward.* If selecting individual category expenses proves difficult, if family members clash, then calmly stop the selection session. A simple, "Now that I think about it, it might work better if we all just contribute what we can to a single bank account or debit card for the wedding expenses. This way, it's more organized." Solution granted.

8. Always, *always* maintain your discretion. What one family contributes to the wedding fund should never be discussed with others. No one should be compared or judged by what they can contribute, and you should never talk to others about the size of your budget. Again, respect your inner circle's privacy and show no other emotion than gratitude at this point.

honey, we can take care of it

Oh, to be able to plan and pay for the wedding by yourselves! If you can pull off this ultimate liberation and dream plan, more power to you. You can then really create the wedding of your dreams. However, remember that money does not buy good manners or considerate behavior. Always give kudos and respect to those in your family who must have it, whether or not they're footing the bill. Defer to their opinions where you can, even when they have no financial bearing on your day.

Once you've taken the financial reins for the Big Day and everything leading up to it, create for yourselves a budget plan and responsibilities list. Many of today's brides and grooms enjoy the autonomy of planning their own weddings, and their freedom from others' input makes the process that much more precious. The day turns out to reflect *them* fully, not others' wishes, and brides and grooms glow, knowing they've created a meaningful, personalized celebration . . . and paid for it themselves. It's their first major "purchase" as a team, and the pride and the process is theirs alone.

from sharon

Gone are the days when a successful wedding was determined by how much money you could spend, how lavish it would be, and how jealous your parents could make their friends with their almost insane level of spending for sheer decadence. While that kind of wedding certainly has its place in the society pages, it's the wedding with meaning, *far more than price, that can be deemed a true success. Who wants to be overshadowed by the décor, the ten-layer wedding cake, and the trappings of the day? A truly successful wedding is elegant simplicity, where guests can see your smile past those fancy ice sculptures . . . and feel the warmth of the moment* for you.

getting great gifts

What better time to talk about the *free* stuff than right here in the budget section. For many brides and grooms, the stress and tension of talking about what everything costs floats away when they think about *the gifts.* At the outset of your plans, before your engagement party, showers, and other events at which you are practically buried beneath festively wrapped presents, it's time to register for everything you'll need to set up house and home. Even if you already have a fully stocked kitchen and linens galore, registering is still a very smart idea. After all, your guests appreciate having an organized and personalized list from which to choose, and they generally want to get you items you'll need. And even if you have all the basics, no doubt there are *some* fancy gadgets or tools you two can use in the future!

When you're ready to embark upon the joint trip to register for your gifts, be sure to keep the following tips in mind:

from sharon

Today's biggest trend in registries is for the men to add their most-wanted items to the list. Why shouldn't they get the goods as well? The new groom wants in on the best new gadgets and toys, and that bagel-slicer just isn't cutting it for him. Now, he may want a George Foreman grill, some power tools to remodel your bathroom, or a digital camera you both can share. Encourage your groom to dream-shop to his heart's content!

1. *Do your homework to find original and unique registries!* Sure, we all know about the wonderful and efficient online registries at Macy's, Tiffany, and Target. But do a little checking, and you'll undoubtedly turn up little-known registries at other stores and small boutiques that might be perfect for you.

2. *Include the groom!* This is one wedding task today's men are getting more excited about, even if it's just because they get to use the scanning laser gun to record product information into the computer database! Of all the grooms we know, this shopping trip gets top ranking on their list for favorite wedding task.

3. *Make registry-finding easier on your guests.* Sure, go ahead and allow your maids to print where you're registered on those shower invitations. Old etiquette rules of yesteryear said they couldn't do it, but today's efficiency rules say they can. Provide the correct

URL for your online registries, and perhaps add a link directly to them from your own personal wedding Web site!

4. *Be specific when you register.* Put exact model numbers and sizes, colors, and description in the details sections of your registry.

5. Provide an address where faraway guests can mail your gifts.

6. *Be sure to say that "Gift Certificates Are Welcome."* Most registries will allow you to print this welcome announcement on your profile, and many guests find this option a relief. They may not know what to choose for you, or they may have signed on too late to purchase all those moderately priced items on your list! A gift certificate can be a welcome alternative to cash for those who are so inclined, and you get the benefit of taking those denominations of gift certificates to the store later on, to fill in sets or gather up the must-have items you really need . . . without spending any of your wedding gift cash! It's a win-win situation.

from henry

When choosing your registry, be practical. Allow for a broad price range so that all your guests can feel comfortable.

7. *Consider including a honeymoon registry.* Another growing 21st-century trend is to establish a honeymoon registry. This service can allow your guests to contribute to your honeymoon trip as a whole, or purchase special treats such as massages, spa treatments, champagne dinner cruises, bike ride tours, scuba lessons, or flowers for your honeymoon suite. This registry adds to your memories of the trip of a lifetime, not to your kitchen cupboards!

8. *Consider requesting personal items.* Another big registry item for the bride who already has all the towels, egg dividers, potholders, and bread makers is *lingerie!* Inform your maid of honor directly and far ahead of time that what you could really use is a lingerie shower . . . boxes and bags full of silk robes, bustiers, camisoles, thigh-high stockings, and other seductive items for

saving money without the savings showing

The smartest of couples make their plans with reasonable budget-saving strategies in mind. Cutting corners *can* be done stealthily, without any of your guests noticing you cut corners. No one will know that you spent half the expected amount on your flowers (they still look gorgeous), that you negotiated extra cocktail hour stations in exchange for the raw seafood bar, or that a culinary student created that amazing ice sculpture for *free* in exchange for a page in his portfolio. For smart but sneaky ways to double or triple what your wedding budget can do for you, check out Sharon Naylor's book *How to Have a Fabulous Wedding for $10,000 or Less.* Even if your expected wedding budget is far more than ten grand, these thousands of road-tested tips are sure to help you maximize your budget, and perhaps get you several amazing wedding services for *free.*

the boudoir. Call it an investment in your romantic life! Be sure to provide your size (small, medium, or large), bra size, plus any preferences you might have (as in, *no feather boas!*).

chapter 4

It's Just Me
with a Great Big Rock!

Little did you know that your rings are the only true and lasting items that stay with you after your wedding. Sure, you can display your wedding photographs in your home, and you can preserve your flowers and gown, but those rings stay on your hands forever, symbolizing your commitment to one another. So selecting the engagement and wedding rings is a momentous occasion. It is perhaps the most intimate moment you will share with your groom throughout the entire planning process. This will be one of those times when your heart flutters.

the sparkler: the engagement ring

By now, you might have a beautiful, sparkling engagement ring on your hand. If your groom is a traditionalist (and don't we love those!), he may have created a romantic proposal scene, dropped down to one knee, and asked you to marry him. He may have had the bubbly hidden in preparation. Champagne corks popped, you felt weak in the knees and perhaps shed a tear, and your promise was delivered with a heartfelt "Yes! I will!" He slipped the beautiful, sparkling rock onto your finger, and you were betrothed.

Few moments in life are as magical as this one. You have entered cloud nine, and the world spins slowly on an axis of love.

Today's grooms know that this is a special moment for both of you, and most give a lot of thought to what would make their bride's dreams come true. From searching the Internet to visiting glittering ring shops to secretly "borrowing" one of your everyday rings to get your size, the groom puts a lot of effort and love into this task.

Of course, the traditionalist may have the ring in hand, but the 21st-century couple often departs from the old ways. In fact, some grooms propose without the ring. We see more and more brides-to-be shopping for their gowns without a rock on their left hand. Many are either waiting for their ring to come in or will soon go shopping for their engagement ring with their groom.

Does proposing without a ring mean today's men are commitment phobic? Absolutely not! Today's groom is actually quite practical and considerate. He wants to allow his bride the chance to choose her own ring, to pick the stone shape and setting design that she loves, instead of one *he thinks* will work. This is an excellent approach for independent women, and we applaud it! The joint trip to the jewelry store can be every bit as exciting and heart-fluttering and romantic as a surprise proposal. We think this new trend takes its place beautifully next to the old.

saying yes to a ringless proposal

Of course, there are other reasons newly engaged women today do not always have rings on their fingers. It might be a matter of career, for instance. We had a surgeon enter our salon the other day, and she lifted her hair covering her ears and said, "Don't you love my engagement ring?" Sparkling on her ears were two dazzling diamond earrings. Her fiancé knew that she, as a surgeon, could not have anything impeding the blood flow to her hands, so the diamond earrings took the place of a diamond ring.

Receiving the Ring

Whether your fiancé surprises you with a ring or you choose one together, whether your ring is big and expensive or more modest, the meaning is the same. Here we offer some facts to remind you how special your rock is, however you receive it.

The Surprise Ring

If your man has gone the traditional route, with the engagement ring and the proposal as a complete surprise, then we cheer with you! We know from the stories of hundreds of brides that this is an adrenaline rush like no other! There is something very beautiful about traditional proposals with the ring. Can you imagine how long and hard he thought about what would make you happy? Every time you look at it, think of the love, care, and research that he put into making your dream come true.

from michelle

When my husband, Peter Roth, proposed marriage, he gave me a gift instead of a ring at that moment. It was the Paloma Picasso "scribble" broach with diamonds. It was such a heartfelt moment! The next day, he took me to the place where we chose the diamond and setting for my engagement ring. I'll never forget that moment; it was classic Peter Roth!

The Joint Decision

Betrothal can happen in so many ways in this liberated decade in which we live. Formula expressions of love are over (thank goodness!) now that today's groom knows his bride better than anyone. Bringing you in on the ring choice doesn't diminish your fiancé's intentions; rather, it's a sign that he respects your independent tastes and knows what would make you happiest.

Men have begun to understand that women have specific preferences in rings, specific views on what shape looks best on their hands. Some grooms know their brides are very particular, and that exchanging the ring for a different one later might be an emotionally wrenching decision, and perhaps an added expense. Your wise choice

Of course we have all heard the many creative ways by which men now choose to propose. A new contemporary approach can leave little opportunity for the groom to go ring-shopping with his bride. Usually, the most outlandish proposals are reported on Valentine's Day when the love radar is up. Reports of messages written in the sky, on-air television proposals, billboards with impossible-to-miss messages, radio station love calls, and many other methods of declaring love have become ways to communicate a proposal in unforgettable style. Mr. Spontaneous may be the man who takes you window-shopping for a ring—or up in a hot-air balloon to ask for your hand. We say this: Go along for the ride, and let the spontaneity of the moment carry you off like a skyrocket!

to make this a joint venture then saves you both from the awkward issue of ring replacement.

The Sentimental Ring: Love Me Tender

Another trend in today's engagement ring choice is the groom's handing down of an heirloom ring from his grandmother or another cherished family member. This keeps a precious jewel in the family and adds additional significance to this lovely gift of commitment. You may either love this heirloom ring as it is, in its original setting, or you may reset the diamond stones into a setting of your choice.

Counting Carats: All That Glitters

In whatever manner you receive your engagement ring, surprise or not, you must remember that the thought he put into it is what truly counts. How much your groom wants (or is able) to spend on the ring is usually his decision. Don't worry that your friend's ring is two carats larger than yours; numbers and sizes do not make that ring more valuable in terms of the emotion it represents. Comparison is

Happily Ever After

Jodi Della Femina, one of our spotlight brides you'll see pictured on page 199, shared a wonderful story about her engagement ring. Jodi's beloved grandmother passed away three weeks before Jodi became engaged to her love, John Kim. When John proposed to Jodi on the beach at her father's estate in the Hamptons, he knew that Jodi had always tried on her grandmother's engagement and wedding rings when she was a little girl. Jodi and her grandmother, after all, had the same size hands. So when John proposed to Jodi, it was all the more meaningful that he presented her with her grandmother's engagement ring. Shortly afterward, they used her grandmother's wedding ring—reset with a new band—as Jodi's wedding ring. These precious family heirlooms, so important and sentimental to Jodi, became the symbols of her own marriage and love-filled future.

futile, as a larger carat count does not make her groom more loving than yours. So put away that measuring stick and see the love reflecting from every precious facet of your ring.

bands that bind

The symbol of wedding bands is culturally one of the foremost signs of unity. The circle of the wedding band means eternity, a never-ending connection that lasts through the ages. A gift between you and your groom, an outward symbol to the world of your commitment, the ring is the definitive symbol of your promises made to one another. Remember the true meaning of your ring; that is what matters.

from henry

All that sparkles is not gold. Whatever the size of your rock, it's the sparkle in your eyes that needs to shine brightest.

Stones

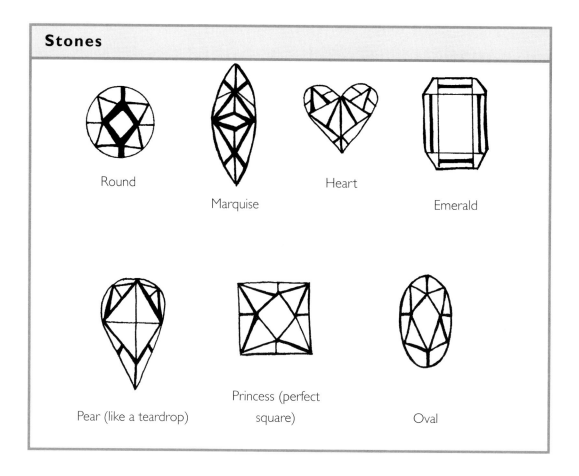

Round

Marquise

Heart

Emerald

Pear (like a teardrop)

Princess (perfect square)

Oval

Radiant, Oval, Princess, or Pear?
Gold or Platinum?

As you flip through those bridal magazines, looking at rings or bands of every size and shape, you may wonder, "How am I to choose just one?" Indeed, the selection out there is enormous, and the level of artistry in designing new rings is stunning. Above is an illustration of what you might have to choose from when shopping for diamonds or gemstones on your engagement and wedding bands.

Once you decide on a "shape," then it's time to look at settings. Engagement rings and wedding bands now feature side diamond and gemstone channels for a little extra sparkle, or you can go traditional

Q&A Bridal

"I'm aware of the 4 C's of diamonds: clarity, cut, color, and carat, but how can we tell what's a good shade of clarity and color for a ring? We can't afford perfection, and we don't even know what grading is perfection. Is there some Web site we can go to in order to learn more about diamonds, gold, white gold platinum, and all the other specifics of rings?"

Of course! Learning everything you can about the specifics of rings ahead of time is the best way to choose that perfect rock for you. So we suggest you surf through the following ring sites to educate yourselves before your shopping trip and then make an informed investment once you're in the "hot seat" at the jeweler's and actually trying on specifically "pedigreed" rings:

American Gem Society: www.ags.org

Blue Nile: www.bluenile.com

EGL Gemological Society: www.egl.co.za

Novell Design Studio: www.novelldesignstudio.com

Tiffany: www.tiffany.com

Zales: www.zales.com

www.adiamondisforever.com

One of our favorite sites is www.adiamondisforever.com for its in-depth ring element explanations and grading sheets, plus its "Design Your Own Ring" interactive tool that lets you virtually create your own ring design and print it out for ordering or crafting by an expert. Bluenile.com also has this ring-building tool, with a wonderful sliding scale that narrows down your choices to your chosen carats, color, and clarity, in a range of designs.

with a smooth platinum or 18K gold metal band. The choice is up to you and your dreams of the ideal ring.

For your stones, the science of gems comes into play. For example, a basic question that diamond appraisers answer is this: "Is it clear and colorless, or does it have a yellowish tinge to it?" With diamonds, the range of acceptable color in the industry is judged by a scale of D (ideal) to J (fair, but visibly colored). Clarity too has its sliding scale, and we encourage you to research the many gradations, ask plenty of questions, and examine each ring carefully to see just what these scientific labels look like in real life. The same applies if you plan to incorporate precious stones other than diamonds in your ring setting, such as emeralds, rubies, sapphires, or your birthstones.

Keeping It a Quality Story

Shopping for your wedding rings together is a uniting effort. As a couple, you are choosing these all-important symbols, so your selection process must take high priority. Not only must you find those stunning rings, but you must purchase them from an extremely reputable dealer. It's not only *what* you buy, it's *who* you buy from.

We can't emphasize enough the value of a top-notch jewelry dealer or designer, one who knows his or her stuff, and one who will take the time to explain those many detailed questions you may have about your rings. Ring professionals will become your best friends as you try on rings, giving you the in-depth news on gemstones, care and handling of your rings, and the absolute truth about a ring's unseen flaws. Diamonds, after all, are like snowflakes. No two are exactly alike.

from sharon

True diamonds become beautiful, priceless, and valuable things after starting out as lumps of carbon and then, after being under tremendous pressure for years, become diamonds-in-the-rough. Through careful tending, pruning, and polishing, that middle-earth find becomes a shining beacon of love. I've always loved the analogy that throughout the wedding planning process, brides often feel like that lump of carbon under tremendous pressure, only to discover themselves polished into a priceless, radiant gem for their wedding day!

if you could see me now

Few moments are as breathtaking as sitting with your beloved in front of a well-lit glass case in the jeweler's showroom, with trays upon trays of dazzling sparklers set out before you. One after the other, you slip the rings onto your hand—platinum bands inset with diamonds or pavé stones, delicate laser-cut swirl designs on one gold band, gold and silver edging on another to match any outfit and any future "in" style of jewelry. If you can stop your mind from wondering what the price tags must be, you are experiencing the ultimate form of dress-up.

Narrowing down your choices is likely to be difficult, so breathe deeply and focus not just on how a ring looks on your finger, but how it feels. Let your fabulous female intuition let you know, "Yes! This is the one!"

As for your groom, he should try on several styles of wedding bands as well. From smooth and chic and simple to ornately edged, from narrow to wide, he too must see which band feels like it's part of him.

✎

On behalf of *Your Day, Your Way*, Sharon interviewed Mara Leighton, daughter and partner of jewelry luminary Fred Leighton, to hear what their famous, infamous, and fabulously everyday 21st-century brides and grooms choose for the eternity symbols of a lifetime:

> **SHARON NAYLOR (SN):** *Mara, what do you see as the growing trend among brides and grooms who come to you for their wedding bands?*

> **MARA LEIGHTON (ML):** The couples who come in want rings that are distinctive and reflect their own style. Today's bride and groom really want to be individual and unique with the bands they choose, but they want comfort as well for their everyday busy work lives. It's not like it used to be, when everyone's wedding rings looked similar, with the same prong settings and the same diamond bands. Now, the look is one-of-a-kind.

> **SN:** *So what are the styles that are attracting these unique brides' attention?*

> **ML:** We're setting a lot of early 20th-century pieces, Edwardian styles, with great detail to the bands. They want old stones remounted in

new settings with a classic Edwardian or art deco look. The mountings have a tremendous amount of intricate detail—not just in the view from above, but also on the sides, under the diamonds, and all the way around for a custom look and feel. These details may not be immediately obvious to others, but the bride and groom know they're there.

SN: *So it's all in the details?*

ML: Exactly. We specialize in the art deco cuts today's brides are going wild over. Such pieces as "lozenge cuts," which is like a marquise with more pointed sides, and elongated diamonds that run from left to right, geometric designs. We're showing a lot of Asscher cuts, cushion cuts, unique shapes, and very distinctive settings and stones.

SN: *So there seems to be a return to "everything old" as a departure from previous decades?*

ML: The run for originality and uniqueness is turning today's brides and grooms back in time to find those original designs. For instance, today's diamonds are all cut to ideal, measured proportions. Back in the 19th century, they didn't do that. They took a piece of diamond rough and faceted that rough into the shape it most resembled. With less technology than we have today, and with less interest in fitting a stone into a perfect round, they would just bring out the shape from that rough. That meant that it was rare to find similarly cut stones back then, which makes all the available old stones we have now incredibly unique and special.

SN: *Are brides and grooms coming in with their mothers' and grandmothers' stones for resetting?*

ML: We don't do that here, but that is an option for a couple who already has a gorgeous, unique stone or ring to redesign.

SN: *No wonder you're so popular with celebrities, with all those incredible jeweled pieces on the red carpets! Celebrities and celebrity brides certainly want incredible pieces to wear, with the originality, the impact, of a beautiful ring or necklace. So tell me, which celebrity engagement and wedding rings have you done?*

ML: We've done many, but the most recent ones we can talk about are Catherine Zeta-Jones's engagement ring, earrings, and that Edwardian tiara she wore at her wedding to Michael Douglas.

SN: *That was gorgeous! She was an absolutely regal bride.*

ML: We also did Joan Collins's 19th-century heart-shaped engagement ring, 19th-century diamond earrings for Anne Heche's wedding, and we did a collection of diamond hair clips for Gwen Stefani from the band No Doubt, plus a diamond bow with a natural pearl accent, also for her hair.

SN: *That was beautiful. I love those extra, unique touches like Gwen's hair clips. Brides of today really want to use jewelry well in their wedding day look. And speaking of using jewelry well, I understand that when the Roths outfitted Shaquille O'Neal's bride, Shaunie Nelson, you did a little something special for her as she chose her wedding gown and wedding day jewelry.*

ML: Yes, when Shaunie was trying on wedding gowns with Michelle Roth, we sent over a collection of pieces—earrings, necklaces—that she could try on with the gowns she was considering. Michelle guided her in matching just the right pieces with just the right gown, so the jewels were a part of Shaunie's gown selection process.

SN: *That's a wonderful idea. Mara, thank you for sharing these great stories and trends with our readers. How can they get their rings from Fred Leighton's?*

ML: Just have them call us at 212-288-1872, and we'll take good care of them.

❧

Your Day, Your Way also spoke with Melvyn Kirtley, group vice president, retail, for Tiffany & Co. (www.tiffany.com) to get another high-style view on the hottest trends in engagement and wedding rings. Here are Mr. Kirtley's top picks for *the* 21st-century look:

- The most popular style of diamond engagement at Tiffany & Co. is the classic round brilliant cut diamond in a Tiffany six-prong setting. Its simplicity and classic elegance showcase the diamond beautifully and the brides-to-be feel that this is a look that will never go out of style or become dated.

- The wedding band is critical when selecting a ring. The band must both be complementary and enhance the engagement ring. Diamond band rings are becoming very popular as wedding bands and display the center diamond beautifully.

- Mixed-cut styles such as our Lucida diamond cut have recently become much more popular. The combination of a square diamond with cut corners and a brilliant faceting arrangement on the pavilion of the diamond gives a very pleasing combination of styles in a more contemporary look. The Lucida setting is light and contemporary and has a matching wedding band that nestles alongside the Lucida engagement ring. Simple, elegant, and comfortable.

- More couples are interested in diamond solitaires with side stones in more interesting and unique combinations using accent diamonds as triangular cuts, trapezoid cuts, and half moons.

- Also, brides are increasingly interested in colored diamonds and are asking to see pink, yellow, and blue diamonds. These are rare, appealing to those customers interested in something unique.

- Platinum is the most popular metal type chosen as it accents the diamond's beauty and is extremely durable. Men, though, often tend to choose 18-karat yellow gold for their wedding bands.

upgrading your ring in years to come

There is always a later. Many women upgrade their engagement rings years after their wedding as a sign of continued renewal and the depth of their marriage bonds. As bride and groom become more precious to one another over time, the changing shape of the ring reflects the growing value between you. In a little bit of "ring plastic surgery," you may choose to have your original setting changed to a more (or less) ornate one. You may choose to have additional stones set on either side of your original solitaire, or you may include the birthstones of your children down the road. We've heard many magnificent stories of wedding and engagement ring upgrades, including the following:

- The original stone (what the groom could afford while he was in medical school) was replaced with a larger, brighter, higher-quality stone after he and his bride started their own medical practice together.

- Two additional stones were added to a single diamond engagement ring to symbolically reflect the couple's "past, present, and future."

- An additional sentiment was engraved on the inside of the rings. Sharon particularly loves this idea: If the couple has had "I Love You" engraved inside their wedding bands, they can add a meaningful "…Still" or "…More" or "…Always" after the original sentiment.

Think of what you two have to look forward to. If your wildest dreams have not been fulfilled with the ring your groom originally chose for you (perhaps his budget was limited or you never told him you preferred emerald-cut over oval), then you have a lifetime to upgrade and renew. Ring upgrades can make an ideal special anniversary gift in your future.

drastic measures

Call 911! We forgot the ring!

Yes, it does happen once in a while; the nervous groom forgets the wedding rings at home after the hustle and bustle of a busy wedding morning. What to do? Improvise for now. Borrow friends' rings, or your parents' rings. Or, ask the officiant if he or she has "dummy rings" in the building. Some places of worship prepare for the worst by keeping a spare set on hand. If you must use rings that aren't yours during the ceremony, be sure to make up for it afterward. In a private "ceremony" of your own, repeat your vows to one another, exchange rings, and seal the deal with a kiss (you can make it a passionate one this time!).

style that leaves them speechless

chapter 5

Aisle Style:
Finding Your Perfect
Wedding Gown

L et's get real.

Your wedding dress—no matter how formal or informal—will be among the most important dresses you will ever wear in your life . . . if not *the* most important! Even if you are planning a second, third, or fourth wedding right now and have already walked down an aisle or two in a fabulous gown, the fact remains the same: *This* is now the gown of your life. Few dress selections will be this important, this exciting, this expensive. Undoubtedly, your bridal gown will be the most symbolic dress purchase you'll make, as well as the most talked-about piece of fabric that will ever grace your body.

The range of styles and options for brides has never been more expansive! With each passing day, bridal style gets more original, more personalized, more beautiful, and more pleasing, with something for each individual bride-to-be. Whether you want a traditional ball gown, a sexy strappy sheath, a strapless number that shows off your hard-earned great arms and shoulders, or a whisper of a sundress for an outdoor wedding, the design choices are all out there, and there's no end to what you can create from individual style elements (which we'll get to in the next chapter).

For the bride who married quietly in a civil ceremony or spontaneously in Vegas and is about to make her splash at a big reception, your choices are still wide open. Even the repeat bride has a complete range of choices now that the stigma attached to second weddings has disappeared! There are no more hush-hush judgments of *"You are not allowed to wear white!"* or *"That dress is too traditional for you."* Bridal dress choices are now based on the tone and theme of the wedding rather than on (shudder) what is *allowed* or on a bride's demure desire to blend. All brides can shine in their own way. The beauty of the 21st-century wedding is that it's *your* day, so when it comes to your gown, have it *your* way.

from michelle

Brides often choose the aisle as their personal fashion runway, letting their own personality and individuality shine through. This is expected of today's bride. However, if you prefer a more traditional dress, go for it. You should feel no pressure with regard to what you wear, except for possible religious considerations (some churches maintain strict dictates of the church and might require that you wear a gown that covers your shoulders or arms, for instance).

taking your first steps with confidence

Even before you open that first page of a bridal magazine or Web site to *oooh* and *ahhh* over the delicious bridal fashions, many thoughts will be swirling in your head. We want you to be calm, cool, and collected when you select your top contenders, so we identify typical issues and offer a few sanity-savers at the outset of your search. You might recognize some of these concerns already, and may encounter others along the way. As you proceed, watch out for these problem areas and keep our pointers in mind:

Michelle Roth bride Shaunie O'Neal, who married basketball great Shaquille O'Neal at a lavish wedding celebration in Beverly Hills (see their feature on page 135), explains her wedding gown vision: "I knew I wanted to be Cinderella, I had always dreamed of a big beautiful wedding gown. I wanted the top of my dress to be soft, but sexy. I wanted to seem as though I was floating down the aisle, so the bottom part of my dress had to be full and flow perfectly, which was successful. I hadn't quite imagined my veil at this point; however, I did know I wanted drama coming from the back of my gown. Still soft and delicate, yet dramatic at the same time."

The Pressure of "Making Everybody Happy"

What people will think when they see you in your gown and what impression you will make on your family and invited guests is going to be at the top of your mind. Know this now and forever: You are *not* going to make everybody—mother, mother-in-law, your fiancé, and ultimately you—happy at your wedding with every decision you make! Someone is likely to have an opinion, raise an eyebrow, or give a thumbs-down on even your most-loved ideas. If you try to please everyone with every choice you make, you'll drive yourself crazy and ultimately disappoint yourself! When it comes to gown selection, nothing makes for a worse expedition than bringing along too many "walking opinions"! After a few moments, you're bound to feel pulled like a fresh batch of taffy, battered like an old pillow, and spun around like a top. The various opinions roar inside your head, and the thrill of gown shopping is gone!

Our solution to this is *balance.* Remember who *you* are, remember that it's *your* day, and remember that how *you* feel in *your* gown matters above all else. So consider only the most important influences in making your dress decision, and try to defer to them where possible. Yes, it's your day so it's your way, but sometimes others' opinions *should* be taken into account. For instance, your reliable maid of honor might be the only one honest enough to tell you that the neckline is too daring or that a particular gown makes you look "boxy." Maybe your mother is correct when she says that one gown is too heavy and formal for an outdoor wedding, and perhaps she's also right in nixing your strapless choice because your house of worship doesn't allow you to bare arms during a service.

Balance is your key. You have entered a decade where you have the last word, yet you don't want to cross that fine line and become a "control freak." A *little* flexibility will go a long way. Trust us!

Body Issues and the Quick Fix

What does my body look like in this dress? How do my arms, my stomach, my back, and my bottom look in this A-line? Is there a bubble of bra fat showing back there?

Trying on wedding gowns can raise issues that go way back, exposing the root of many a raw nerve from puberty that achieved full bloom in adulthood. Brides tend to become overly self-critical, making themselves and those around them absolutely miserable.

If you are considering a drastic quick-fix makeover, think again. You may just do it and lose those pounds overnight. However, unless you go into a program that addresses your weight issues for life, you will drive yourself and others around you nuts. What is the point of losing weight if you'll just put it back on after all is said and done? To be honest, severe diet regimens are very 20th-century bride. They provide short-term solutions at extremely high personal and image costs. By all means, adopt a program for life and make this your turning point, rather than just making the wedding a be-all, end-all date. After all, there is life after a wedding. You'll read more about the weight issue in chapter 13.

How you will look in your gown is, of course, important. We don't expect you can erase your body sensitivities just because we say so, but we do encourage you to join the ranks of the 21st-century bride and embrace your body as it is by finding a gown that makes the most of

© Debby Brown

© Debby Brown

Carrie's Story

CARRIE YOUNGBERG, a Michelle Roth bride from New York City, says, "I had major anxieties about getting a wedding dress. I'm a petite size 12 to 14 and always thought I'd look like a white whale at my wedding. I was sure I wouldn't even put my wedding picture on my desk! When my mom and step-dad insisted that I have a real wedding dress, I started doing some research, and my anxiety level skyrocketed! I was never going to look like a bride in the bridal magazines, plus I heard that for a wedding dress I'd need two sizes larger than I usually wear. I've worked hard to ensure that I never see a size 16!

"When I went to Michelle Roth's studio, the consultant I worked with, Cathy, showed me so many flattering options for gowns—just the right shapes and styles to make me look great. When I finally found the dress, I felt like a princess, and dress size did not matter at all. Then when I went to the fittings, two or three people made detailed changes that made me look even better. Not once did anyone suggest that I diet or mention that I was not skinny. It was an amazing, freeing experience."

Q&A Bridal

I'm planning to lose fifteen pounds before my wedding next summer, so I'm thinking of ordering my gown in the size that I'll be then, an 8. Is this going to save me money on alterations?

Slow down, honey! Never, never, *never* order a gown that you *plan* to fit into. If there's one eternal fantasy we hear as we help our brides get ready for their big days, it's the dream of shedding pounds in time to wear that 8, 6, 4, or 2. And what happens most often? Dress suicide. If the weight doesn't come off, you and your seamstress have a big problem. Order for your actual size and continue to maintain or reduce your weight within reason. A last-minute alteration can pull your seams in . . . and that's far more encouraging than letting out seams after wedding stress regularly led you to the Krispy Kreme counter. Don't invite disaster.

your favorite features, that accents the positive! As Carrie Youngberg's story (page 63) illustrates, magic can happen with the right gown elements, expert design, and careful tailoring. You can look gorgeous, no matter what your size or shape.

Unless, of course, you have the opposite dilemma. The pregnant bride must consider the weight she's going to *gain* before her wedding, how her body will expand and change. Shaunie O'Neal turned that dilemma into a showcase of blessings as she and Michelle Roth created a gown that would work for her (see Shaunie's feature on page 135).

Money, Honey

Oh, the expense of a fine wedding gown! Sometimes brides find it hard to justify spending so much on a dress they'll only wear once. There is often a real tug-of-war between your desire to create lifelong memories and to stick to your budget. Once you start looking at dresses, you may have second thoughts about the priority you placed on your wedding dress relative to the rest of your wedding expenditure plan.

This is the time to *set your boundaries* concerning what you are thinking of spending on the dress. Allow for a safety margin, but try to stay around the figure you imagined. Remember to include the veil, headpiece, accessories, crinolines (for A-line and ball-gown styles), alterations and pressing. Budgeting isn't fun, and money can certainly limit your options, so research the prices of gowns you love, then determine a flexible range and try to stay within your limits.

Image and Your Sense of Self

How you want to portray yourself and the setting you choose—from contemporary to classic, from The Pierre Hotel Bride to Maui Beach, from a chic New York City loft to a natural country-style wedding in Missouri—is an important consideration. Ceremonies and receptions have almost become *bridal safaris.* With the newfound freedom they have been afforded, 21st-century brides can select a setting that has tremendous meaning or portrays a unique sense of style. It is vital for you to factor in your style and setting when you start your dress-hunting mission. Dressing in the style of the wedding you create is your opportunity to make a statement.

While it's vital that you consider these points when determining the final look you want to achieve, tackle each issue one at a time rather than bundling them into one insurmountable mountain. You can avoid a potentially bewildering obstacle at this point by becoming the best bridal dress detective in town! Get to work researching what's available in bridal gowns even before you decide how you are going to find *the* dress.

from sharon

One suggestion I've made in many of my wedding books is that you "shift" your initial budget figures. If you fall in love with the gown of your dreams, but it's $500 more than you'd budgeted, find another budget category from which to take the money! Cut out the pricey favors and guest hotel gift baskets or go for more moderate choices (perhaps chocolates in nice wrapping rather than silver-engraved frames), and then shift that $500 to your gown budget so you can fulfill your gown dream.

it's all about hue

A defining trend in 21st-century bridal gowns and accessories is color. In days of old, no self-respecting woman would dare wear a gown that wasn't virginal white. To do otherwise would have been a mark of shame or ignorance, even a symbol of defilement. *Please!* Yes, white was symbolic of purity, of virginity, which was expected of "proper"

bride 101

Before you set foot in a salon, do your homework:

- Research books, magazines, Internet services
- Cut out pictures of dresses and information on designers you like
- Print out hard copy pictures from Internet sites
- Create your dress binder
- Talk to married friends to get their recommendations
- Become acquainted with price points, shapes, and silhouettes of gowns (see page 89 for Michelle's primer on styles of gowns)
- List designers whose dresses you would love to try on

brides in the old days. But again, let's get real. White is and may always be the primary color for wedding gowns, but the old meanings are *passé*.

Now, second-time brides can wear white, and first-time brides can wear ivory, blush pink, baby blue, lilac—whatever you like. A wonderful trend these days is to include bright-colored or pastel accents to the bodice, train, even the veil. Look through any bridal magazine, or visit www.michelleroth.com, and you'll see a display of wedding gowns that infuse the old and the new—traditional white ball gowns with intricate, colored beading or floral embroidery. Sharon's favorite gown in one of Michelle's past collections is a blush pink gown with light green accents and a cluster of pink roses at the bottom of a plunging backline. Another of Michelle's pink gowns was recently featured on *The Oprah Winfrey Show* as an example of how wedding gowns are waking up to color.

So don't turn away when you see color. If you adore a gown with color, don't worry yourself with *"what will people think?"* Why should your maids have all the fun with hues and tones? Stand tall as a bride of the 21st century, and if color calls out to you, answer the call!

your bridal binder

Once you have started paging, cutting, clicking, and printing contenders for *the* dress, you will need to house all this information somewhere. For the ultimate in organization, insert all your material into a bridal binder. Grab any binder from the office supply shop, label it your "can't-live-without-it carryall," and fill it with images of your favored designs. Create these three easy categories:

1. Straight dresses and their price points
2. Princess/empire line dresses and their price points
3. Full-skirted/ball-gown-shaped dresses and their price points

Include your notes, questions you'd like to ask, the Web site at which you discovered your gown of interest, sketches you make in your downtime, and any other pertinent information regarding your gown hunt. Keep a record of where you found each one, and slip business cards into a pocket holder for easy retrieval later. Leave plenty of blank pages for additional notes and phone numbers, and use this handy tool to keep all your details in line.

becoming the belle of the ball

Trying dresses on is the most important step to buying one! No matter what your venue or what option you choose, you'll never know unless you go! You'll want to make the experience fun, exciting, and everything you dreamed it could be when you were a little girl. Some of the fantasy should remain, as that little girl is still inside you! But, try as you might to live your fantasy, you will be awakened to the reality of what dresses are available, what they cost, and what they look like on you when you begin trying them on. Adjusting to reality is good since living in a fantasy world is a one-way ticket to disappointment. Fortunately, there's plenty of room to keep the process light, fun, and relevant.

The dizzying array of options for gown-shopping is at once thrilling and overwhelming. Where do you go first? Should you plug into a designer's Web site to search for retailers that carry your gown? Should you make an appointment at a designer's salon? What about department stores? Going off on a million tangents, or pulling yourself in a dozen different directions, will detract from your joy. Again, that snowglobe of yours has received another major shake-up! Allow the thoughts to settle, and then plan your attack. As a "gown detective," you'll soon scout out the best places to investigate and will undoubtedly discover the gown that's been waiting for you.

Before you grab your bridal binder, car keys, mom and maids, and credit cards, here are a few clarifying tips:

- *Find out where your friends searched for their wedding gowns.* Word-of-mouth is the best predictor of quality, so ask your recently married and engaged friends whether they can recommend a fine gown supplier . . . and name any that you should avoid at all costs.

- *Research the gown shops.* Determine which salon or store has designers who have caught your imagination and admiration, whose dresses you dream of wearing. Check out their Web sites or step through their doors, noting the general atmosphere and looking at the stock they carry. You can tell a lot by a first impression, and even more by exploring firsthand.

- *Know your realistic dollar figures.* Your budget will have a big say in where you end up going, and how you will arrange the purchase (or perhaps loan) of the dress you'll wear in your wedding. This is the time to firm up your numbers. Do consider stretching your budget a little for *the* dress. After all, it will remain with you longest in mind, photographs, and video or digital imagery. However, stretching does not mean leaping. Don't tempt fate by going to a salon or store where you know you couldn't afford even a hairclip, let alone an entire bridal wardrobe.

- *Go when you have stamina.* Are you a morning person or an evening person? Do you have a flexible schedule that leaves you available to cruise gown salons at 3:00 P.M. when most people are hard at work in their offices? Shopping for gowns when you're tired is a drain, and can seriously injure your objectivity, patience, and drive for this important task. You wouldn't want to buy the first gown you see out of sheer exhaustion. So schedule your gown expedition when you know you'll be at peak performance, bright-eyed and sharp-minded, enthusiastic and energetic. It's the only way to go bridal gown shopping.

- *Don't settle.* Sure, that first gown you see may indeed be *the one.* You knew it the moment you slipped it on. Plenty of brides cherish their personal tale of "It was the *first one I tried on!*" Even so, we encourage you to try on a range of gowns, just to get a *look* at different styles. After #6 or #7, you may be even more sure of #1. It's kind of like dating . . . you may have to "try on" several to find the perfect one, perhaps finding that nothing beats the original . . . or that everything beats the original.

- *Don't turn looking for a dress into a career.* There is such a thing as overdoing the gown shopping. Make a reasonable plan for a limited timeframe, visit the best salons or shops for your tastes and budget, and choose your gown from a finite selection of options.

- *Don't include a cast of thousands while choosing.* You may be wise to set off on your first scouting mission with one assistant, perhaps your maid of honor. Too many opinions at this early stage will only slow you down. You can bring Mom and Mom-in-law and the girls in on the action once you're down to two or three choices.

location, location, location

Sometimes finding just the right shop leads you to the gown of your dreams. You know as soon as you enter. The sales assistants are personable, the dress selection is amazing, and the brides shopping there are handled with care. You can indulge your fantasy of being treated to petit fours and champagne while seven sales associates cater to your every whim (who wouldn't love that royal treatment?), or left to your own exploration with minimal fanfare. The shop you choose should offer what you're looking for and correspond to who you are, and you might be just as happy at a consignment shop, antique store, upscale chic salon, or a department store during its Memorial Day sale.

Here, then, are some tips on finding the right source for your treasure.

The Designer Flagship Salon: Bride's Delight

Many designers run flagship salons where you can schedule an appointment to see their entire collection. This is an excellent way to view a collection that keeps coming up among all your clippings.

Such salons are typically run by appointment. A good reputation means high demand, so prepare to wait for your scheduled appointment at the best salons. Make sure you book well in advance, as the most popular and well-established designers can be fully booked for months ahead. Be aware, the flagship salon is normally based in the city in which the designer lives. As expected, Manhattan has now become the Mecca for the flagship salon, and many a bride follow the confetti trail to New York City for a trip to "Bridal Disney."

You may even get to see the actual designer running around, tape measure in hand, sketching out requested design accents and presenting fabric swatches to lucky brides. Participating in its very creation can be exhilarating and make your dress even more precious to you! Your gown will need to be special-ordered so leave plenty of time to find, purchase, order, accessorize, and commence fittings of your gown.

Specialty Bridal Salons: Bride Candy

Not every bride wants or has the time, inclination, or budget to go to New York City to take the ultimate bride ride. Across America and around the world, a variety of highly specialized bridal salons have emerged, representing many of the best American and international designers available. The specialty salon is just that. Because they deal with brides daily, they understand your particular requirements. Again, prepare in advance, as they typically take appointments only and will need to special-order the dress of your dreams. Make sure you don't find yourself in a time crunch.

Large Bridal Stores: Bride-o-Rama

These stores normally carry the dresses of many designers and tend to be less personal than specialty bridal salons. You will find a much broader price point here, so prepare for hustle and bustle as a large gathering of brides and their entourages may be whisking through the racks and lining up at the dressing rooms. These stores normally require appointments for individualized service, and sell both ready-to-wear and you-must-wait special-order dresses.

The Department Store: Dreams and Lingerie—Second Floor

Many larger department stores devote a portion of their floor space to brides' and bridesmaids' fashions. These departments work almost autonomously from the rest of the store in that the personnel understand the bride's very specific requirements and avoid paint-brushing the service code without adjustments as other departments typically do. Department stores, especially those that have a good reputation

Aisle Style

For a much greater selection of appropriate wedding dresses found in department stores, be sure to check during the peak seasons for stocking formal and informal gowns in both the wedding and the dress areas of these department stores. That would be pre–prom season of February to May, and during the winter holidays and post-holiday sales.

in larger cities and regional centers, offer a nice variety of dress and accessory options. You may need an appointment for bridal attention, although you're likely to get plenty of help as a walk-in, and they just might carry dresses by the designer you are itching to try.

Large Bridal Discount Stores: Bride Idea

You need to do your homework before you go to large bridal discounters. Knowing exactly what designer or styles you are looking for is extremely helpful, as these mammoth stores tend to cram in a range of dresses from high-quality designers to less than stellar manufacturers. For such a large discount, you'd better be ready to work your arms at those dress racks, pushing aside heavy gown bags and elbowing away that girl who has her eye on the same gown. If you've made an appointment, it's likely to be rushed. Be prepared for high-speed service at a discount, depending on how crowded the store is when you go there. You can either purchase dresses ready to wear and or on special order.

Dressmakers: Bride Ambition

Having your gown made from scratch can fulfill your ultimate dream. You may have definite ideas about the fabric, the style of train, the neckline, the back detail, and the amount of lace and embroidery, but you haven't seen anything in the salons, stores, or catalogs that matches your vision. Your solution: Hire a quality dressmaker to custom-create the gown of your dreams.

If you go this route, be aware that many dressmakers will say they are willing to make your dress. However, it's important that you ask to see a portfolio of the dressmaker's work to be sure they *specialize* in bridal dresses (and we mean specialize!) and speak to several clients the dressmaker refers you to. This option can end well, but you need to do extensive homework and allow plenty of time for the dressmaker to complete your gown. Also, be advised that what you think will look good, even when sketched, can be very different when the dress is completed and you try it on.

You need to understand issues such as the way the fabric and linings fall, whether the dress is cut on the bias or straight, the importance of an internal bustier, embellishments, color of linings, sleeves that may restrict movement—especially if you venture into the world of gown design without a fashion degree! It's not a good time for you to learn the intricacies of dressmaking; you must be confident that your seamstress really knows how to make your vision a reality. Proceed with caution, and consider that you may be better off requesting stylistic changes to an existing, well-made gown at a quality salon.

Vintage: Bride Epic

Certain brides of the 21st century refuse to think of anything but vintage for their wedding gowns, and you know who you are! Very specific brides choose vintage dresses, often lace sheaths of olde rather than true wedding dresses, to make a highly romantic statement. Classic dresses may include beautiful slip satins, pleated laces, and lovely hand embroidery, often in warm tones of cream and ivory. This particular style of dress can be found at vintage stores and is often teamed with netted hats, laced veils, or hair jewelry. Although very 1940s, such dresses can have a rather contemporary and stylish feel when worn with the right attitude.

To find a store that sells vintage dresses in your area, check the Internet or Yellow Pages of your phone book. You may, however, be lucky enough to stumble upon a vintage dress at your favorite open-air market. If the vintage dress you love fits you well and is in excellent condition, you are likely to spend less than you budgeted for your dress, as vintage dresses should not cost more than about $1,000, and typically average between $600 and $700.

This option suits the very particular bride who wants to create an entire look and feeling that complements the vintage theme. Whatever you do, make sure you carefully inspect the condition of the dresses, especially the dress you decide on. With age comes wear and tear, so investigate this gown fully before committing to it. When doing the vintage look, make sure you go all the way with your theme. A vintage-style dress can look out of place if it is not in the right context, so consider all your wedding elements, including bridesmaids' and men's outfits, invitations, reception decoration, and music. When thought through carefully, the look can be breathtaking and leave a lasting impression of you and your groom.

Mother's or Sister's Dress: Bridal Ties

Some brides choose to go down the aisle in the dress previously worn by their mother or a sister. This can be beautiful and sentimental as well as a budget-saving selection. To make the most of this emotional choice, we urge you to consider these suggestions:

- When you unpack the dress, be sure that it is in excellent condition.

- If the dress has age and wear marks, get expert advice from a reputable cleaner. If the cleaner is unable to remove all the stains, check with a tailoring expert on how to obscure marks with well-placed appliqués, accents, or embroidery.

- Some portions of the dress fabric may have decayed through age. Replacement is sometimes possible, depending on where the problem lies and how easily the problem area can be camouflaged.

- Try on the dress to be sure it's not too big, too small, or simply does not suit you.

- If the dress is in excellent condition, basically fits you, and has only stains that can be removed, it will normally need alterations and additional restyling to update or fit in with your ideas of how you wish to look.

Aisle Style

Only a very few people specialize in restyling services specializing in bridal gowns. Visit michelleroth.com and enter "restyling" for more information.

If you do take the family heirloom gown route, keep this in mind: If you do not love the dress when you try it on, it can be difficult to tell your mother or sister that you don't wish to wear her dress after all. They may be so caught up with the meaning of your wearing one of their gowns that your decision will disappoint them. We have full faith that you can break the news gently and diplomatically, explaining that her gown is simply different from *your* idea of your dream gown, and that harmony will return along with lasting goodwill due to the fact that you considered their fine gown in the first place. Offer to have their gown represerved for future generations. This gesture shows your consideration of their feelings, as well as great pride in the dress as a family heirloom worth packaging with care.

Something Borrowed: Bride Beware

Some brides borrow a dress from a friend who has already taken her glide down the aisle. This happens due to traditional or religious reasons, as a form of goodwill or charity, or as the perfect answer to a budget crunch. If you borrow a wedding dress, be very clear what the friend loaning you the dress expects.

Is it yours to keep or should you return it? If you're to return it, how does she want it returned? If the dress is only on loan and not yours to keep, be sure your friend realizes that you may need to alter the dress. Are alterations acceptable? What is your agreement should you accidentally stain the gown? Will you be expected to pay for stain-removal services? If the stain proves permanent despite your efforts to return it in perfect condition, will your friend accept the fact that her precious gown just might bear a cherry-red mark for all eternity? Answer all these questions before you even try the dress on. Best friends have become estranged over borrowed wedding dresses, so weigh future risks against present favors. It might not be worth the savings.

Consignment Stores: Bride Be Savvy

Consignment stores often have a variety of ready-to-wear dresses. They are pre-loved gowns that are being sold on consignment by the owner for a fraction of the original cost. Her castoff becomes your treasure! Speaking of good fortune, some consignment stores are linked to charities, in which case you know that your money is going to an excellent cause. The dresses can be in good to fair condition and, of course, will normally need additional alterations. If you are comfortable with the setting, are *not* uncomfortable with the idea of a pre-worn dress, and find a dress you love, you could walk away elated with the perfect dress in hand.

Sample Sales: Bridal Budget

Most salons or bridal stores have an annual or biannual sale of actual gowns the store has had on the racks to provide examples of particular styles. Typically, dozens of brides have tried these on before falling in love with a style and ordering a fresh new one directly from the designer. When the new season's bridal gown collections come around each year, the stores get rid of these sample dresses, which are now "old merchandise," by marking the price off at steep discounts.

If you can actually find your dream dress at a bridal sample sale, you are sure to save hundreds and at times thousands of dollars. However, be equipped to face snaking lines and a crazed atmosphere. With all those gorgeous gowns on sale, veritable busloads of brides from all over the area will swarm the place to find a designer treasure at consignment prices. For your own protection, we recommend you get set before setting off for a sample sale. Here's how:

- Call the store to verify the date of the sale and exact time the sale commences, and to find out whether there are any special requirements (for example, the store may take only certain credit cards, or require cash and cards—no checks).

- Get lots of sleep the night before. You are going to need it!

- Get a head start on your bridal sample sale sisters by getting there as early as possible.

- Educate yourself before you go as to which styles, shapes, color, and fabrics suit you best.

- Be aware that most samples offered come in a size 8 or 10. If you wear a larger size (and let's face it, many of us do), there is no point in trying to squeeze into a fabulously discounted dress that you have no hope of wearing for your wedding. If you are a tiny 2, the available dresses are likely to be too large, and altering them might be a huge headache for your seamstress. When

Aisle Style

When you go to a sample sale, keep in mind that stains or marks may be permanent. Ask yourself, "Could I walk down the aisle with the stain or mark?" Of course, the location of the stain or mark is critical. Floor dirt that has accumulated around the skirt or train is easily removed by either dry cleaning or shortening the dress. If the gown is already long on you, a simple alteration can cut away the entire problem. Or, if adding extra beading or lace can camouflage the mark, you will have no problem. So when you see a scuff on the train, consider whether or not it can be made invisible. *No problem.*

you take into consideration the construction and flow of a gown, it's always best to buy one that's close to your actual size.

- Expect to find marks and stains on sample sale dresses. Don't delude yourself into thinking that you're the first bride who has located, touched, or tried it on. You're likely to find lipstick marks at the neckline, scuffmarks on the hem, deodorant stains under the arms, and other assorted marks and scrapes.

- Tears, missing buttons, and missing beadwork can also be characteristic of sample sale dresses. If you, your mother, or your family dressmaker is confident that you can work magic on your dress, you have sample sale insurance and your problem is solved.

- Wear clothing that is comfortable, easy to remove, and has no extra buttons, ties, or encumbrances that will slow you down. We are talking dress for speed! Some brides-to-be are happy to wear gym-appropriate sports bras and bike shorts for easy, modest quick-changing with minimal fuss.

- Wear appropriate lingerie. The undergarments you wear when trying on dresses at a sample sale can be important. If you are going for a strapless dress, wear a strapless bustier. Slinky sheaths are your desire? Then you need a good supporting bra. Try to wear the type of lingerie that your dress style requires so you can get a better look at the fit of the gown.

- Take along shoes with an approximate heel size and the approximate accessories you are thinking of wearing on your wedding day. Leave as little as possible to the imagination.

- Throw modesty out the door. You may need to undress in front of a bevy of brides-to-be and their entourages. This may require the ability to try on the dress where you are standing—not a comfortable situation for the blushing bride. Just pretend you're wearing a bikini at the beach and stand tall.

- Take your mother or your best friend only. You will need to make accurate, quick decisions, and must get immediate feedback from someone who will tell you the truth. Bringing a group of friends into *this* scene is cruel to both you and them.

- Be prepared to be subjected to stringent final sale and non-refundable policies. You are likely to be wedded to your decision, so think clearly before you jump.

Many a bride has found the dress at a sample sale. Whatever you do, don't compromise, otherwise you will be haunted with misgivings. Choosing your gown should *not* be something you'll regret.

keeping your perspective

Pack a good dose of bridal reality, an excellent sense of humor, and a flexible attitude before you set out on the sample sale experience. Know that you either will or won't find the dress you love, the one that meets all your criteria, at a dramatically reduced price. If you don't walk away with the ideal dress, the experience will certainly provide you with a deeper understanding of what you do want for your wedding dress.

Bridal Rental Stores: Bride-to-Go

Brides today also have the option of renting their dresses. This is an entirely different experience from purchasing, borrowing, or buying on sale. Remember that the dress you try on in the rental store may not be the actual dress you'll wear on your wedding day. The store will have you try on a variety of dresses in the styles you are considering, and they typically have duplicates of every style to fulfill bookings, especially over the summer.

As long as you know that and have the right attitude, you are sure to save tremendously. However, if you can't allow even tiny imperfections on your dress, then steer clear of rental shops. If you are unhappy with the dress when you pick it up two days before your wedding, you can do very little about the flaws. Rest assured that the many lines of small print in the stores' terms, regulations, and conditions will have them well covered.

how will i know?

Of course, the big question on every bride's lips is: *How will I know when I've found "the one," the dress of my dreams?*

You want to make the correct decision, right? This is your once-in-a-lifetime wedding dress choice, and you want to get it 100 percent perfect. Well, hang in there . . . *we are going to help you do just that!*

chapter 6

Knowing When You've Found *The Dress*

The dress. Your wedding dress. Sweet dreams are made of this.

A milestone in your wedding preparation process is finding a gown in the fabric and style that encompass your dreams. The path that leads you to the front of the aisle takes a lot of diligence, especially when it comes to finding the perfect dress.

Okay, you have done your homework—enthusiastically studied the bridal magazines, visited your favorite Web sites during lunch break, spoken to girlfriends who have recently married, seen a plethora of bride-themed movies, rented your favorite love story DVDs, and watched taped segments of bridal design fashion shows. You are primed and pumped and in the mood. So let's go shopping!

If you have not already landed on *planet bride* after receiving your engagement ring; booking your ceremony and reception; speaking to your priest, rabbi, or celebrant; or having friends bombard you with detailed questions for which you have no answers to right now, then get ready, because here it comes.

now entering the bridal zone

No other dress purchase has such significance or follows so much unwritten ritual as buying your wedding dress. The atmosphere that you will encounter in a bridal store may indeed seem like another planet. You'll hear unfamiliar terminology bandied about as if it were commonly used by the rest of the world, *except you.* Phrases such as "cathedral length veils," "three-tier crinolines," "tiaras," "corsets," "bustling," "blusher," "drop-waisted princess-line dress," "charmeuse fabric," and "silk white" are casually spoken in hushed tones. In addition, you'll hear talk about headpiece appointments, the alterations schedule, swatches for matching color, dress sketches for the cake decorator, and themes for the invitations that may leave you befuddled.

from henry

A wedding dress is far more than fabric, beading, crinolines, and lining. A bride pours her dreams into her dress, which is why those who watch her walk down the aisle can feel a magical aura.

Be not befuddled! A bride with knowledge is a bride in control. So let us take you through what can be the most magnificent part of your entire wedding planning process—finding *the dress.*

On Your Mark, Get Set . . .

When should you start? You may have heard through the grapevine that stores and designers make up ridiculous lead times to pressure you into ordering the first dress you try on.

The truth is that special-order dresses can take four to six months to arrive, and some from international designers sometimes take as long as six to eight months. We recommend starting the process a year in advance, if possible. Whether you buy a ready-made dress off the rack, special-order one, customize a couture-designed dress, rent, buy vintage, consignment store shop, or the like, start looking as soon as you can. With so many choices today, you may need the extra time just to decide which route will best serve your needs and requirements.

When you special-order, you can't go wrong with a twelve-month timetable. Figure that you want the dress in the store two months before so you can commence fittings about six weeks before your wedding date. Often, designers require six to eight months to actually complete the gown from the date of its order, and it is wise to have a two-month buffer just in case you need it.

Twelve months is the optimum time to allow yourself freedom of choice and to minimize rash or harried decisions. Oh, we hear brides from all corners of the globe whining, "But I don't have twelve months!" We understand that not every bride has the luxury of a year, and that many need to condense the process. Fortunately, designers, salons, stores, and dressmakers can usually speed things up. (See page 104 for Danielle Dobin's story of her rush order, custom-made gown.)

If, for whatever reason, you need to arrange for your special-order dress close to the date, most stores and salons and designers charge an express fee between 5 to 20 percent, depending on how close your wedding is. Some dresses—especially beaded dresses that require longer lead times—are simply not orderable if the wedding is less than three months away. Most express fees will start *three* months out from the wedding date. So please, don't put yourself through the extra expense and stress. Leave plenty of time to fantasize, shop, and decide.

Of course, how much time you'll need depends on the method you choose for finding your dress. As you would expect, buying off the rack requires much less lead time than custom-ordering—*if* you can find what you want! Even rental stores that have a great selection experience peak periods over the summer when high demand drains the store of its top designs. The sooner you make your booking, the sooner you know your choice is in place.

We will concentrate on the store experience (broadly speaking) and what you can expect throughout the process. Whichever way you go, remember *time is of the essence.*

Making the First Phone Call

When you contact your initial shortlist of salons and stores (if you are going that route), most will want to work by appointment. Although some will work with walk-ins, it's best that you book an appointment. This way you're more likely to receive the ultimate personalized service from the store's staff, and can enjoy a more relaxed atmosphere and a non-rushed block of time to peruse and try on the gowns.

Appointments and Walk-Ins

Stores that take both appointments and walk-ins are typically more budget oriented than appointment-only salons. You can certainly find the dress of your dreams in a "walk-in" store, but don't expect full service. For many brides, what they *experience* at the shop makes the gown itself more precious to them. If you give up royal treatment for convenience or savings, you lose a lot of service and a bit of the magic.

i don't like your tone of voice

When you call a bridal salon, even if just to find out their business hours and directions, note how the receptionist handles your call. Keep in mind that you will be working with these people to select your most important clothing purchase ever. You will be interacting with the store's team in many instances, so start your assessment of each company's kindness, courtesy, and patience factors from the first "hello."

Your First Visit to the Store

Many a time we have seen a weary bride enter our salon crumpled and exhausted, as if she has just completed a marathon. Most likely, she's trying to cram too many appointments into a single day—or one at the end of an already draining day. How can she possibly enjoy this? Simple answer: She can't. She's taking on too much too soon.

We can't fault this bride, though. The 21st-century motto seems to be "Rush, rush, rush!" Many brides cram schedules from early morning 'til late at night, answer a constantly ringing cell phone, and simply haven't enough hours in the day. Even so, our advice is this: Don't even *try* to complete your gown-shopping expedition in one day. Block off several days, several weekends if you must, and devote that time to the individual shop you're visiting. No one is timing you with a stopwatch; no one is clicking a fast-forward button on your visits to salons. Spread out your appointments, take your time, *breathe deeply,* and look around you. Your first visit should *not* be rushed.

Have Airline Ticket, Will Travel

Of course, how you space your appointments will depend on the locations you plan to visit, at which store or salon you schedule your first appointment, and what your schedule is like. Some brides like to shop locally, some will drive to a nearby city for the best their region has to offer, and others will fly to a distant big city for the ultimate fashion salons. Michelle Roth has brides flying in from Florida and California, and even from Australia, Hungary, London, and New Zealand, for appointments, which illustrates how much some 21st-century brides invest in this once-in-a-lifetime gown search. In our experience, great distances are no impediment to a bride's determination.

Your Gown Shopping Entourage

Brides can exercise many options concerning who they wish to accompany them on their first bridal appointments. Here are a few common choices:

Just Me

Some brides decide to navigate their first appointment alone. These brides want to concentrate on their own impressions—without the opinions, judgments, or interference of well-meaning mothers, maids, sisters, or friends. If you are one of these relatively rare but increasingly common brides who prefer to keep the initial appointment focused yet relaxed, be proud of your liberated status and rejoice in your freedom.

Going solo may be for you if you are fiercely independent, already know what suits your body shape, and know what you want to achieve on your wedding day. The solo-shopper normally makes tremendous initial progress because she is truly focused. It's *her day, so she'll do it her way!* She knows herself best, so she seeks her own initial reactions. We recommend this method of trying on gowns in private, then narrowing the selections down to your favorites. At *that point,* if you wish, you can invite in your "opinions committee" for constructive feedback, enjoy the proud and beaming looks of admiration from family and friends, and watch for that tear of joy from your mother or other dress confidantes that helps you make a final decision.

Some new-generation brides bring along a unique bridal gown committee including aunts, brothers, fathers, even fiancés! Of course, not all brides require a group review; many make their decisions solo (at

Happily Ever After

Jodi Della Femina, a favorite Michelle Roth bride from New York City (see her feature on page 199), says she was aware of the old theory that "if your mother cries when you try on a dress, that's the one." Well, Jodi tried on at least forty dresses, and the theory didn't seem to be working. She went from shop to shop, expecting to have fun choosing a dress but finding nothing but disappointment. "I didn't feel welcome at some stores," says Jodi. "Some salespeople had an attitude, so the experience was just no fun at all."

Then she found the right salon with the right attitude: Michelle Roth's salon in New York. "This was the experience I'd been hoping for," says Jodi. The first dress she tried on at Michelle's was just okay. But when she stepped into the second dress . . . her mother's eyes filled with tears. And that was when Jodi knew she'd found The One.

By the way, Jodi was searching for an appropriate gown for her beach wedding. She didn't have a complete vision in mind at the outset, but what she found was perfect: a white A-line dress with organza three-quarter sleeves decorated with crystals to look like sparkling water drops to suit her oceanside theme. With her matching veil, also with crystal "water-drops," her dream wedding gown became an actuality.

least until the credit card comes out!). Such self-assured brides can make their gowns a surprise to not just their grooms, but to all their loved ones and guests on the wedding day! Talk about a grand entrance!

The rules of old have bent to accommodate real people, and we love the fact that we can rejoice in newfound freedom yet simultaneously soak in various cultures and traditions on this new Planet Bride.

Mom and Me

The most traditional, tried, and tested appointment attendee is Mom. She's dreamt of seeing you in your wedding gown since before you played dress-up with a pillowcase "veil." Knowing that this is one of Mom's greatest dreams and visions as well, most brides happily invite their mother to attend the dress appointments as a trusted adviser. Like Jodi Della Femina, many brides look for Mother's eyes to tear up, signaling *this is the one!*

Because families of today are often spread far and wide, it is not unusual for mothers to fly in for gown appointments, or for brides to fly to her. Should this be the case, the time you can spend looking together will often be limited and you're likely to condense your decision-making to fit into the time you have together. If you must ship Mom in, it is advisable to arrange appointments to view your short-listed collections first. You've searched, scouted, and tried on a selection of gowns and have narrowed the list to your top three, or five, or ten favorite dresses for Mom to see. This is probably the best way to avoid stress if your time together is short.

My Best Friends and My Dress

Sometimes brides invite best friends and close family members besides Mom to come along on initial appointments. Who and how many supporting cast members you invite to your first appointments can make the difference between getting constructive or destructive feedback. When brides walk in with noisy exuberant groups, the bride often leaves dazed and frazzled. Your sales consultant or assistant will find keeping track of the varied opinions and group dynamics difficult. Not only can a large group intimidate your consultant, but the participants may take your search less seriously than would a more diligent support cast.

We recommend a limit of three people besides yourself, consisting of your mom (or Mom substitute), your sister(s), and your true best friend for the first appointment. Groups that include more than three plus yourself are more likely to incite bridal party politics, as in "You invited Maud's cousin but not me!" Such scenarios gallop back to you via the gossip trail, and no bride needs that additional headache. This is supposed to be *fun* and meaningful.

first-appointment essentials

Keep a checklist of what to take with you. At a minimum, it will include:

- *Shoes:* If not *the* shoes you'll be wearing on your day, then bring along another pair of the precise heel height you plan to wear.

- *Lingerie:* Wear or pack a solidly constructed standard bra, and a strapless bra if you're considering a strapless dress.
  (*Note:* Some salons and stores keep a varied supply of both shoes and bras on hand for bridal gown try-ons.)

- *Your binder of clippings.* Carry your "can't-live-without-it carryall" so you can refer to what's in it and add new information.

- *An open mind.* Please do *not* go to your first appointment with a strong predisposed opinion. Yes, you may certainly have the shape, color, and style at the top of your mind, but keep your mind open in case there are even better ideas out there. Learn from the experts what color, fabric, quality, and silhouette suit you best.

  So often a bride comes to Michelle Roth asking for one look and leaves with another. The reason is simple: She never considered some of the many creative gowns available that look stunning on her. If a dress style you hadn't considered takes your breath away when you try it on, why fight it? After all, that's the reaction you want from your groom, family, and friends.

It can be just as productive to put on dresses that you *don't* immediately fall in love with as ones you do. Half the dress decision is knowing what you *don't* like and why.

- *Knowledge of your silhouette and body shape.* Come to your appointment equipped with essential information and descriptions on gown silhouettes. Some tried and tested shapes work best for certain body types. We also strongly encourage brides to try on various shapes to determine what suits them best and what they feel beautiful in. This is your time to be Cinderella at the ball.

Which Silhouettes Suit Your Body Type Best?

Broad shoulders (see sketch 1): Broad-shouldered brides may want to veer from halter and off-the-shoulder necklines, which tend to accentuate the shoulders. Try strapless and scoop necklines.

Fuller busted (see sketch 2): Brides who are fuller busted must make sure their undergarments do them justice! A firm corset is essential! We then find that scoop and square necklines cut straight

Sketch 1. Broad-shoulder gown.   *Sketch 2.* Fuller busted gown.

Sketch 3. Heavy arms.

Sketch 4. Hourglass.

Sketch 5. Pear-shaped.

across the front with straps tend to diminish fuller busted figures and present more flattering necklines. Stay away from bateau and jewel necklines, as they overemphasize the bust. (Refer to our primer of necklines on pages 92–94.) Be sure the neckline is fitted properly. Strapless is still okay, though too much cleavage can be inappropriate and unflattering.

Heavy arms (see sketch 3): Nearly every bride who comes to the salon mentions her arms somewhere in the process. Either, "Now I'll really have to work out on those arms!" or "How can I cover my upper arm without making the dress look too heavy?" One way is to find a dress that gives the illusion of covered arms using fabric that's either completely sheer or includes some beading or embroidery. In solid fabric, usually three-quarter or long sleeve works best as it elongates the line of the arm. The cap sleeve, off-the-shoulder sleeve, or sleeves that finish just above the elbow make the upper body look wide, which will overemphasize the upper arms.

Hourglass (see sketch 4): Two-piece and corset dresses enhance the hourglass figure. Anything that accentuates the bride's waist is in. Again, the correct lingerie is essential.

Pear-shaped (see sketch 5): The best silhouettes for pear-shaped figures are often fitted bodices, complemented by A-line and/or ball-gown skirts that define small waists and disguise fuller hips. A chapel length veil or train will add longer, sleeker lines, again accentuating the bride's waist. Avoid slinky, clingy fabrics such as charmeuse, silk-knit jersey, or chiffon. Such fabric tends to gather around your hips.

Petite (see sketch 6): Clean, unbroken contours without too much fabric tend to elongate without dominating the petite bride, so the A-line shape and sheath usually work much better for petite brides than big ball gowns. Long, clean veils without heavy trims or decoration ensure that the petite bride is framed delicately rather than visually overwhelmed.

Pregnant (see sketch 7): The best shape here is the princess line or Empire waist with an A-line skirt. Michelle says, "I usually take the initial measurements and ask the bride to return twice to remeasure her as the body during pregnancy will change in ways that no one can predict. Some pregnant brides are so proud that they wear a dress of more body-conscious fabric that shows their form."

Tall: Most silhouettes are great for the tall bride, who has the advantage of being able to carry almost any dress style. From smaller to full cathedral trains, the tall bride can be toned down or as dramatic as she wishes.

Thick-waisted: Princess-line, Empire, and Basque waists are most flattering on the thick-waisted bride.

Sketch 6. Petite.

Sketch 7. Pregnant.

Fabulous Fabrics

Just as your wedding dress style must be appropriate to your setting, so too must the dress fabric. The season will determine the type of fabric that will be most comfortable for you (see table 2 for a breakdown of which fabrics work for you). First, here are details on the composition of wedding fabrics:

- **Silk:** This natural fiber is the most frequently used fabric for wedding dresses. The texture and weight of silk vary in density.

- **Manmade fabric:** Polyester, acetate, and rayon can sometimes resemble their silk counterparts.

a primer on necklines: finding the perfect shape

Necklines really define your dress. Suitability is everything, so take a quick look at our A–Z neckline guide. Here's a basic primer on the most popular styles of neckline shapes for your use:

Bateau (see sketch 8): Wide neckline following the line of your collarbone. This adds a lift to the bustline.
    YES: smaller busted
    No: fuller busted

Halter (see sketch 9): Straps are tied to the back of the neck. Neckline extends up to encircle the neck, then may plunge down in back.
    YES: brides who want to show off their shoulders and backs
    No: brides with narrow backs

High Collar (see sketch 10): Neckline reaches to top of the neck.
    YES: modest and religious dressing; great for elongating the neck
    No: brides with long necks

Jewel (see sketch 11): A rounded neckline that scoops just above the collarbone.
    YES: conservative, modest brides; brides with smaller busts
    No: bigger busted brides

Sketch 8. Bateau neckline.

Sketch 9. Halter.

Sketch 10. High collar.

Sketch 11. Jewel neckline.

a primer on necklines *(continued)*

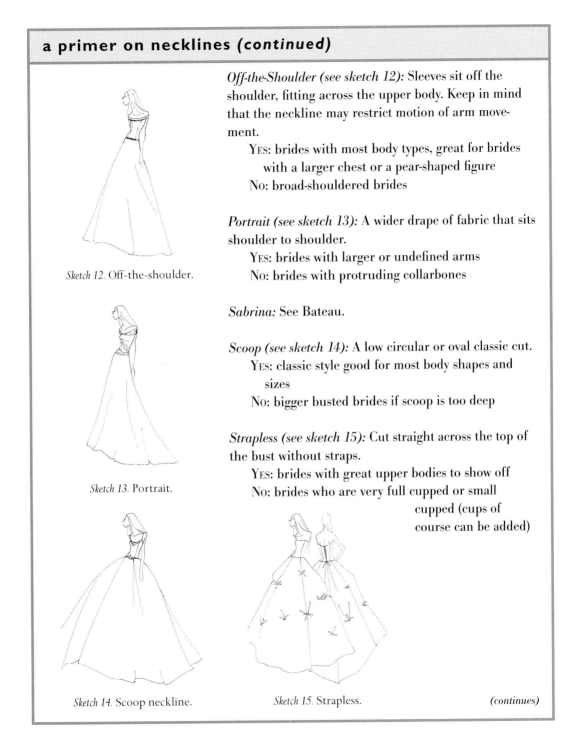

Off-the-Shoulder (see sketch 12): Sleeves sit off the shoulder, fitting across the upper body. Keep in mind that the neckline may restrict motion of arm movement.

 YES: brides with most body types, great for brides with a larger chest or a pear-shaped figure
 No: broad-shouldered brides

Portrait (see sketch 13): A wider drape of fabric that sits shoulder to shoulder.

 YES: brides with larger or undefined arms
 No: brides with protruding collarbones

Sabrina: See Bateau.

Scoop (see sketch 14): A low circular or oval classic cut.

 YES: classic style good for most body shapes and sizes
 No: bigger busted brides if scoop is too deep

Strapless (see sketch 15): Cut straight across the top of the bust without straps.

 YES: brides with great upper bodies to show off
 No: brides who are very full cupped or small cupped (cups of course can be added)

Sketch 12. Off-the-shoulder.

Sketch 13. Portrait.

Sketch 14. Scoop neckline.

Sketch 15. Strapless.

(continues)

a primer on necklines (continued)

Sweetheart (see sketch 16): A heart-shaped neckline that dips to reveal décolletage.
YES: brides with décolletage to show
No: too many cups may runneth over

V-Neck (see sketch 17): Sharper shaped in a V-cut.
YES: brides with thicker hips and bigger busts
No: brides with narrow shoulders

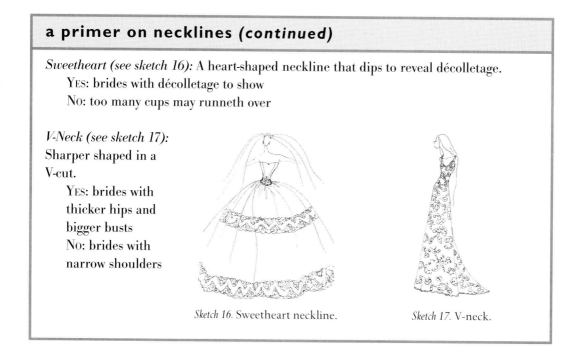

Sketch 16. Sweetheart neckline.

Sketch 17. V-neck.

veils

Our favorite accessory to the bridal gown is the veil, which adds atmosphere as the bride walks down the aisle. However, brides should consider tradition, personal taste, and appropriateness when deciding whether or not to wear one.

Veil Lengths

A key decision for brides who choose to wear a veil is what length is best for them. Here are descriptions of the major choices:

- *Blusher:* One layer of tulle to cover the face, then flipped back at the end of the ceremony. Either worn throughout the reception or removed after the ceremony.

- *Cathedral:* Usually 3½ to 4 yards long. Dramatic.

Table 2. Wedding Gown Fabrics Appropriate for the Seasons

Fabric	Spring	Summer	Autumn	Winter
Brocade Textured, distinct pattern sometimes highlighted with metallic thread	✔		✔	✔
Charmeuse Luxurious and lightweight fabric with a sheen. Often associated with glamour of the '40s	✔	✔	✔	✔
Chiffon Sheer, ethereal, soft fabric	✔	✔	✔	✔
Crepe and satin-back crepe Soft fabric, more dense than charmeuse	✔	✔	✔	✔
Duchesse satin Dense weave fabric, also called silk face satin. The most popular of bridal fabrics	✔	✔	✔	✔
Dupioni and silk shantung Ranges from smooth to textured	✔	✔	✔	✔
Faille Very small-ribbed texture	✔	✔	✔	✔
Gazar Light, crisp fabric	✔	✔		
Georgette Lightweight fabric sometimes confused with crepe	✔	✔	✔	✔
Illusion Sheer fabric such as veil net. Used as part of a dress (sleeves or back, for example)	✔	✔	✔	✔

(continues)

Table 2. Wedding Gown Fabrics Appropriate for the Seasons (*continued*)

Fabric	Spring	Summer	Autumn	Winter
Mikado Stiffer fabric with slight sheen that has gained popularity	✔	✔	✔	✔
Organza Sheer fabric with more body than chiffon	✔	✔	✔	✔
Silkface satin organza Similar to but more opaque than organza	✔	✔	✔	✔
Taffeta Light crisp fabric sometimes mistaken for faille	✔	✔	✔	✔
Tulle Fabric used for veils and ball-gown skirts	✔	✔	✔	✔
Velvet Dense luxurious fabric			✔	✔

- *Chapel:* Usually 2½ yards long and placed directly behind the headpiece.

- *Circle veil:* Cut from one piece of tulle in the shape of a circle with a comb in the center, this veil can be worn as a blusher. Length can vary according to effect desired.

- *Fingertip:* Usually two tiers, the longest of which is at fingertip level.

- *Floor length:* Usually measured to fall an inch above floor length (with your wedding shoes on), this veil can be worn throughout the reception.

---

when shall i remove my veil?

When you remove your veil is entirely up to you. Some brides like to leave their veil on throughout the reception, others wear their veil for the ceremony only, and other brides prefer no veil (just hair jewelry). All combinations are acceptable. The bride's choice depends on her traditions and the effect she wants to create.

- *Mantilla:* A long veil trimmed all the way around, usually with lace.

- *Pouf:* The height of the pouf depends on how much of the veil is gathered to the comb. The more gathers, the higher the pouf; fewer gathers means less height.

shoes

A moderate heel height is always advisable for your wedding day, as you are going to be on your feet most of the day and night! If you're not a towering-stiletto woman, definitely avoid this style on your day. If your wedding will be outdoors, go for thicker and wider heels to avoid sinking into damp grass. Your style of shoe is again completely up to you. You might choose simple white satin pumps or lace-up Victorian boots, or even step into a pair of bridal sneakers when the dancing begins. Hidden discreetly beneath your gown, those sneakers and slip-ons will save your feet! Plus, you can get adorable styles of decorated bridal sneakers or skimmers with glued-on lace appliqués.

accessories

Your chosen accessories might be as simple as jeweled hair ornaments to be revealed after you remove your veil and headpiece, or you might consider your wedding day jewelry your final touch for the perfect wedding look. You might wear diamond earrings, or a draping Tiffany diamond necklace, or pearls. In many cases, the bride wears the groom's gift of jewelry, or she might wear her mother's or grandmother's jewels in the family name. Whatever your chosen style of jewelry, be sure you consider the cut of your neckline, style of your gown, and the hairstyle you plan to wear so you can choose jewelry in shapes and sizes that are perfect for your wedding day look.

carrying yourself across the dress threshold

Whether you enter by appointment or simply drop in to a bridal salon or shop, pay attention to your first impressions. Is there a hushed atmosphere? Are you greeted graciously by someone who seems genuinely pleased to see you? Are you catered to in any way—offered a seat and magazine, and perhaps water, juice, champagne, or coffee? Do the consultants look relaxed and comfortable? Are you treated like a special guest? Do you feel special in this little corner of the wedding universe? This can be a major indicator of how an establishment is run.

So often, brides tell us that feeling comfortable influenced their final dress purchase. The reason is simple. Brides are investing tremendous confidence in the designer, salon, store, or dressmaker to turn their dreams into reality. The only track record they can really go on is word of mouth, gut instinct, and finely tuned bride radar. A bride sees all!

Of course, nothing is quite like stepping through the threshold of a bridal store for your first, initial appointment. You see gowns displayed like museum pieces along the wall, spot-lit from above, and jeweled tiaras waiting on glass shelves or in display cases to be perched on your head. Perhaps another bride stands on her pedestal before a full-wall mirror for her first look after her final fitting. The entire salon has an air of dreamlike perfection and indulgence. If you have traversed this hallowed ground before as a bridesmaid or for your own sister, you will be surprised how different it is for you. Yes, this is happening! We have heard from many a bride that some bridal stores, salons, and rental shops can be outright intimidating.

Once Upon a Dress . . .

At first meeting, you must convey to the designer or person assisting you the fundamentals about your wedding. Knowing where your wedding will be held, the formality level, the style and theme, even the signature hues you've selected as colors for your maids, décor, and flowers gives your gown stylist *fundamental* information to help you select the gown that will prove the most important piece of your wedding puzzle, the center piece to which so many other pieces must connect. And you thought this was just a dress!

Information to be shared with your consultant should include the following:

- The wedding date

- Level of formality

- Number of expected guests

- Location of the ceremony

- Location of the reception

- The type of wedding (outdoor wedding, indoor wedding, beach wedding, church wedding, etc.)

- Theme and feel for the wedding

- Particular gown shapes and fabric you have found appealing so far (Bring out your trusty binder!)

breathe in through the nose, out through the mouth . . .

You have now set up a series of appointments that you'll go to alone, with Mother, or with a combination of Mother, sisters, and best friends. Whatever the aggravations of your day, week, or month, let them go, and set out for your appointment as fresh and as relaxed as you can be. You're likely to feel nervous, anxious, excited, overwhelmed, or some combination of these. You are embarking on what can be a magical experience, not knowing what to expect.

- What you see as your best features (such as arms or waist) that you may wish to make the most of

- The level of family influence and involvement

Try to summarize your thoughts on the dress of your dreams. Use your own words to present a focused picture of what you want, and your consultant will understand far better than you think.

Mirror, Mirror on the Wall, Which Shape Is Best of All?

After you and your consultant build an "Identi-kit" of your wedding gown wishes according to style, theme, formality, and preferences, it's time to go "bridal bungee jumping." Free float while you allow the consultant to bring out or direct you to the dresses she or he thinks may hit the mark. Honestly, the number of brides who say, "This is nothing like I thought I would end up with" is staggering.

Sometimes the bride comes in with a misconception of what suits her and her body best. Even if you have done a lot of evening and formal attire shopping, which is quite different from buying your wedding gown, you aren't expected to know what will flatter you. As your consultant starts pulling out the dress confections for you to salivate over, you are one step closer to making the decision in finding *the one.*

from sharon

If you can produce color photos of your ceremony and reception locations at this point (and some couples do plan the settings out first!), all the better! Gown designers and fashion consultants are usually familiar with the most popular ballrooms and wedding locales in your area, but by seeing pictures of the site that you downloaded from the Internet or were given by location managers, your gown consultant can better visualize the best dress for your wedding.

First Dress Is Best?

Is it possible that the very first dress you try on could be the one?

It happens far more often than you would believe. Brides can be instantly drawn to their gown by their own gut reaction. Without analyzing, they have made a choice based on a subliminal attraction to their dress. If this happens to you, we recommend that you try on other dresses to be sure. Still, the path can lead right back to the first dress you tried on. We see it all the time: Love at first sight.

Narrowing Down the Choices

A more likely scenario to your first series of appointments is leaving with two or three dresses noted and quoted that you are seriously "in-like" with. This is also the time to make sure you get price quotes for all the items you like—veils, headpieces, shoes, jewelry, lingerie—as well as alteration and other charges, *and* to personally record each item and its price in your bridal binder. Get a solid grip on where the prices lie relative to your budget. At the end of your first round of appointments, you might have bought *the* dress, or gone away to do some serious consideration.

Round Two

After visiting all the stores on your shortlist (and do try to keep it short!), whether with or without your mother or advisory committee, you are ready to make the deciding round. You have gone through your "seriously in-like" list of dresses and condensed it to a "could be in love with" list. You call for appointments (or have already made return arrangements) and are ready for serious decision-making. Keep your judging panel as small as possible. Not everyone invited to your first set of appointments needs to be schlepped to your second ones. Keep it easy, joyful, and pressure-free. Most important, keep focused.

The Career Bride . . . or Night of 1000 Veils

Brides searching for their perfect dress can understandably fall into the trap of "Career Bride." There is nothing wrong with exploring the universe of bridal options available, and why shouldn't you? However, at some point you not only run yourself ragged, but may end up more confused than before you started. Soon, you *hurt* your chance of finding the ideal gown by convincing yourself that it's impossible for you to make a decision. You may think: *With hundreds of possibilities, how will I ever decide on just one?* Or even more frustrating: *There is not one dress that I just love!*

So what adds up to too many dress selection appointments? Only you can answer that. However, spare yourself the anguish of expending so much energy on selection appointments that it becomes a task rather than a delight.

Some brides also go through tremendous loops by cost-comparison shopping. Generally, we all want to spend our money wisely—even more so during the planning of a wedding. This gets tricky when stores carry the same designers, but some offer a price incentive while others don't. You may think that ending up with the same dress from a retailer that offers a price incentive rather than the store in which you initially had your appointment makes good sense. However, sometimes going with the original store of your favorite designer who worked hard with you is best, whether you receive a discount there or not. Inevitably, they will have more vested interest in taking care of your needs throughout the dress choosing and fitting process. And trust us, you *will* need professional care!

Consider service and quality equally important to price while you weigh your options.

Let the Dress Speak

At your second set of appointments (or sometimes third and, yes, sometimes more), you will get a sense of which dresses "speak to you" and will begin to envision yourself walking down the aisle. Pay attention to the distinct difference between your former fantasy of yourself walking down the aisle and your picture of yourself since you began trying on actual dresses.

In most circumstances, you will have your very nearest with you, you will be floating on a raised podium of some sort (your feet won't touch the ground!), you will be looking at every angle of the dress in mirrors that give you a 360-degree panoramic view, swirling, swishing, preening, and . . . you will feel everything . . . or nothing! This is a turning point when many brides feel some element of confusion, or perhaps a tidal wave of emotion. You may feel overtaken by the moment, overwhelmed as time for your decision descends. Some brides simply refuse to listen to their hearts, instead feeling conflicting emotions that manifest as a pure adrenaline rush along with protective numbness. Brides can so fear making the wrong decision that they feel nothing instead of that adrenaline rush.

We witness such feelings many times a day. They are normal and natural. So here's our advice for handling the tidal wave of emotion that rises when you're *this close* to choosing your dream dress. First, *look.* Stop whirling around and *look* at the image in front of you in the mirror and *project* yourself walking down the aisle in the dress. Next, *listen.* Listen with all your heart to the inner you. Remember what you want to create for yourself. The same process that helped you decide on your groom will be put to good use right here. Once you have analyzed all your options, let your heart take control. The final verdict should come from the jury of your heart.

I'll Take That Bodice . . . and This Train . . . and That Embroidery

Why choose just one from among your three favorite gowns, when you can take the best features from each and custom-design your own dress? Yes, it is possible to have the best of all dress worlds by picking design elements from three or four gowns, provided your consultant's trained eye confirms that combining these elements yields a unified, flowing look. We kid you not when we say that the 21st-century bride is independent, assertive, and a true individual. She doesn't limit herself to designs placed before her, but chooses what she wants with great self-knowledge (and perhaps a bit of extra budget). Danielle Dobin from New York City, a recent Michelle Roth bride, did just that (see the profile on page 104 for her story).

© Wendy Brant

© Wendy Brant

Danielle's Story

DANIELLE DOBIN had a big problem. The dress she ordered a year before her wedding in a size 6 came in way too large for her, in a size 14. There was nothing any seamstress could do to fix the problem, and the original dress designer was a nightmare. It would take sixteen weeks for a new gown to come in, the designer said, and they were unwilling to give her a price break on a replacement. To make a long story short, Danielle wound up at Michelle Roth's studio for attempted "plastic surgery" on her gown. Not possible.

So Danielle needed to choose another gown in a hurry. Looking for just the right elements for her new, rush-order gown, she selected the box-pleat ball-gown dress she loved at Michelle's studio, but requested the flattering scoop-neck top from a second dress, and the design of embroidery from a third dress. With elements from three different designs "woven" into her dream gown, she placed her order for delivery with just weeks to spare before her formal wedding at The Breakers in Florida, where she married the very handsome and dashing Christopher Smith (who has quite a story of his own in chapter 10). As you see in the photos, no one was the wiser—and Danielle looked as beautiful as ever.

The 50-50 Split

Often, the choice comes down to two dresses, and here the final vote takes place with almost biblical implications. There is one bride and two gowns, each beautiful in their own way—perhaps similar, perhaps vastly different. When the decision gets this close, we direct our brides to go within and ask themselves:

- "Which dress do I love?"

- "How do I feel in the gown?"

- "Do I feel like *me* in this dress?"

- "Am I playing dress-up, or do I feel like a bride?"

The deciding factor could be everything or nothing. Often one dress is slightly more suitable for what you want for you. Or, as we said earlier, the true winner may "speak" to you. Your gut feeling when you try it on *one more time* is that it just feels right; it belongs on your skin.

Of course, you may have competing views from those who have come to help you make the final decision. Remember that 21st-century brides are blessed with freedom of choice. Mother's final word has subsided and today's brides are seldom caught up in a self-perpetuating cycle that went something like this: Bride wears dress that Mother wants for her. Bride goes down the aisle in dress chosen by Mother. Years later, bride's daughter grows up and gets married. Next-generation bride wears the dress that her mother wants her to wear, thus first-generation bride makes the choice that was denied her when she got married. Thankfully, that barrier has been cast aside.

The bride now listens to Mother's/sister's/best friend's/step-mother's opinions, but keeps healthy boundaries. We hear mothers telling us that their daughters are free to make their own choice. This change of decision-making has had a major impact on the way weddings are planned *as a whole,* with the weddings themselves becoming more a reflection of the bride and groom than the bride and her mother. The ramifications for the 21st-century bride as Mother graciously steps aside and allows the bride to have her say for her day . . . in the gown salon and elsewhere . . . are enormous.

We are also not naive. The dress decision is an area in which bridal politics can be explosive. We recommend that you balance and involve your nearest with the decision and really listen (*yes, listen!*) to their thoughts. They do have good *intentions,* which at times lie underneath what at first seems critical, bossy, judgmental, or controlling. In the end, whatever and however loud their opinions, you must go with your gut instincts. Balance *your* needs of the day— the dress most appropriate for a beach wedding, which shape is most flattering on your pear-shape figure, the one that makes you feel beautiful, that makes you feel bridal (however and whatever that means to you!).

Only one question remains to be answered at the end. *Do you love the dress?* Your answer may be: *Yes, but I love the other one too!* That is possible, but one will suit the day of your wedding, your personality, your style, your budget, your setting, and your heart best. Answer yourself honestly, and emotions will be released. If you have answered every question about the dress, you are ready to commit.

This Is the One!

And so, you have made one important, pivotal decision that will serve as the foundation of your aisle style. Your dress decision will influence what the mothers, bridesmaids, and men will wear, what the decorations at your reception will look like. Now you can select your color themes, unleash your creativity, and design your wedding with your own personal stamp. With your gown chosen, the heavenly doors sweep open to the vast and wonderful world of wedding plans that awaits you.

© Selima Ani Photography

Karri-Leigh's Story

I HAD GONE DRESS SHOPPING with my mother in California, thinking I'd have one of those "This is it!" experiences the moment I put on the dress that was meant for me. It didn't happen. But during a Christmastime visit to New York City, I went with my mother and sister to Michelle Roth's salon for a different experience. All along, knowing I used to be a bit heavier in college, I had been trying on ball gowns with full skirts, something that said "bride-like." But my sister asked me why I wasn't trying on different styles. Why was I afraid to step into something a little more fitted and straight?

So, even though a fitted gown wasn't what I'd pictured for my wedding day, I tried on gowns of different styles than that full skirt. The first one looked great, but when I tried on the second one, I saw the look on my mother's and sister's faces. This was it! I just needed to step out of my preconceived idea of what I should wear, and go for a totally different dimension. And I just felt it. It felt completely right. This was my dress! And quite amazingly, that was when my bridal vision came together. I could actually see myself on my wedding day, wearing this dress. That night I dreamed about my wedding for the first time, seeing every detail clearly. Having "the one" completed my experience.

But the best part was, I went into my bridal binder where I'd stashed a collection of bridal gown photos I had torn out earlier in my gown-shopping process. . . and there it was! I wasn't aware that I had torn out a picture of that exact dress months and months ahead of time! As for the dress itself (and I love telling people about it), it's a strapless dress. It had sleeves originally, but I had them taken off. It's covered with beaded Swarovski crystals, an A-line with a little dip in the back, a short train, fitted and sparkling. It's just incredible.

No Finer Moment!

As you make your deposit at the front reception of the store, soak in the moment. Tears, laughter, shock, surprise—all are good. Flushed or stunned—all reactions are natural. There is no one way you should behave. Celebrate the occasion, whether over a celebratory lunch with your mom and maids, an appointment for a pampering pedicure or massage, or a quick martini toast at a lounge. Take a moment from your busy schedule to smell the roses! This, dear bride, is your once-in-a-lifetime moment come true.

Wait a Minute . . . Did I Make a Mistake?

When you've made your final choice, avoid second-guessing yourself. If you need extra assurance, make another appointment, visit your dress, and address any and all questions you have so you can leave knowing you have the dress to match your finest moment of going down the aisle with the groom of your dreams!

Dressing Your Maids, Moms, and Men

Few items of clothing can conjure up greater controversy and ridicule than the revered and feared bridesmaid's dress. The minute you think about the stereotypical designs of yesteryear, you still think of pink, poufy, squeaky dresses with those classic leg-of-mutton sleeves! Articles and even entire books have been written about history's most hideous bridesmaid's outfits, social groups sponsor national "most ugly" *competitions* awarding owners of the most atrocious style and obnoxious color dress, and we are certain that you or someone near to you has an ugly-dress tale! Bridesmaids' dresses of the past have been relegated to the backs of closets, never again to see the light of day. Ah, but we're speaking of the distant past here, in fashion's dark ages before high style was associated with bridesmaids' gowns. Thankfully, the bridesmaid design world has caught up, and today's styles for maids are every bit as thrilling as are the styles for brides.

Now you'll see daring backlines, sophisticated lines, beautiful strapless sheaths with ethereal wraps, shimmering colors—fashions worthy of a head-turning stroll not just down your wedding aisle but down the red carpet at the Oscars or Golden Globes. Bridesmaids of the 21st century are lucky women indeed! There has never been a better time for bridesmaid fashion. Your girls are lucky and honored indeed that this will be their day to shine, though not as brightly as you!

so, who wears the bridesmaid's dress?

Just as the bridesmaid's dress has had a complete makeover, so have the rules for *who gets to wear these fashions.* The rules concerning those invited to your Bridesmaid's Inner Circle have relaxed, and this area is now greatly affected by the gown-specific issues of protocol, dress codes, style, and color. And just as well. Many a tear has been shed in the past over who to invite into the blessed circle and in what to dress them. But the trepidation doesn't stop there! Add in the money factor, as these dresses may be expensive! *Then* there is also the responsibility for shoes, accessories, and wedding day beauty rituals! *And then* add in what role each bridesmaid is to execute before, during, and after the big day, and you may be looking at an emotional cocktail of potent proportions.

And you thought this would be a simple thing . . .

Let us traipse delicately through the confetti-strewn path that leads to Bridemaidsville to discover exactly where you stand with the maid of the 21st century. Just as well this is not 1973.

Bridesmaidsville: Who Should Attend the Party?

For many brides (and this may include you), the selection process for your inner circle of bridesmaids and maid of honor is a done deal. Perhaps you've known since age ten that you'd have your younger sister as your maid of honor, and your three closest girlfriends as your maids.

Choosing your maids may be something you checked off your to-do list before you got your engagement ring! If so, congratulations! However, choosing your maids is certainly not as cut-and-dried as it used to be.

Lifelong friendships have been shattered over a bride's choice not to include said friends in her bridesmaid lineup, and family battles have erupted over a wise bride's choice *not* to include all female first cousins as attendants. If she had caved in and said yes to all, she might have fifteen bridesmaids walking ahead of her down the aisle! Everyone around you, it seems, has emotions invested and strong opinions on who you should add to your bridesmaid list, and you have the unenviable position of letting some people down. The day you say "No" (or say nothing) to those who believe they should be on your list is a trembly day in your wedding experience.

You might wonder, *How could it get this intense?*

How are you to choose which longtime friends to include, especially if you've drifted apart from some of them? How are you to choose between the sister you're not particularly close to and the best friend who has been *more* of a sister than your blood relative? What about the distant friend who inexplicably asked you to be in her bridal party eight years ago? Are you obligated to return the favor?

We could go on for hours citing sticky interpersonal issues that may send you straight to the nearest Ben and Jerry's, but instead we'll provide a few solutions for the 21st-century bride. At the start, you might assume that, since bridal parties are for the closest family members and best friends, those who are not invited will totally understand. This myth needs to be addressed immediately, as not everyone is thinking rationally and considerately at this time. For some, being selected is like winning a popularity contest.

Being left off the roster, then, may be misread as a signal of rejection delivered right to their egos. No one likes being left out, so at this point you need some deep thinking and good people skills to create harmony after you announce who will join you down the aisle. Here are some golden rules about picking your chosen few:

- *Determine your number.* Decide about how many attendants you want in your bridal party. Just two or three? Five to seven? Ten plus?

- *Prioritize.* Start with the main players. Who will be your maid of honor, and who will be his best man? If the choice isn't obvious, such as your only sister or well-known best friend, and his older brother or longtime friend, then select according to your heart. It always knows what's best once your head quiets down.

- *Be flexible!* Let 21st-century rules come to the rescue! In the past few years, wedding couples have solved their "top spot" dilemmas by choosing *more than one* best man or maid of honor, and that trend is picking up steam these days. Can't decide between your sister and that dear-heart best friend? Crown them *both* maids of honor. Even better, if one is married and the other single, one gets "maid of honor" and the other gets "matron of honor" status. No one stands above you with a sword, demanding that you choose one or the other! Problem solved.

- *Let tradition be your guide.* If you are a traditionalist and have the budget and the inclination, then a large party of, say, five to ten maids is not only impressive, but can certainly help you out of a "numbers fix." Eventually, your decision may be based partially on an emotional and numbers game basis, and that can be difficult.

- *Make a rule.* Limit the bridal party to family only, for example. If you are able to keep your maids/matrons and flower girls to family only, sending this message out to your friends could help you avoid a friendship collision course. It is always appropriate to give priority to sisters and sisters-in-law. Nothing can substitute for family. If relationships among some of you are strained, then a wedding can be the perfect opportunity to melt away hard feelings grown over months or even years.

- *Welcome new members.* Another fun (and loving!) trend we're seeing now is opposite-gender members of each side's attendants. That means the bride's best, platonic male friend stands on her side as one of her attendants while the groom's longtime female buddy stands as one of his attendants. The male bridal attendant, of course, wears a tux to match the men, while the female attendant can either wear what the bridesmaids are wearing *or* an elegant black dress to blend in with the groomsmen's black tuxes. We've seen both choices enacted successfully, and we love the fact that brides and grooms are not limiting their choices according to gender. Such freedom of choice is calling to 21st-century brides and grooms in growing numbers.

A Word About Step-Sisters

When you think about Cinderella's positively obstructive step-sisters, the term conjures up negative connotations. With the onset of blended families, many a bride of today must deal with the issue of step- and half-sisters, as must the groom with any acquired siblings. Cinderella's blended family set a bad example, one that's far more the exception than the rule these days, so we are going to end the quarrel right here. Whether your "sisters-by marriage" came through your mother or father, let it be known that they have a status in your life (and the same goes for the groom and his blended siblings!). Whether you are close or not really involved with each other, the 21st-century bride adheres to a different code of ethics.

> ### we are family...
>
> Inviting all your sisters and sisters-in-law-to-be is most important. If you have a large family, you should be used to doing things in big groupings anyway. If you gained a larger group of sisters-in-law, count them as your own, and by all means think about what including them in your bridal party now would mean to your future relationships with them. Inclusion leads to harmony, whereas exclusion at this point might get you off to a rocky start with his sisters (especially if he's close to them and values their input and happiness as well).

If the decision is right for you, if there are no long-held, truly bitter battles between you, take the initiative to invite and include. It is appropriate out of respect to your birth mother or father and your blended parent to respect your sisters/matrons by marriage. Be bigger than the rest. That is what marriage and maturity is all about. If they choose not to take you up on your invitation, accept it. There is always going to be an existing level of comfort between you, and you must honor the realities of that relationship. And that makes it a personal choice for you alone.

Yes, inclusion now can set the stage for the erasure of long-held and unspoken tensions, but only if the seeds are there for such a reunion. Let them make the final decision. It is amazing how appropriate behavior invites appropriate responses most of the time.

Move Over, Matron

While we are at it, let's talk about the married woman who holds the honored position of your top female attendant: *matron-of-honor*. The term sounds a bit dowdy, doesn't it? This is not the decade where women look or feel matronly. Providing naming options is forward-thinking and another mark of the 21st-century bride. And so "Best

Happily Ever After

Your personal formula of who gets invited onto your attendants list is very much contingent on the actual number of family, future sisters-in-law, and very dear friends in the equation. You may wish to devise a very fair system of invitation that has spiritual and emotional significance.

One of the Roths' staff members, Tammy Kreiter, created a genius formula in relation to her wedding party list. She invited her two future sisters-in-law, her oldest friend, and her newest friend to be part of the bridesmaid's contingent. This created harmony and intelligent decision-making, and it worked perfectly for Tammy as she fulfilled much meaning and honor in her choices. Whatever formula is best for you, make it meaningful to yourself and those around you. Thinking independently is how a 21st-century bride adds her personal signature to her big day.

Lady" has been introduced into bride vernacular, as the more acceptable counterpart to the "Best Man." Matron of Honor or Best Lady—the choice is yours.

Just Two Surrounded by Children

Another growing trend is to name just one honor attendant each, a maid of honor and best man, and then fill out your bridal party by having all your favorite little children, dressed in their most adorable white party dresses with color-coordinated sashes and wearing floral wreaths on their ringlet-covered heads. From your nieces and nephews to your own kids, to your friends' children, to the kids you teach at school or at ballet class or soccer practice, choosing to surround yourself with the exuberance of youth lends a wonderful look to your day, as well as the sheer joy and laughter you envision in your future life together.

Positions of Honor Without the Frock

If you do have many friends around you and theoretically would love them all to be involved, you can do just that. Not everybody needs to be a bridesmaid to be involved with the wedding and feel extra special.

Dear, close friends could be invited to sing or read a poem, or to be greeters, program distributors, musical performers during the cocktail hour, or any of a myriad of other special roles. Providing each with a role allows all who are near and dear to hold a meaningful position and bask in a spotlight of appreciation, and it also keeps everyone as happy as possible.

Ego Meltdown!

If some friends do feel insulted when you explain that you cannot include them in your bridal party because of your budget or space considerations, personal preference, or whatever reason you offer, ask yourself what the true state of your friendship is. Perhaps it is time you move on, or maybe this will test the strength of your mutual understanding and flexibility as friends. Yes, some will get bent out of shape, and we hate to see that happen, but this is one of those harsh realities of the bridal world. Some people have very fragile egos, and a wedding magnifies that. Sad as it is, it's best that you recognize what this low level of adversity brings out in some people. And then you can focus on the many around you who *are* gracious and understanding of your decisions. Those are your truest of your true friends and family.

Willing, but Unable

Be prepared when you ask a dear friend to be a member of your bridal party that she may decline your invitation, for any of many good reasons. She may not have the financial resources to contribute as she might wish to your shower, to buy the dress, the shoes, and accessories you choose. She might live far from you, and may know she has limits to being there for you and fulfilling her expected roles to the best of her ability. So, graciously, she must say no.

This is *your* time to be understanding, since she's undoubtedly nervous about hurting your feelings. It's your turn to extend the same graciousness as did those friends you were unable to invite. Give her a peaceful exit from the obligation, and promise her a less demanding role of honor if she's able to attend your wedding, perhaps the reading of a sonnet or psalm during your ceremony.

Popping the Question . . . It's Your Turn!

Few moments with your closest friends and family will be as exciting as when you ask them to be in your bridal party! Of course, when you invite your maids or matrons and flower girls, do it directly and diplomatically. Personally invite those you would love to have join you, sharing the moment by phone if not in person. Some things are far too precious to do through e-mail! But make sure you do the inviting on the same day, so other friends and family do not learn through secondhand sources.

Once each wedding party member has confirmed with a "Yes!", plan a little meeting for drinks or coffee to celebrate and to "gather the troops" for your first official time as a wedding circle. Toast the moment; it has a wonderful bonding significance.

fashion forward!

In days gone by, the bride simply decided, with little if any discussion, what she wanted her bridal party to wear. With little thought to others' budgets, body shapes, and coloring, the bride of old tore out a page from a bridal magazine and circulated it to her maids with this message: *This is what I've chosen.* Then, more liberal brides began to give maids two or three options, all the same style, to review and choose from. Of course, that often meant one or two bridesmaids were less than happy, as they had to squish into the style that suited the majority. Fortunately, that is no longer the case. The influence of fashion and major dress faux pas has enlightened the bride of today, and the dress selection process more often left to the bride's and maids' discretion. Some brides are even saying, "Wear whatever style you like, as long as it's black/red/some shade of mint."

from michelle

The days of the Pepto-Bismol bridesmaid in puffy sleeves and polyester everything are over! Fashion has fortunately taken over, rescuing bridesmaids from fashion no-nos. The ugliest thing a bride and her maids need to watch out for is discord and disharmony. Nothing can camouflage that!

Why has this become the case?

Brides often remember dresses they did *not* love, perhaps those they wore in friends' weddings or saw at weddings they attended. In defense of brides past, their choices were limited by the costumey approach most fashion designers took to bridesmaid style. Fueling this non-fashion conspiracy, the bridesmaids didn't want to upset the bride by telling her how ghastly her choice was, so they went along with it, thinking "Friendship is thicker than fashion." Thus began bridesmaids' horror stories.

Fortunately, today's brides generally take a more flexible approach to every aspect of the style of the wedding, including offering bridesmaids a variety of choices. At the same time, the bride still orchestrates how she wants the bridal party to look by giving her bridesmaids certain stipulations:

- *Traditionally speaking:* The dresses must be in the same style, same color, and chosen by the design and color numbers at the store. The maid of honor or best lady has a bit of flexibility to set herself apart, perhaps another style in the same color as the rest of the bridesmaids, or the same style in a deeper color that still coordinates with the group. Overall, the look is uniform by design.

- *Style supreme:* Brides sometimes tell their maids: "You can wear any style as long as it is black, *BUT* the skirt must be floor-length and the dress must have long sleeves." This gives the bridesmaids the option of choosing the skirt style, neckline, and bodice that flatters her body and is comfortable to wear. (The advice in chapter 6 applies to bridesmaids as well, so flip back for details on bodices, skirt lengths, and other gown elements.)

- *Fashion replay:* A fashion-forward approach focuses on dresses that can be worn after the wedding: "You can choose different styles by a certain designer in one particular color, or the same style in varying colors that coordinate, such as a range of mahogany." The main idea is that the dresses all complement each other. The look can be stunning, with colors in a range off a palette.

  As we pen this chapter, the latest look for bridesmaids is all white. (We kid you not!) It can look incredible, especially if the wedding is set on the beach. Remember, this is fashion. Whatever you agree on, make sure that it is classic in some way and will withstand the test of time. This is the ultimate in bridal fashion freedom, as your maids will be able to wear these dresses again and again and again.

- *Non-compete clause:* The bridesmaids' dresses should essentially complement what the bride is wearing, without in any way competing with her. If possible, ensure that the bridesmaid's dress is different in style and spirit from your gown, so that your maids complement *you*. In no way should their dresses be more ornate, more attractive, or more formal than yours.

Communication between brides and bridesmaids can be more direct when the bride allows her maids to make their own choices. It becomes a respectful interchange, and the best path to harmony within your group. Here are style suggestions and some basic rules to keep everyone proud to walk down the aisle in a dress of her own choosing.

from sharon

No more uniform looks for the women in your bridal party! We were all blessed with individual shapes and sizes, heights and bra sizes, and we shouldn't be crammed into a dress that looks perfect only on your size 6 bridesmaid. Now, allow your maids the freedom to choose their own tops, ballgown or skirt designs, even level of allure (within reason!), and you'll undoubtedly be voted "Bride of the Year."

Six Essentials for Bridesmaid Dress Magic

1. *Consider shapes and sizes.* The maids must honestly assess their body shapes and sizes and get an expert's input on which styles will emphasize their best features.
2. *Select for the setting and season.* Whether deciding on the one style or any combination, make sure it's appropriate to your setting and season of the wedding—and that it complements your maids' coloring.
3. *Determine what's appropriate.* We all have our own definition of what makes us look sexy in a dress. Unfortunately, some women blur the line between sexy and tacky. If one of your maids is popping out the top of her dress and likes it that way,

then reserve the right to veto her choice and ask that she choose a more appropriate style.

4. *Plan and confer.* Sit down with or conference-call your brides-maids and discuss your approach for selecting dresses, your time schedule, and your goals. They'll appreciate your having a plan that includes timelines they know in advance.

5. *Set the foundation.* Choose your bridal dress and plan your reception before you set style guidelines and schedule appointments to shop with your bridesmaids, best lady, flower girls—in fact the entire party. Your dress and the style of your wedding are the foundation for every decision that follows.

6. *Include long-distance maids in the selection process.* You can include maids who live in other states or countries in the dress selection process by giving them local store names and Web sites where they can get a good look at what they might be wearing.

Money Matters

Don't forget to note those price tags! As you search for ideal brides-maids' dresses, price as well as style matters. Remember, your maids are volunteering to take on what can be a tremendous financial investment (if not burden) to honor you on your day, so do keep gown prices in the moderate range. The most gorgeous designer gown with an inflated price tag is likely *not* the way to go.

Unless you pay for your maids' dresses (which some brides generously offer to do), be sensitive to your bridesmaids' budgets and be open to their suggestions. You might even give *them* the freedom to find gowns within their budget ranges by allowing each maid to choose what she wants to wear in an acceptable color range. Or if all of your bridesmaids except one agree on a pricier designer gown, you can save the day for that cash-strapped maid by offering to pay the difference between the group's selection and what she can afford. This kind of forward thought shows that you have your priorities in line and will endear you to all your maids. Remember that it's all about surrounding yourself with your most loved female friends and family . . . no matter the price of their wardrobe.

Shop 'Til We Drop

The group shopping trip to try on bridesmaids' gowns should be an enjoyable experience. Whether it proves to be so depends on your setting the right tone. Part of being a contemporary bride is taking into account your maids' sensitivities and making sure they'll all be comfortable. You don't want someone thinking, *Ugh, now I have to get undressed in front of all these skinny women, and I am having a fat day!*

Whatever your maids' mindsets, these tips should help you take care of this task efficiently and completely:

- Choose the bridal gown attire store whose dresses you love, and make an appointment for everyone.

- E-mail or send out-of-town maids a photo of the dress so they can see what's "in store" for them.

- Let your maids know that the seamstress will use a tape measure to get specific dimensions of their chests, waists, hips, arms, and for the length of the dress. Tell them to trust that the consultants will know what size to order. Even if they normally wear a size 8, a size 10 or 12 might be necessary in a particular style since designers use different measurements. Some run small (particularly dresses by European designers), and some are roomy. Keep your maids focused on fit rather than dress size.

- Have your distant maids go to a local seamstress for a professional measurement session.

---

credit card scorchers for bridesmaids

Unless the bride offers to pay for her maids' gowns and other items, the average bridesmaid must pay for these items:

- Gown
- Shoes
- Accessories
- Appropriate undergarments (such as a strapless bra)
- Her share of the shower bill
- A shower gift
- An engagement gift
- A wedding gift
- Travel
- Lodging
- Phone calls (to stay in contact with the bride during the planning)
- Hair styling, manicure, and makeup application
- Bachelorette party expenses
- Any other wedding plan expenses she volunteers to assume

We highly recommend that a tailor or a dressmaker take official measurements. They know just where and how to position the tape to get the most relevant and correct dimensions for gown sizing. A do-it-yourself job is a lure for disaster; paying for a professional measure is worth every last penny.

They can then send or fax an official size sheet to you or to the dress shop for the optimum dress size ordering.

- Keep the tone light. Few people beam when they hear their actual waist or hip measurements, especially with others in the room! Discreetly ask the seamstress not to announce the measurements out loud.

- Order all your dresses at the same time from the same store, so they are cut from the same bolt of fabric. Otherwise, dye lots from different rolls of fabric can vary in shade, perhaps causing some gowns to look a bit faded or "off."

- Submit your order with plenty of time to spare so you can be sure your maids have their gowns four to six weeks before the wedding date, when alterations take place.

- Remind your maids that their health is more important to you than their weight. If any of your maids are determined to lose weight before being paraded down the aisle, encourage them to eat healthily and remind them that a good alterations department is there to fit you perfectly.

Shoes, Bags, Wraps, and Accessories

Outfit your maids in not only flattering gowns, but with modern accessories. Gone are the days when shoes were dyed to match the dress. Today's bridesmaids put on stylish shoes in wearable colors (who will ever wear lilac-colored pumps again?), luxurious wraps around their shoulders in colors that complement the dress, smart jewelry and hair accents, and round off their look as perfectly polished, poised, and picture-worthy.

Your maids will thank you later.

mother, you look gorgeous!

After you have your gown selected and outfitted your maids to complement you, it's the mothers' turn to step on the fashion runway and try on beautiful gowns designed for mothers of brides and grooms. And these styles, too, have come a long way, baby. No longer are mothers' gowns frumpy and matronly. Beaded jackets are now stylish, and mothers are free to flaunt their figures in necklines, gown lengths, and arm styles that flatter. The explosion of dresses for mothers fortunately takes more cues from the fashion pages. In fact, the wedding fashion industry has responded to the proliferation of body-conscious women worldwide with beautifully cut and slim-line silhouetted dresses that show off their best figure features. From pastel colors to bold plums and navies, formal black to glittering ivory, mothers can shine . . . without outshining the bride, of course.

At this point, you may or may not direct the mothers in to their gown choices. Some brides have very particular taste, especially when it comes to the statements they'd like their own mother to make. If Mother has been supportive of your own gown decision, let her choose something she feels comfortable in. As long as Mom has a swatch of your dress and the maids' dresses, let her choose a color and style appropriate for her.

It's important that Mom consider your wedding style and the reception décor, just as you did when choosing your gown. She must fit with the formality, style, and theme of your wedding, as well as with the general feel of your bridal look. Mothers should take into account colors that suit their complexions, so encourage her to test out a range of colors rather than prescribe one to her. Mothers and grooms' mothers usually don't choose the same color dress, but are likely to consult with each other to determine colors that complement. Ultimately, that is their decision, again according to their individual coloring preferences and bride parameters.

The days of mothers never wearing suits are also over. Depending on the time of day and location of the wedding, a magnificent crisp suit that she adores might just be her bridal ticket. After all, every mother has her personal style.

And where does Mom find her dress of the 21st century? It might be at the bridal salon a few feet from where you discovered the gown of your dreams, but it also might be at a specialty or department store. Don't count out department stores, as many have a wonderful range of women's formalwear, especially during the months before and after the winter holidays. That is when she'll find an array of formal and informal gowns and dresses in lovely tones, with stylish wraps and jackets, fabulous accessories that bring out the color of her eyes, and great shoes to complete her wedding-day look.

Your wedding day is a very special once-in-a-lifetime day for the mothers as well, so they too deserve to glow, to shine, to look as wonderful as they feel. Thank heavens Mother's wedding-day fashions are every bit as glamorous as your maids' in this century. As pivotal women of the wedding day, mothers deserve nothing less.

. . . and all the bride's men

Goodbye penguin suits! *Au revoir* 1990s prom tuxes. The look for men—the groom, his groomsmen, the fathers, and even that charming little ring-bearer—is dashing and debonair, smooth and sophisticated with a bit of a James Bond feel. The 21st-century groom wants to look and feel stylish (though he's unlikely to actually say that out loud!).

Men seldom subscribe to the tremendous emotional and fashion roller coaster as do women involved with the bridal party. Women tend to be more intense about fashion and friend politics than men. Whether the wedding is black tie formal to smart casual informal, be sure of this: Check that socks match and shoes are shined. It's a guy thing.

Now that we've covered the controversial socks issue, let's dive into the subject of wedding day wardrobe for the men. Flip through any bridal magazine, and you'll see sharp-dressed male models with chiseled jaws and piercing eyes standing confidently in black or gray tuxedos. Tear yourself from those eyes for a moment, and notice the details of the tuxedo: those pinstripes in barely-there color, the shine of the fabric, the line of the lapel. Top fashion designers for men provide the most current directions in suit cuts and colors, and the growing trend in male wedding-wear rightly follows the same upscale looks in tuxedo design and details.

from henry

Whether he is a jeans man or a Wall Street high-flier, watch out for the groom's socks. Men love to strike out at weddings; they hate uniformity!

To Tux or Not to Tux?

Formal and semiformal weddings prescribe tuxedos for the groom, his men, and the fathers. Just like your gown and the maids' attire, men's wedding wear also looks to the rules and etiquette of matching the formality and style of the big day. So once you have *your* gown picked out, it's time to figure out whether your men will buy or rent tuxedos, or whether you'll have them dress in classy street suits, or in khakis and crisp white shirts. To help you assess the right menswear for your formality and style of wedding, we've assembled the following guide:

Formality Guide

Ultraformal Evening: Usually a "white-tie" wedding; black tailcoat and pants, white wing-collar shirt, black vest, white bow tie, gold or silver cufflinks and accessories.

Ultraformal Daytime: Gray pinstriped pants, gray cutaway coat, gray vest, white wing-collar shirt, gray tie or ascot, appropriate cufflinks.

Formal Evening (most common): Usually a "black tie" wedding. Black tuxedo, white wing-collar shirt, black vest or cummerbund, black bow tie, cufflinks.

Formal Daytime: Black or gray tuxedos or tailcoats with matching pants, matching vest, white spread-collar shirt or wing-tipped shirt, black or gray (to match) tie, ascot or four-in-hand, cufflinks.

Semiformal Evening: Dark suit or dark tuxedo with matching vest (white jacket appropriate for summertime), long tie, white shirt with wing- or turned-down collar, accessories.

Semiformal Daytime: Suits work well—black, navy, or gray— plus white jackets in summertime, white shirt, tie optional.

Informal: Suits are fine, as are khaki pants with white shirts and navy blazers, as is dress to fit the theme of informal weddings.

Ultra Informal: Everything from linen to Hawaiian shirts. As long as it is crisp and smart and works with your theme, then the sky is the limit for how you'll dress your men.

It's Raining Menswear!

So many styles, so many colors, so many ways to let your men stand out in the crowd! Start looking early at all the tuxedo and suit styles out there, and plan to reserve any rentals at least five or six months in advance. At peak wedding times, of course, the best stores have already rented out their best stock. That's why you and your groom should scout the most reputable formalwear rental agencies near you, surf the Internet to look at style concepts, and flip through bridal magazines to gather names of your favorite designers and where you can find their products.

When you do find the right rental agency or men's department, speak to the men's style experts there to select just the right fashions for your men. This means not just choosing an attractive tuxedo style that suits your formality, but also in styles that suit your men! Some tuxedo styles look more flattering on taller men, stockier men, or men with a little extra around the middle. You can choose tuxedos that make the most of your individual men's appearance, and still suit the style of your day. Look for these and other individual fashion details.

Tuxedo Styles

- Two-button tuxedo

- Single-button tuxedo

- Three-button tuxedo

- Double-breasted tuxedo

- Shawl-collar tuxedo

- Specialty tuxedos such as Oscar de la Renta's Silver Cloud and La Vida styles (the La Vida, for instance, has a long four-button jacket and a smooth satin-accented collar . . . very stylish!)

- Tuxedo fabrics listed as Super 120s, a comfortable worsted wool fabric blend that's ideal for events year-round

Vests

- Five- to eight-button vests

- Shiny, shimmering fabrics

- Deep colors

- Geometric patterns

- Fun solid colors, patterns, and theme designs (such as patriotic wear for a Fourth of July wedding, shamrocks for Irish or Saint Patrick's Day, wine bottles, chili peppers, and more for the ultimate personalized and theme-appropriate look

- Color-coordinated vest-and-tie sets

- Adjustable belts, some with the belt inside the vest for a smoother appearance

- 100 percent silk vests for that dapper sheen

- Besom pockets

- Stylish cummerbunds with pleating facing up

Shirts

- Wing-collar formal

- Spread-collar formal

- Crossed-collar formal

- French cuffs

- Pleating

- Informal fold collars

- Luxurious silk microfiber blends

- Cool 100 percent cotton

Ties

- Classic bow ties in 100 percent silk or silk blends

- Pre-tied bow ties with clasps in back

- Silk long ties

- Ascots

Shoes

- Formal patent leather shoes, all matching

- Matching toe boxes to the shoes (all round or all to a slight square toe)

- Matte-finish formal leather shoes

- *And don't forget the matching black socks for all your men!*

Cufflinks and Accessories

- Gold or silver cufflinks

- Gold or silver studs

- Black onyx cufflinks and studs

- Diamond- or rhinestone-accent cufflinks and studs

- Design-cut cufflinks and studs

Aisle Style

Here is a sampling of the more upscale tuxedo and men's wear designers:

After Six	Lord West
Andrew Fezza	Oscar de la Renta
Calvin Klein	Perry Ellis
Frederick Leone	Ralph Lauren
Geoffrey Beene	Tallia Uomo
Hugo Boss	

- Classic black button covers
- Classic black button covers with rhinestone accents in the rounds
- All-silk suspenders in shiny black, stripe, or design
- Pocket squares

fathers of the bride and groom

Fathers of the bride and groom should also be fitted for tuxedos so they match the men of the bridal party. With this unification of style and sophistication, your fathers will indeed look the part of "man of the hour" and will blend well into your wedding portraits. A nice touch for fathers is to present them with a unique style of boutonniere, such as a sprig of lily of the valley if the rest of the men will wear stephanotis sprigs. This little touch sets the fathers apart with style, class, and something special.

Measuring Your Men

All your men need to be measured professionally for the ordering of the right-size tuxedos, so you might plan a "guy's night" for just this task. Distant ushers, groomsmen, and fathers can be professionally measured at their local tailors, and e-mail, fax, or call in their dimensions to the one person placing the tuxedo rental order for the group. Remind far-flung men to have their neck sizes measured for bow ties as well! Payments can be made when tuxes are ordered or when they're picked up.

When the men go for their fittings before the wedding, they must also pick up the appropriate accessories and shoes, to unify their look as a group.

If rentals must be returned, designate one return man to collect all the rented tuxes, shoes, and accessories the day after the wedding, and get everything turned in before the clock strikes the deadline . . . and late fees begin to pile up.

If you plan an informal wedding without tuxedos, avoid the most common male fashion faux pas! If khaki pants are the rule of the day, send all the men to one store to pick up their pants together. Because the shades of khaki vary tremendously from store to store, you might otherwise wind up with a lineup of men wearing pants that range in color from dark cream to true khaki to light green! To ensure a unified group, send the men pants-shopping together!

groom style standouts

Today's groom knows how to set himself apart from the crowd. From ceremonial wedding robes of African, Korean, Japanese, Indian, and Nordic origin to tuxedo vests of a different stripe from the rest of his men, the 21st-century groom wishes to stand out and make a statement, as will you in your gown. Here, then, are additional ideas your groom might consider as his stylistic spotlight:

- Groom wears a cutaway coat while his ushers wear standard tuxedo jackets

- Groom wears a double-breasted jacket while his men are in single-breasted

- Groom wears a satin-sheen lapel while his men are in matte or plain lapels

- Groom wears a white vest while his men wear black, gray, or patterned vests

- Groom wears a white bow tie while the rest of his men wear long ties

- Groom wears a different boutonniere than the rest of his men (a single white rose and white stephanotis, for instance, while the groomsmen wear single white roses or sprigs of stephanotis)

- Groom wears ethnic garb, while the rest of his men wear standard tuxedos

- Groom wears his military uniform (if applicable) while the rest of his men wear tuxedos

And another way the groom can stand out (but only for his bride in the privacy of their honeymoon suite after the wedding): Wear heart-themed or red silk boxer shorts, or a stylish temporary tattoo applied where the bride will find it eventually.

The Final Word

Undoubtedly, bridal party attire has come into its own, giving you far greater scope in creating a dashing look and style that is both coherent and elegant. Whatever you do, do it simply. Overstyling is overkill. When in doubt, it's better to dress with less fuss and more dash. Over-accessorizing and over-labored styles can look out of place; keep it clean, simple, and meaningful, and enjoy creating a magnificent masculine look.

chapter 8

Tiny Visions:
Your Child Attendants

Few wedding images are as adorable as precious little flower girls scattering rose petals before the bride's path—or a smartly dressed groom Mini-Me (otherwise known as ring bearer) with his hair slicked back and a miniature rose in his lapel. Adorable, just adorable. (No wonder ad geniuses on Madison Avenue feature kids to pull at our heart strings!)

Yet as endearing as these little darlings can be, some also become holy terrors on the wedding day. Flower girls with fear factor. Ring bearers as rebels with a cause . . . often to attract as much attention to themselves and their discomfort as possible. Of course, we don't speak of all flower girls and ring bearers; some are proper little ladies and gentlemen. But kids of all ages present a big unknown to a day already filled with many uncontrollable elements. Will the child throw a tantrum? Will she refuse to walk down the aisle as instructed? Will he turn on the tears, or charm your crowd? Will she run around in circles laughing hysterically, or remain in control? Again, it's unknown.

While you're selecting your little angels and ninjas, it's also important to evaluate them carefully. Some brides love the look of six flower girls and only one maid of honor, which increases her odds of at least one of them throwing a dramatic tantrum (it just might be the maid of honor! Who can tell?). Whatever the numbers, whether you'll have one flower girl and one ring bearer, or several of each, consider these factors when you make your decision:

- *The child's age.* We won't set a number in stone (such as, seven is ideal, while six is too young). Children are individuals, and we've seen many well-behaved five-year-olds carry off their wedding day tasks beautifully, with no tears or tantrums.

- *The child's maturity level.* Even that nine-year-old might become a handful, so look at the child's behavior and level of responsibility. Make it an individualized decision.

- *The parents' assessment of the child's readiness.* Talk to the child's mom and dad and see whether they think Junior can be responsible on your big day. Parents may, of course, so desire the spotlight for their child that they say yes without considering the truth, but many will be honest and forthright about their child's readiness, and *about their wishes should they not wish to have the child included.* They may politely decline because of money issues, the child's schedule, or any number of factors. So consider the parents' decision objectively. Of course, the children in your bridal party may be *your own,* as in the case of a blending family where both the bride and groom have children from previous partners, or children of their own. What, then, could be better than having the children attend the wedding and share in the special day? In this case, the previous considerations are your own to make, as you assess your children's readiness and the ideal roles for them to play on the big day.

photographs by Andrew D. Bernstein/Steve Sherman

Shaunie's Story

To have our children there meant *everything* to Shaquille and me. There was no way we could have not had them there with us. Even though they're young, we definitely wanted them to look back at pictures, videos, etc., and see that they were part of Mommy and Daddy's very special day. We were a wonderful family before December 26th, but an even better one after. Plus, who better to serve as your ring bearers than your own sons (Myles, 6 and Shareef, 3), and your daughters as flower girls (Taahiriah, 7 and Amirah, 1)? Plus I think Amirah stole the show, with her big entrance in her "cloud on wheels" [a cloud-designed bassinet that made her entrance a rolling success].

enter *stage mom*

Believe it or not, family politics can rise up like a tropical storm over the selection of child attendants. If you're in the unenviable position of having a dozen nieces and nephews, do you choose your "favorites" or the oldest ones who can handle the pressure and performance requirements for the day? What do you do when the mother of the nine-year-old niece you select also demands that her "entitled" four-year-old also must be in your lineup? How do you say no to that?

Ah, it's a tricky business choosing child attendants, and everyone is ready to add their "unbiased" opinions over it: Why not *my* child? If you have one child, you have to have her sister/cousin/step-sister/imaginary friend as well!

Happily Ever After

Shaunie O'Neal, our model Mom Bride (featured on page 135), shares the solution she and hubby, Shaquille O'Neal, arranged for keeping their children well-entertained at the wedding: "Well, I have to give all the credit to Mindy Weiss, my wedding planner, on that one. All I could tell her was that I needed the children to have something to entertain them at the reception because I didn't want them running around either playing or bored. I didn't know how she was going to achieve this without making a children's play area. So she came up with having the kids sit at a kid-size table that was exactly like one of the adult tables. Their names were placed on their plates, and on the back of each of their chairs was a special personalized bag for each of them. Inside each bag were little toys and gifts that fit each one of their personalities. From Power Rangers to Barbie dolls, coloring books, and crayons. It was great, the children were thrilled! And best of all . . . it worked!"

Pretty soon, the children are off playing a videogame peacefully, while the adults are acting like five-year-olds! Tantrums abound that don't come from the children! What is a bride to do?

Your answer lies within you. You can crown either all or none of the children as bridal party members. You can stick with your original selections, and tell the parents that you choose by age-appropriate limits. The other children, you might suggest, will get a different title. Perhaps they can be Masters of the Bubble-Blowers, with the very important job of handing out those post-ceremony bubble bottles. You must be creative and diplomatic here, as you must appease both the children and their parents. Don't be surprised if you must defend your position, if you must stand firm against an icy glare or attempted manipulation. You may be shocked at the spine you must show in this seemingly innocuous decision. *Hey, it's not full-paid college tuitions I'm handing out here! It's a requirement to dress up and act nice for a few hours. Geez!*

what's a child to do?

Once you've weathered the storm of naming your child attendants, what comes next is determining their roles. Theoretically, it's simple: Flower girls walk down the aisle in the ceremony procession, either holding hands or scattering rose petals, stand quietly during the ceremony, then walk back up the aisle at the end. Case closed.

Ring bearers either walk down the aisle in the procession, or stand in one place holding the pillow with the rings. Done.

After that, all that's left is for the little darlings to stand still and smile during pictures, and then they're off to enjoy the reception. Not so fast! The bride of the 21st century may choose to involve children much more in her wedding.

Let Them Be Seen and Heard

If the child in question is *the bride's* son or daughter, or a step-child about to welcome the bride into the new family circle, it may be wise to pay some extra attention. Perhaps the children will participate in an extra set of family vows, or light a candle, or perform a reading. Some ceremonies are so informal and so personalized that the child might perform a song or a dance in honor of her parents. The child might be the one to release doves or butterflies after the ceremony.

If you have special children in your lives, think about the possibilities. How can you make this child a very special part of your day? Display framed photos of your family? Feature on your program covers a picture of the two of you with the child, your first portrait as a new family? The options are endless and joyous, and we encourage you to find new ways to make your flower girls and ring bearers, even if they're not your own children, a fun and light-filled part of your big day.

Handful Kids

Although you may have decided to go the traditional route and have your flower girls and pages take on important ceremonial roles, they may have other ideas. You need to prepare yourself for any scenario, such as these:

- *The Runaway Flower Girl:* What about the runaway flower girl who decides to run up and down the aisle before you've had your chance to step onto the white carpet, all stiletto'd and steady?

- *Pageboy Indians:* How do you react to the page boys deciding to play cowboys and Indians around your beloved three-tier, Tiffany-style, hand-crystallized $3,500 couture cake?

Here are some tips for maintaining kid control:

- *Liberate spontaneity.* Draw a distinction between fabulous spontaneity and out-of-control kid-jinks. Do factor in a certain amount of child exuberance and absolute joy, but make a distinction between overexcited and over-the-top behavior.

- *Designate child monitors.* Make sure you have two or three responsible adults and give them time-out guidelines concerning appropriate kid behavior, and suggestions such as "Say it; don't scream it," playful interaction without brawling, maintaining order during important phases of the evening such as portrait-taking time and sit-down dinner hour. By appointing child monitors, you can enjoy the exuberance without getting your silk-gloved hands dirty!

- *Anticipate kids' needs.* Provide kid-friendly menus, and have an optional time-out room and sleeping quarters ready in case your affair lasts into the wee hours.

Planning Ahead: The Playful Pow-Wow

We recommend setting up a time to talk with your child attendants. Call it a Playful Pow-Wow, where you gather the kids for a mini-grownups meeting, a pint-sized version of the ones you're having with your parents and bridal parties. At this meeting, with as few distractions as possible (in other words, not at a kids-gone-wild restaurant with dancing characters and arcade games), let the kids know what they'll be doing on the wedding day, and what you expect of them. Describe it in as fun a manner as possible. For example: "You get to dress up like a fairy princess and walk in FRONT of the bride!" will get a shy flower girl to see this as an adventure, a fairy tale, a game of dress-up.

Allow children to have a say in the decisions as well. When you describe their tasks, allow them to ask questions, and give them small decisions to make on their own. The ring bearer, for example, can decide whether he wants to be part of the procession, or if he'll stand up front with the men. The flower girl can decide whether she'd like to scatter rose petals, or would just like to carry a small bouquet. Giving children a sense of autonomy, within reason, can get them to see their part in your wedding as something they *want* to do, rather than something they *have* to do. And being "consulted" makes the children feel special and grown-up.

ribbons, bows, and blazers

The picture becomes complete when you decide what the little ones will wear. And again, it's up to you what your level of involvement in this decision will be. While some brides point out exactly which flower girl dresses she'd like her little maids to wear, others give the parents a general instruction, such as "A pink party dress will do." Others go to the childrenswear shop with the flower girls and their parents and allow the girls to choose the dresses they'd like to wear.

from henry

Kids can add to the festivity of your day! Allow for exuberance, but let them know well in advance who is boss.

Allow some flexibility. Just as your maids were free to choose the tops and skirts that make them happy, you might also allow your fashion-conscious flower girls to choose their own styles of appropriate dresses. Your five-year-old might like one frilly party dress with ribbons and a sash, while your ten-year-old will roll her eyes at the ribbons. So coordinate the girls' dresses to complement each other's, and still work with the look of the rest of the bridal party, and your image will take shape.

Remember to take the formality of your wedding into account. Your child attendants, whether flower girls or junior bridesmaids, should *not* be dressed in miniature versions of what the bridesmaids wear. The style may be too adult for them (we don't care what the hot new pop singer wears these days!). But you're likely to find children's styles in the same fabric as your maids' styles. Investigate child

© Kim Hummel

© Kim Hummel

Amber's Story

A T AMBER PARSELL LYNCH'S May wedding, her bridesmaids wore celadon silk chiffon dresses with a draped cowl back that complemented the bride's gown, while the flower girls coordinated as well in ivory dresses with celadon sashes and pearl and silk ribbon headbands, plus ballet slippers with rosebuds on them. Her ring bearer wore an ivory pleated shirt with matching shorts and white knee socks and oxfords, and he carried an ivory pillow with ribbons.

Aisle Style

You can "dress up" and color-coordinate plain white party dresses with your bridesmaids by adding a matching sash at the waist of each child attendant. Flower girls might even be able to wear clean, almost-new white party dresses they already own, giving the parents a price break.

attendants' dresses both in and outside bridal boutiques for the widest range of options and prices.

For your male child attendants, you have the option of matching them exactly to your groom and groomsmen by renting a child-size tuxedo, and either matching the vest and tie to the men's or giving the child some style of his own. At one recent wedding Sharon attended, the ringbearer's vest color-coordinated with the men's style, but with a fun and friendly print that set him apart. Or, you can dress down your boys in plain black suits with white shirts, again saving the parents money.

Speaking of informal, some weddings are truly on the comfort-wear level. The bride and maids wear pretty pastel sundresses, while the men are comfy-casual in khaki pants and white button-down shirts. Kids at these weddings can comply with the same dress code: sundresses for the little girls, and matching khakis and whites for the little boys. Tuck a flower behind the flower girl's ear and some shades on the ring bearer, and you extend the beach-ready style to the kids.

Childrenswear experts we spoke with all gave the same advice: *Dress the children for comfort, not just appearance.* Avoid stiff or itchy fabrics, awkward bows, tight sleeves and collars, and other fashion features that will only add to the child's fidgeting and discomfort. Keep the temperature of the day in mind, so your kids won't be boiling underneath heavier fabrics and jackets. Be a cool bride who allows the kids to whip off their jackets after the picture-taking and maybe even change into more comfortable shoes. Comfy kids are better-behaved kids, so being flexible on fashion points once the most important moments of your day are over make you a smart child-attendant wrangler and a wise woman indeed.

The Care and Handling of Dressed-Up Children

Allow for a major case of wedding dishevelment. Untucked shirts and skewed bows are normal. Outdoor wedding? Expect grass stains. Serving cherries jubilee? Expect fruit stains. Kids get into everything, so anticipate marks and mars to what they're wearing. This is one reason it's important that you allow parents to seek price breaks when they purchase kids' wedding-day attire. This outfit might never see the light of day again, and that will be fine with a relaxed bride. A tight traditionalist is likely to demand that the children stay clean and presentable all day and night. Which kind of bride do you want to be? Don't set yourself up for disappointment. Allow for leeway.

One trend that's sweeping the world of tiny attendants is allowing them a wardrobe change. Yes, just like the most fashionable and famous of brides, kids are switching into different outfits for the reception. This can be a smart move if the flower girl is wearing, say, her First Communion dress (with a colored sash tied at the waist) for your ceremony. Talk ahead of time with the child's parent and allow them this flexibility. Some parents would not otherwise know this option was possible, or that you would be open to it. Again, it's all about comfort and the realities of children in fine clothing, so do consider allowing the little ones to change into formality-appropriate outfits of their own choosing for the rest of the long event ahead.

It's All Child's Play

Plenty of brides attest to the blessings of having children's activities lined up throughout the wedding day and wedding weekend. At some weddings, kids are taken aside or into another room to be entertained by babysitters, puppeteers, magicians, and story-tellers. Some visionary couples set the kids up for movie screenings of their favorite DVDs or cartoons. Others who plan informal outdoor weddings set up inflatable children's rides, pony rides, full carnival games, and face-painters. At beach weddings, supervisors can lead the kids off to take part in a sandcastle-building contest, volleyball games, or crafts activities such as gluing seashells to wooden picture frames (or all working together to make one big seashell frame as a gift for the bride and groom). Providing activities for kids makes the day even more exciting for them, and good supervision for their kids will enable parents to fully enjoy the day as well.

from michelle

Make your wedding child-friendly. Have a child coordinator or games and entertainment set aside especially for them. Contented, well-behaved, and thoroughly entertained children make for a magnificent wedding. Involve the kids with your festivities as much as you can!

Outside of movies and guided activities, since your wedding may be too formal for pony rides and face-painters, make a game out of good behavior! Create a competition for the best-behaved flower girl and page boy, with the "winner" to be announced at reception. Before the wedding, you might tell them that the best-behaved child during the day will get a special prize, such as a new videogame or music CD. Although you might see this as bribery, the promise of a CD can work wonders in encouraging children to be on their best behavior.

In the end, you'll announce that all the kids were so good that they're all winners. The children receive special gifts for their behavior, which happen to be the special gifts you got them for being part of your bridal party: silver lockets, tickets to a movie or play, or specialized gifts such as the microscope your niece has been begging for and an autographed baseball your nephew will treasure. The choice of reward is up to you.

And if your promise of a new CD or microscope is not enough to entice the child into good behavior, and the tears flow or screams drown out your vows, all is not lost. Let them cry. Believe it or not, child's play and even inappropriate behavior add to the spontaneity and warmth of the wedding. It's reality. If you see guests giggling at the funny faces your ring bearer is making at your crowd, or if your flower girl runs down the aisle to get the lollipop you taped to the first pew as her reward, accept their behavior as a true display of excitement, not a violation of your instructions that ruin your day!

Children are wonderful, impulsive little beings who can charm you into submission, blurt out blunt honesty, and make you suppress a smile when they're being very, very difficult—even when you're very, very angry. Children can't be guaranteed to behave well, so toss that expectation out. Kids can bring spontaneous laughter to your day, unstaged displays of emotion, and reminders of affection to all. In the end, your flower girl's tantrum may have you and your sweetheart giggling years from now . . . and will make a great story to tell her future boyfriend or husband.

planning details

chapter 9

Flawless Touches and Exceptional Flair

A quiet revolution is taking place in the "bridal boardrooms" of the world, where brides and grooms are overturning the way weddings are planned. You, dear couple, are a part of it!

Weddings of the 21st century are filled with individualized, stylistic, flawless touches and exceptional flair . . . your personal accents in everything from the exotic flowers to the architectural masterpiece of your wedding cake to the beautiful lavender silk seat-back covers at your reception to the favors your guests take home. This is where you have license to stretch your creativity to the boundaries of your personal tastes, to reflect who you are as individuals and as a couple.

The question you may be asking yourself is, "How do we reflect the theme of our wedding and the symbols of who we are in inanimate objects? How do we keep our wedding elegant and sophisticated, whether it's at a restaurant or the Regent?" Whatever stylistic parts of your day thrill you, this section will lead you through the leaps and bounds of the aesthetics of your big day. We'll start with some general advice:

- *Focus on a theme and style.* Keep your wedding's style and theme real, uncomplicated, and focused. Focus on the tiniest of details to create a masterpiece of style.

- *Feel it and believe it.* If you're uncomfortable with some feature, however traditional or unique (such as the father-daughter dance or an element of cultural significance), don't have it at your wedding.

- *Use your senses.* Define not only what your wedding will look like, but what it will smell like, taste like, and sound like.

- *Take it step-by-step.* Don't freeze in the "bride option dilemma," but take action methodically. Attack each style element separately. Don't attempt to lump all your planning into one basket, but keep tasks bite-size, bride-size.

- *Choose with discernment.* Along with the new freedoms comes an explosion of wedding-day vendors to provide every wedding-day whim. As we've mentioned, some only want you to do it *their* way. Here we open your eyes and minds to the possibilities wedding plans can offer you, and also remind you of this: *To thine own self be true!* Remember what *you* want to achieve, and your choices become easier.

- *Stimulate your style.* Attend bridal expos to pick up new bridal trends and ideas in every stylistic segment for your wedding day.

- *Choose your assistants well.* Whether you're making these planning decisions with the help of a wedding coordinator, your mother, or your groom, be sure you work with a person who has the time and dedication to partner with you, and understands and is loyal to your sense of style.

Note: Mothers are still the major planning partner for brides. If you work with your mother, give her plenty of direction and listen carefully to what she says. If your groom will partner with you, as can be the case for 21st-century weddings, communicate well. Use the experience to liaise, discuss, determine, compromise where needed, and bond. When you dispatch an assistant—perhaps your maid of honor, your sister, or a friend—to do some research or arranging, whether for color patterns or table settings, be sure she or he knows your preferences and can speak and decide on your behalf. Working with someone who isn't invested in your wishes will be something to regret.

Now that you have the basics and know with whom you'll be partnering, here are the main style elements to consider:

from henry

During your reception, however elaborate or simple, grand or low key, what needs to be on "high volume" is your warmth. Your love, not the glow of the Cartier chandeliers, needs to be the focus of your day and all your planning.

❧ wedding websites ❧ invitations ❧ flowers ❧
❧ reception and all the trimmings from menus to drinks ❧
❧ toasts and tributes ❧ photography and videography ❧
❧ grand entrances ❧ favors and gifts ❧

a word about wedding websites

Wedding websites offer the bride and groom a unique way to interact with wedding guests before the wedding. By featuring graphics such as video streams of the proposal and captioned photos of fun moments throughout the wedding planning process, personalized wedding websites give your guests a glimpse into Planet Bride, and encourage them to e-mail one another. You can highlight your flair, individuality, and wedding style well before you send the first invites by personalizing your site with calendars, countdowns to the wedding day, and stylish graphics.

We'd like to create a wedding website, but don't have a background in graphics or Web design. A friend offered to make the site for us, but we want to design and update it without always calling our techno-savvy friend. Should we hire a professional Web designer?

If you don't possess website design skills but want an exceptional site that's personalized, beautiful, and functional with the best interactive tools, then look for a professional's help. Sharon Naylor spoke with Todd Meikle who, with his wife Krista, runs www.wedstudio.com, a specialized wedding website creation service where you can use existing templates and easy-build interactive tools to create your own site from start to finish even without much computer knowledge.

"When Krista and I were getting married," says Todd Meikle, "our family and friends were scattered all over the country, so we wanted one centralized location where everyone could easily get the information they needed, see what was going on, and find out more about *us*." If your groom has many far-flung family members and friends, some may never have met you, and some of your loved ones may not have met your fiancé, so this is a good way to give your guests a more in-depth look into your relationship, not just the details of your wedding.

Todd states, "With wedstudio.com, you can use the templates, design your own layout, write your own 'About Us' story, provide your registry links and travel information, and keep track of RSVP's. And you can easily update information whenever you'd like as your wedding plans progress." Clearly, the Internet has become a helpful tool for all couples planning a wedding, and even without a shred of Web design experience, you can design a beautiful, professional website through services such as Todd and Krista's.

Top tools and menus on today's wedding websites include:

- Wedding day details, from the time and place of the ceremony to the time and place of the reception.

- Directions to ceremony and reception sites, as well as hotels and other wedding weekend activity sites.

- Wedding weekend activity itineraries.

- Links to your registry.

- RSVP setups for the wedding and additional wedding weekend activities.

- Links to area hotels so guests can easily make their own lodging arrangements.

- Links to area attractions for guests' downtime.

- Special pages for the wedding party, both as an icebreaker site complete with pictures and short bios of fellow bridal attendants, but also for organizing the workings of the bridal party itself. For instance, changes to fitting schedules can be posted on the site, on a page specifically for your maids, so your ladies can keep themselves on track—without your pager going off fifty times a day!

- An "About Us" page that contains the story of how you met, your courtship, and engagement details.

- A video stream that plays videotaped footage of each of you as children, moments as a couple, perhaps scenes from the marriage proposal, special moments during the planning, the shower, or (later) from the wedding itself.

- A photo album where you can post pictures throughout the planning, as well as pictures from the wedding, as a lasting memento for you and a way for those who couldn't attend the wedding to see it all!

Whether you're techno-savvy or not, a wedding website is perhaps the brightest idea for those who want to be efficient, have fun, and leave a lasting impression on their guests.

invitations to inspire and excite

Your wedding invitation is your way of welcoming guests into your wedding world. Not only does your printed card in its crisp envelope convey the essential facts—date, time, and place—of your wedding, but the wording, format, individuality, and color of your invitations set the tone for the occasion. Guests get their first glimpse at the formality and style of your event through the unique or strictly traditional way you express yourselves via the invitation.

Traditional

While the 21st-century bride has stretched the bounds of Old World etiquette in many categories, such as her gown's design, wedding location, and alterations to the wording of the ceremony, invitations *for the most part* have remained untouched by the winds of change. For traditionalist brides and grooms, age-old custom still stands when it comes to proper invitation wording, and etiquette still has its say on the level of creativity you may take with formal invitations. Following are the essentials regarding wedding invitations, from formal to informal.

Invitation Decisions

- *Stock.* For ultra-formal and formal weddings, invitation design leads you to the well-known, elegant styles of ecru invitation card stock with black lettering in formal script.

- *Print.* Formal invitations may be printed with standard thermography, or with the more-expensive option of engraving, which raises the letters and gives an indelible impression of up-scale panache.

- *Style.* Formal invitations follow a strict code of preferred style, often limiting you to a narrow range of design options, such as a thin or swirled black "frame" or outline around your wording, inset or raised borders, or slightly frayed edges to the card stock.

- *Dash and bow.* For a dash of color to a formal invitation, you might design it to have a colored ribbon tied in a bow at the top of a single-panel invitation, or the same ribbon bow enclosing a double-panel card.

- *Outside the classic box.* Stretching the boundaries, you might choose a pearlized border around the outside of your invitation edges, or even intricate laser-cut lace patterns to make the invitation card even more impressive.

- *Overlay.* For an added layer of sheen and style, you might follow the growing trend of choosing an invitation with a vellum overlay, an opaque sheet that covers the invitation page and is perhaps tied with a ribbon for more effect.

- *Informal.* For more informal invitations, the stratosphere is the limit. You might choose from among thousands of styles in patterned or flower-embedded invitation card stock, colored papers, imported Asian rice papers, recycled papers with confetti colors embedded into the paper during the creation cycle, or with watermarks.

- *Graphics.* Formal and informal invitations might be stamped with various theme borders, such as rows of delicate daisies bordering the wording of the invitation, or starfish or sand dollars featured at the top, bottom, or corners of the card.

Should you choose the formal-invitations path, do so with conviction. It makes a statement as much as a relaxed theme does.

from michelle

No other marketing tool better primes your loved ones and guests for the wedding than your invitations, which essentially declare, "Here we come!" Have fun creating a theme that starts with the invitation and runs throughout your wedding. Always be tasteful, even if you're using one of the fun, nontraditional options out there.

We marvel at the selection out there today and encourage you to research the thousands of options in wedding invitation design—endless samples in thick sample books and never-ending picture pages on Web sites. As always, invest yourselves in this process, and request in-print samples from invitation companies so you can inspect the elegance of a glossy card stock and run your fingers over those pearlized borders. Experiencing the real thing is a must here, since your invitations set the tone for your wedding.

Custom

Forget tradition, we're going custom-made!

Here comes the 21st-century bridal couple—personalized all the way! *Cream-colored papers? Not for us!* Why go standard when you can go custom? Why choose invitations from a giant samples album when you can create custom designs with the help of a professional? Your wedding is one of a kind, so you might want your invitations to reflect that too.

"In years past, young brides came in with their mothers to order their invitations," says Ellen Weldon, owner of Ellen Weldon Designs, who specializes in creating today's hottest invitation styles for celebrities and individualistic brides. "The mothers chose what was 'proper' and the bride went along with that. Not anymore! Now the bride and groom come in, and they have a wonderful sense of who they are, what they want, and how far over the 'proper' line they're willing to step when it comes to their invitations."

Below we list the main trends and tips of how you, too, can turn a simple wedding invitation into *the* must that has your guests buzzing well before the day.

A Dash of Color

We love the paper-invitation expert Ellen Weldon's uses for invitations today. The trend began several years ago and continues to bring new designs and styles to the forefront. Consider these real-life examples:

- *Wedding #1* was an ultra-formal black-tie affair at the St. Regis Hotel in New York City. Normally, such a formal event would call for the traditional, expected cream-colored invitation with formal black lettering, but the couple chose instead to have Ellen design their invitations on ice blue paper with platinum ink. The look was captivating, unique, and true to the color theme of the wedding.

- *Wedding #2* brought the couple's romantic red-and-white theme (as used in their flowers and reception décor) straight to the invitations. For this black-tie formal wedding, they used bright red paper with silver ink. "This couple had great courage and a sense of style with their invitations, and that translated to the wedding itself," says Ellen.

So, color is *in* now for even the most formal invitations. Take note! You're free to choose between the bounds of custom with off-white papers, or go bold with brights and pastels. The choice, quite rightly, is yours.

Paper Freedom

Ellen Weldon goes on to say that the mark of the unique and personalized wedding invitation, that little something extra special that today's couples are looking for, is all in the paper the invitations are printed on. The color-and-patterned-paper trend began several years before we entered the 21st century. Handmade papers with bits of dried flowers embedded in the paper texture quickly gained popularity—but they are so three years ago! Now, Ellen lists a few of the new, hot trends in invitation papers, which she specializes in finding from around the world and from individual paper artisans in the United States. "These artists are now coming to me, sending me samples of their wonderful, unique papers, so there's no end to the supply of gorgeous paper materials to work with on custom invitations and wedding card packets," says Ellen. Here's her short list of great new trends in papers for all your wedding weekend print needs (more on this later in this chapter!):

- Wedding papers are more contemporary and edgier in how they incorporate special design and print elements on unique papers.

- We're seeing more line drawings on invitation papers, such as bunches of grass for outdoor weddings and beach weddings.

- We use papers from around the world, bringing the best of the international markets home for unique use—India, Thailand, Australia, Indonesia, Japan, China, South Africa, Egypt, to name a few.

- We're using texture in papers and ties, such as Japanese caning paper.

- We just created a unique hand-embroidered invitation for a wedding in Maui. This one will be a scroll to be rolled up and placed in a custom-made box covered with silk.

Color My Letters with Passion

With a world of papers at your disposal, and true artistry going into your invitations, menus, place cards, and programs, we also encourage you to look at the diversion from formal black lettering. Here again, you have a choice! You can use unique papers, but hold fast to the tradition of formal black script lettering, or you can listen to Ellen Weldon once again and replace that black ink with color! From charcoal gray to deep navy, a tea-colored brown to a deep purple, turquoise to burgundy, now the color of formal invitation print can match the color of your flowers, the color of the ocean in St. Lucia . . . or the color of your eyes! It's completely personalized, and a welcome burst of beauty in the world of formality.

Fonts with Flair

Fonts, too, are more contemporary—no longer limited to the two black, swirly script prints that are stamped "proper." Now, you can get unique with your style of font, going nontraditional and keeping the print in tune with the style and theme of your occasion.

Linda Zec-Prajka of An Invitation to Buy—Nationwide (www.invitations4sale.com), a company based in Orland Park, Illinois, says that fonts have literally exploded in style and availability. When Linda got married in 1989, she had only about twelve fonts to choose from! Now, you'll find an unlimited number of fonts. And the best part is . . . you don't have to choose just one font for your invitation. Here are Linda Zec-Prajka's top tips regarding fonts:

- First things first: Choose fonts that are legible. Some are so swirly and detailed that they will be hard for your guests to read.

- It's absolutely vital that you check out how the numbers look in your chosen font. In some forms of script, 0's can look like 9's, 1's can look like 7's. If you're having trouble discerning the numbers, then your guests—particularly your elder guests— will have trouble reading them too.

- Next, be sure to look at the capitalizations of your most important letters, such as those of your first and last names. Go one-by-one through the letters that will be capitalized, and be sure all are legible and attractive. Some fonts are so artistic that a T can look like an F.

- Now you can order double fonts for your invitations. This has been a growing trend for the past five or six years. You can have the wording of your invitation in a straight manuscript font, but have your names in a different font to set them apart. By the way, your invitation stylist or company should not charge you extra for this.

Show Me Proof!

Linda Zec-Prajka offers this key piece of advice when you're ready to select the font and style of your invitations: Order a proof. This may be news to you, but you can order one copy of your invitations so that you can see exactly what your chosen invitation style, font, colors, and wording will look like before you spend hundreds of dollars on your full order. It's well worth spending $8 to $25 on a proof before you make such a big investment so there are no disappointments when the finished products arrive.

"Most invitation companies will send you a print-up on plain paper with an outline of your invitation designs drawn in," says Zec-Prajka. "Birchcraft is the only invitation company I deal with that sends a real proof on an actual invitation card. It's a little pricier, but worth it to get the full effect and see the real thing first."

Note: Check to see if the invitation company you choose will automatically send a real proof or a photocopy, or if you'll have to request one specifically; different companies have different policies and practices on this matter.

Finding the Right Words

Does this artistic new freedom with invitations extend to their wording? No, and rightly so. Tradition and the dictates of etiquette stand firm when it comes to the actual wording of formal wedding invitations. As Ellen Weldon says, "The rules of wedding wording transcend the ages," and we couldn't agree more. It's fabulous that today's weddings have stretched the boundaries of what used to be accepted in so many areas, but some things should remain untouched. The wording of formal invitations is one area where tradition has its place, so follow the rules.

You, the Diplomat

It's a simple card with a few simple sentences, but so much family diplomacy comes into play here. Which set of parents will be listed first on the invitation, as the grand hosts of your event? What if the groom's parents paid for less than half of the wedding expenses? Should they be listed as co-hosts right up there with the bride's parents' names?

And if the two of you will plan and pay for the wedding, is it disrespectful to list yourselves as hosts, mentioning your parents halfway down the invitation as just that . . . your parents? How do you deal with the emotional fallout from parents who still think it's 1965 and carry that decade's reverence for the bride's family? How do you list step-parents? Divorced parents? Newly discovered adoptive parents or the grandparents who raised you? It's enough to make your head spin, and not in a way that helps your hairstyle! Who knew a simple line on an invitation could provoke a family feud, hurt feelings, the silent treatment, and threats not to attend your wedding or walk you down the aisle?

Sadly, it's true. The wording of wedding invitations is a major stress point for families and a common subject of questions Sharon gets through her online wedding Q&A column at www.nj wedding.com. To help you envision the wording layout for a formal wedding, look at the following script that Amber Parsell Lynch (featured on page 141), who married George Lynch III in Charleston, South Carolina, shared with us. This wording mixed with the layout of her elegant formal invitation conforms to the eternal standards of etiquette:

Mr. And Mrs. Thomas James Parsell
Request the honour of your presence
at the marriage of their daughter
Amber Lee
to
Mr. George Philip Lynch III
Saturday, the fourth of May
Two thousand and two
seven o'clock in the evening
First (Scots) Presbyterian Church
Charleston, South Carolina

In this invitation, Amber's parents are listed as the hosts. Since we know this is the 21st century, with both sets of parents now sharing equally or to some measure with the planning and paying for the wedding, look to these variations to suit your own personal invitation wording needs:

When the Bride's Parents Are Divorced ...

Mr. Alexander Elliott

And

Mrs. Renee Simmons Elliott

[or Mrs. Renee Simmons if she has reverted to her maiden name]

request the honour of your presence

at the marriage of their daughter

Alexandra Jane

and

Mr. Thomas Scott Jenkins

son of

Mr. and Mrs. Arnold Jenkins

Saturday, the twenty-fifth of May

. . .

When Both Sets of Parents Are Hosting ...

Dr. and Mrs. Reginald Sunata

And

Mr. and Mrs. Kelvin Brown

request the honour of your presence

at the marriage of their children

Evangeline Anne

and

Mr. Kenneth Brown

Saturday, the fifteenth of May. . .

When Multiple Sets of Parents Are Hosting

This includes adoptive parents, birth parents, step-parents, and the very common situation of both sets of parents being divorced and re-married yet hosting as a group of *four separate* sets of parents . . .

The loving parents of
Kenya Daye
And
Warren Marshall
request the honour of your company . . .

When the Bride and Groom Are Hosting

Ms. Julia Anne Sage
And
Mr. Oliver Michael Jeffries
Request the honour of your presence
As they unite in marriage
Saturday, the twenty-fifth of May . . .

With Honour and Favour

The most formal of invitations allow you to become British for the day. When you express "The honor of your company is requested at . . . ," you may substitute *honour* for honor (or *favour* for favor) . . . just as the Queen would. Ellen Weldon, our invitations expert, explains the ruling guide for this important phrase, the actual extension of the invitation as such:

> For a wedding that will be held inside a house of worship such as a church or synagogue, the correct wording is " . . . request the honour of your presence" (or "honor" if you choose not to use the old-world wording). For a wedding that will be held outside of an official house of worship, you would use "request the pleasure of your company."

Similarly formal and elegant wording is used throughout the rest of your invitations and envelopes. Titles are spelled out, such as "Captain" and "Master," and all abbreviations within an address also get the elongated treatment (as in "Street," "Avenue," "Boulevard," and the full names of cities and states where your wedding events will occur). It's a matter of proper addressing, as well as one area where formal weddings do not let you exercise creative control.

Come Join the Fun

For informal invitations, you may veer from centuries-old etiquette as you will—get funky, fun, playful, and creative with the wording if your informal wedding allows you the opportunity. For a less formal invitation, your chosen wording will obviously depart from the formal word use. You might instead choose to "invite you to attend," or it might follow a completely casual style of wording as follows:

Come with us to the sun and sands of Jamaica
As we join in marriage
at sunset
Saturday, June 24th
Wedding beach attire and shades a must
Maureen and Sam
RSVP by June 1: 555-8269

Some brides with artistic flair create poetry, use their own line drawings or watercolor art, or have their wording done in the most decorative fonts possible. Digital pictures of the couple can be featured on informal invitations, and even children's artwork has graced cards inviting guests to the weddings of blending families. Ethnic designs find their way onto the papers, and unique vellums laid over the tops of floral invitations lend an ethereal look to your packets. The Queen and diehard etiquette mavens might fan away their surprise when they see your irreverent designs, but you can beam, knowing this invitation design is truly *you* in your own unique and informal way.

Love in Any Language

The 21st-century world is multicultural and multilingual, so wedding invitations may be as well! With so many weddings combining brides and grooms of differing ethnic origins, religions, and languages, a beautiful, unifying gesture is to create wedding invitations in both of your family's native tongues. Ellen Weldon brings this idea to your attention, and encourages you to consider it. She has done Spanish-English invitations to great acclaim, including singer Marc Anthony's media-covered wedding celebration with his bride Dayonara. Their wedding invitations were in silver and white with silver organza ribbon. Even if you're not internationally known, you can be international in the wording of your wedding invitations.

Invitation Inserts

Within the pockets and folds of your well-chosen invitation packets, you will include any of the following:

- Reception card

- Response card

- Response envelope

- Printed notice of hotel reservations and contact information

- Printed notice of your wedding website (if applicable)

- Printed directions or a detailed map to your ceremony and reception sites

Be sure your add-ins conform to the style and formality of your invitations, whether you order them professionally along with your invitation package or create them separately on your home computer.

Punchy Papers for the Day

It's become almost universal for brides and grooms to provide beautiful printed wedding programs for their day. They might be formal single cards, program folders, or even the very stylish and unique look of six or seven individual long cards attached at the top by a color-coordinated ribbon.

The program will, of course, outline the elements of your ceremony, list everyone's names—from your parents, to bridal party members, to the officiant, to the musician—and gives you two an opportunity to print an indelible message of thanks to your guests, pay tribute to your parents, and announce that the flowers stand in memory of your departed family members. This take-home keepsake, printed as attractively as possible, becomes an eternal reminder of the people who played special parts in your day. When your guests get their first glimpse of your program on the wedding day, they get a feel for the class, style, and sophistication of your wedding and the excitement ahead.

We Wish to Announce

For wedding announcements, use your chosen sense of style and formality. As mentioned earlier, save-the-date cards are essential for destination weddings and weddings to be held during the popular summer months. And as a reflection of today's wedding spontaneity, we've seen beautifully designed and whimsically worded announcements of a couple's elopement. Again, Ellen Weldon has an example: "We did one wedding announcement that read along the lines of 'Woulda, Coulda, Shoulda . . . But We Eloped!' Such unique and personalized announcements share your great upcoming or past news with flair."

How lucky to have such freedom to choose—freedom to be yourselves and have your say with the previously untouched hallowed grounds of wedding details.

flowers that won't make you wilt

Flash back for a moment to when you played bride in Mom's heels; an improvised veil; and always, yes, a little nosegay bouquet, even if it was scrunched-up stems from the garden next door. Fast-forward and here we are! Nothing signifies pure celebration in quite the same way as does a profusion of flowers.

Flowers complete the wedding dream. Now, you might choose a collection of white roses with a sprinkling of blush florals; a dramatic burst of color—all red; a range of deep purples; or a sunny collection of daisies for an informal, outdoor look that's blooming with innocence. Color, foliage, fruits, and more entice you to mirror your passion by bringing floral fantasies in beautiful, living color.

The Bridal Bouquet and Me

Deciding on your bridal bouquet and the flower arrangements of your day is one of those moments you deserve to indulge yourself. We say let yourself swoon, smell, and be seduced by your blooms of choice. We have some magnificent advice on how you can transform that branch of twigs you clutched in childhood into your bridal bouquet and floral display, so let's get to work:

from michelle

The bridal bouquet of only pure white or demure blush roses is over. Brides can walk down the aisle with truly original and colorful creations. The flowers you choose can set you apart from the millions of brides before you.

- *Snap open that bridal binder.* Like most significant elements of your wedding, your bridal binder should be filled with ideas that inspire you. As always, gather ideas on just the kind of floral bouquets you want, as well as concepts for your wedding day flower décor.

- *Flower.com and albums anon.* Check out websites and bridal magazines, and browse through portfolio books at your appointments with the floral pros. Be ready to describe the style and formality of your wedding, and provide a picture of your gown to your floral designer.

- *Take your wedding scheme to a florist.* Today's florists artfully weave their designs into the tapestry of your day, making sure that every floral piece they design works with your total wedding scheme. A photograph, sketch of hyperlink from your dress designer's website, plus pictures of your maids' gowns will cue floral designers about the lines and style of your dress so they can design a bouquet that coordinates with your look. Even more important, the designer can choose the right size of bouquet for your stature and the accents of your gown. Make sure you're not hidden behind a too-large arrangement that takes you over like a *Dynasty* mid-80s look. The delicacy of your gown should be visible behind the flowers you carry. You need to work it, not it you!

To illustrate the concept of your bouquet working with the look and style of your wedding, Sharon Naylor spoke on behalf of *Your Day, Your Way* with renowned floral designer Michael George, whose

Happily Ever After

When Amber Lee Parsell Lynch married George Lynch III in the bride's original hometown of Charleston, South Carolina, the couple created a theme of a Tuscan garden (see their feature on page 141). Their colors were celadon and lavender, which they carried in theme from the ceremony to the reception and all of the details in between. Her bridal bouquet was white vendella roses with green hydrangea, and her bridesmaids' bouquets were sterling roses with green hydrangea and blush purple flower accents. The mothers carried small bouquets of white vendella roses, and the flower girls carried purses of sterling roses with celadon ribbon around the wrist.

company has a top name in wedding flowers (www.michaelgeorge flowers.com):

> SHARON NAYLOR: What would you say is the new, hot trend in bridal bouquets, and how have bouquet styles changed from decades past?

> MICHAEL GEORGE: Styles go in and out over the years, just like in fashion. But there is one major change right now: Traditionally, brides have always imagined and planned to have cascading, over-scale dramatic bouquets to fit the style of their elaborate wedding gowns. But now, in fashion with the gowns themselves, the look is less traditional and more couture. So the bouquets have changed to be more tailored and couture, to match the entire look of the gown, hairstyle, and mood of the wedding.

> SN: So you look at the dress and the style of the wedding to design the bouquet?

> MG: We tune in to the dress, see what the silhouette is, and also look at such elements as the lace and beading. We might take some of the extra lace fabric from cutaways of the bottom of the dress and use that for the handle of the bouquet. Or we might use pearl beading in the bouquet design and handle to match the beading of the gown for a unified look.

Sharon also spoke with Michael George about the new looks in bridesmaids' bouquets (they too have a more couture look that matches their gowns) and about the hot selections for boutonnieres. Michael George shared a story of how, long ago, grooms would pluck a flower from the bride's bouquet and insert it into their lapel slit. Now the groom's boutonniere flower choice is a matching look with the bride. If she has a bouquet of stephanotis and gardenias, he might wear a stephanotis boutonniere so that the bride and groom match. Similarly, the other men of the bridal party will wear boutonniere

David Coake, editor-in-chief of *Florists' Review*, seconds the notion of designing the bouquet according to the shape and style of the dress, but he also says that today's florists are looking at the *bride's* shape as well. "It's just like how a hairstylist looks at the shape of the bride's face to create the ideal haircut for her," says Coake. "Professional florists look at the bride's shape and features to determine which style of bouquet will most flatter her."

flowers of a type that matches those carried in the bridesmaids' bouquets. "The coordination of these matched flowers," says Michael George, "provides a careful, tailored look for all."

Wish List

Plan your flowers with precision, choosing not only the colors you want, but the individual varieties of flowers and greenery you'll carry into your wedding day vision. Visit flower Web sites if you must, to explore the wondrous world of buds and blossoms. Among the usual wedding-type flowers such as roses, lilies, lily of the valley, stephanotis, and gardenias, you might discover ranunculus, camellias, and foxglove. It's a fragrant floral universe out there, so explore your options.

One 21st-century trend that's blooming is choosing premium flowers for all your bridal arrangements. Even for more informal weddings, couples are choosing quality blooms to give their weddings an elegant and natural feel, staying away from the noted "inexpensive" flowers and opting for a higher class of flowers . . . even if they'll use fewer of them. David Coake of *Florists' Review* says there's a big push for highly scented and exotic flowers: oriental lilies, hyacinths, gardenias, orchids, stephanotis, and of course a variety of roses—the eternal bridal favorites.

Aisle Style

Some blooms are in season and plentiful at certain times of the year, and may be rare and imported (and thus more expensive) at other times. Sometimes it's best to let Mother Nature decide for you.

Symbolic Fleurs

Find out the symbolic meanings of flowers, too, in case you'd like to imbue your day with sentimental sayings or select the flower of your birth month (and your groom's too!). You may feel strongly about honoring the matriarchs of your family. Having the same flowers your mother, mother-in-law, or grandmother had at their weddings will honor them to no end. (Michelle Roth, for example, chose her mother's gardenias to show respect and as a symbol of good luck.) Or, go international and give a nod to your heritage by using the traditional flower of your ancestors' homeland.

Bouquet by Design

Cascading, fragrant gardenias, grapes, and champagne roses were Michelle Roth's choices for her walk down the aisle, and there is nothing like creative bloom. David Coake says this: "The trend is moving away from the small knots of flowers and densely packed round bouquets that have been in for the past few years and giving way to more of a cascade arrangement. Not the huge, opulent enormous cascades of decades past, but smaller designs with an elongated oval or teardrop shape. Round bouquets are still popular, and they're growing a bit more in size now."

from sharon

A bouquet with personal meaning won't be shown in any florist's design book. This is your chance to paint a custom bouquet that's blooming with meaning and tribute.

your bouquet directory

Make sure you've pre-designed every item you include on your shopping list for wedding flowers. Start with this list and make it bloom and grow as you wish:

- Your bouquet
- Bouquets for your bridesmaids
- Bouquets for your maid of honor, matron of honor, or best lady (Add a little stylistic flourish, such as roses of a different hue from the maids' bouquets.)
- Boutonnieres for the groom, his male attendants, fathers, and special male guests
- Corsages for the mothers, grandmothers, and special female guests
- Décor for the ceremony site
- Décor for the reception site
- Your throwaway bouquet for reception fun

- Any floral tribute arrangements (such as a special, flower-ringed portrait of a departed family member, or a special wreath to float off into the ocean in memory of loved ones who've passed on)
- Flower petals for the flower girls to scatter
- Extra flower petals for table décor, such as those to be sprinkled on tablecloths around your centerpieces
- Floral arrangements to decorate your getaway car or horse and carriage
- Floral arrangements to perk up restrooms
- Fresh flowers your baker will use to decorate the top of your cake
- Flowers for your hair, or your maids' or flower girls' hair

One trend in floral design today is including unique additions to floral arrangements that set you apart. It might be tall, flowering branches standing up from your arrangements . . . perhaps cherry blossoms for your springtime wedding. Your florist might add ginger blooms, cactus blooms, berry sprigs, sugared fruits, nuts, unique greenery, or filler so your arrangements have visual impact. When it comes to flowers for your wedding day, creativity knows no bounds. Do, however, recognize the bounds of taste. Go traditional or go unique, always making sure you've pre-designed your entire shopping list.

Accents upon Accents

For the bridal bouquet, consider accenting your flowers. This trend was popular in the 1970s and 1980s, and it's making a comeback in 21st-century bouquets. We're seeing pearl and bead accents applied *within the flowers themselves,* by inserting pearl head corsage pins in clusters in the centers of rose heads. These pearl or crystal heads can be traditional white or off-white, or in a coordinating pastel to unite the hues of the bouquet. You'll want to see photo examples of this accent, as the effect is elegant and stylish, bringing something extra to even the most modest collection of blooms. Ask your floral designer about accenting your bouquet, as well as others, using netting with crystals embedded, ribbons, and unique creations for your bouquet's handle.

Backup Choices

Wedding day disappointments can occur, and we want to help you avoid them. Yes, of course you should be able to walk down the aisle with exactly the flowers and elements you planned for. Yet you must also be prepared for "on the day" changes. With uncertain weather patterns, anything can happen to a crop of tulips in the Netherlands or the Bird of Paradise supply in Hawaii! So prepare a Plan B that names both the type and color of flowers your florist can substitute if necessary, providing leeway on the day of preparation. An approved substitute list will leave you delighted at the altar and not wilting from disappointments if for some reason the florist's order of lilies doesn't arrive on time.

from henry

I don't believe you can have too many flowers at a wedding, wherever the ceremony and reception. They are such a symbol of happiness and festivity, and truly set the tone for a special day. However, if the particular type of flower you ordered is not available on your wedding day, avoid disappointment and upset—you'll laugh when you look back!

Very important: Write up a detailed list of which floral arrangements are to be delivered where and when. For example: "Bride's

Q&A Bridal

What do we do if some flowers aren't delivered to the ceremony site in time?

This actually happened to Sharon! (Or rather, the florist dropped off the box of boutonnieres in the front of the church, but none of the men saw it.) "When I got to the church, my men were without boutonnieres, and had already seated the guests! My bridesmaids snapped some roses out of their bouquets and stuck them in the ushers' lapels for the ceremony. We replaced them later with the *real* boutonnieres from a box set right on the altar. My maids' quick thinking saved the men's appearance . . . at least during the ceremony."

If something isn't delivered, whether it's your boutonnieres or, worse, your bouquets, improvise! One bride had her limousine stop at a florist's shop on the way to the church to buy single white roses with filler for each maid (and the bride) to carry. You can fight with your negligent florist later—just save the day with quick thinking!

and bridesmaids' bouquets to 2345 Main Street by 9:00 A.M. SHARP!" And "Men's boutonnieres to the Intercontinental Hotel, Room 203 by 10:00 A.M. SHARP!" Be sure you include exact street addresses and your cell phone number so the florist can reach you in case of emergency, such as a locked church door or no one at home while you and the girls are at the beauty salon (add an alternate note, such as: "Take the boxes next door to the neighbor. Don't leave them outside, not even in the shade!").

Pre-think the flower delivery plan, and have all delivery instructions spelled out clearly in your contract with the florist. Together with your designer, plan set-up timing so the atmosphere is complete well before your guests arrive.

When you speak to the floral designer, find out who will be doing the decorating with your chosen flower pieces. Will the designer personally be on-site to instruct and create your wedding day look, or will the design team arrange your reception décor? Do they plan to drop off, or will they tie the floral pieces to the pews and place the altar décor on the altar? Be specific about such details in your contract, and give your flower co-coordinator (a helpful friend overseeing the floral delivery and setup) a copy to have in hand.

Flowers are festive, organic, visually joyful . . . and sometimes magnificently fragrant. But remember that too much fragrance can be overwhelming. Subtle elegance is best.

making the reception right for you

The celebration is often the most defining, exciting, and style-influencing element for today's couple. The key to a great celebration is location, location, location. The reception is when your wedding becomes unquestionably Your Day. Not only has there been a major shift in officiants' willingness (and ability) to marry you at a reception location of your choosing, but the new, imaginative locations for receptions has in turn had a major impact on your theme, and how your wedding will actually look.

As you'll see throughout this chapter, coordinating all your wedding elements—from the cake to bridesmaids' dresses to invitations to favors—has the most impact on wedding style. Your reception is where it all comes together.

As with all other elements, your reception should be truly *you*—an unmistakably personalized affair that pays unmistakable tribute to your family, to your partnership (and your children, if you have them), and perhaps even to your heritage. In the sections that follow, we'll guide you through building your reception wonderland—a place of beauty, class, and elegance—by sharing what's new and red-hot in reception style. Take notes! You'll want to apply exceptional flair to your day with some of these flawless touches!

Your Menu

Your reception menu is prime territory for creating flair that leaves your unmistakable signature. Fortunately, brides today can break free of what is visually expected at a wedding.

The menu options out there for every wedding type, from the ultra-formal to the ultra-casual, could fill several phone books, so we won't venture to list appetizers and entrées from A to Z. We will tell you that today's wedding couple is sophisticated when it comes to menu choices, from cocktail hour through dinner and on to desserts. Every caterer and chef we spoke to said essentially the same thing: Today's bride and groom have excellent tastes for gourmet, exotic, and cultural foods, and they know exactly what they like and what will thrill and satisfy their guests.

That said, we encourage you to research potential caterers and chefs well by checking with professional catering societies, asking plenty of questions, sitting down for tastings to sample their food, and creating your menu list with your wedding style and theme in mind.

Trends

The hottest trends today include ethnic food stations, multiple stations at elegant cocktail hours, and unique combinations of gourmet dishes for the dinner hour—all stepping away from the decades-old standards of "chicken or beef" to explore wondrous and romantic flavors and spices in sauces, soups, salads, and sinful desserts. Choose dishes that your guests can't get elsewhere, brilliant blends of traditional and eclectic tastes that will pique their taste buds.

Delving deeper into the world of reception menus, Henry spoke on behalf of *Your Day, Your Way* with Robert DeMaria, director of catering at the Hotel InterContinental in New York City about the ideal selection of wedding fare. DeMaria suggests the following steps for making your tasty and taste*ful* menu decisions:

- Meet the chef from the very beginning, so that he or she knows your individual preferences and needs.

---

a menu fit for wandering

Amber Parsell Lynch's Charleston, South Carolina, wedding (see her feature on page 141) reflects a growing trend that is spreading from the South across the country. They had a buffet-style reception, not seated, which is the tradition in the South. The hors d'oeuvres and meal were plentiful, but never cumbersome, leaving the couple's guests free to socialize and dance without being tied down to one table all night. Scattered chairs and tables gave guests appropriate places to rest, sit, and chat, but no formal seating was required in this very freeing and flowing reception style that we hope will continue to grow.

- Have the chef attend your menu tasting, so you can make direct suggestions and requests regarding the preparation and presentation of your menu choices.

- Have the chef work with you on offering special food pricing based on seasonal availability, and also "piggy backing" off a menu from an event that is happening the same night as your event. (For example, if the chef will be making special dessert crepes or pastries for another event that evening, then it's quite efficient to have the same items at your wedding.)

- Ten years ago, people liked to eat a LOT. Menus consisted of heavy sauces and overkill cocktail hours. Now, today's couples are more educated and know what they like. They also know what the current food trends are, which is likely to lead them to more stylized menu choices that might be more health-conscious.

- Challenge the chef. If you don't like what you see listed on a menu proposal, ask for other options.

- Ask plenty of questions: "Can we do this instead?" "What are our options?" "Do we need this?" Smart wedding couples customize their menus without worrying.

- Couples need not do what their parents did at their wedding 40 years ago. Think outside the box. Be creative. Incorporate ethnic cuisine. Mix the menu. There are no laws on what you have to serve.

from sharon

On behalf of Your Day, Your Way, *I spoke with Edward Stone, executive chef and partner at the Bernards Inn in Bernardsville, New Jersey. His eagle-eye view of the state of affairs in wedding menu building is this:*

> *Menus are far more sophisticated than they used to be, with requests for complicated dishes and appropriate wine-pairings instead of traditional banquet-hall reception fare. People are more knowledgeable about food and wine these days, so they want greater input on the menus. Even though chicken, beef, and salmon dishes are still popular, we're getting more and more requests for unusual entrees such as halibut, pheasant, venison, and lobster ravioli. An unusual dish can make the reception more memorable.*

Food Presentation

You might choose to have tuxedoed waiters wearing white gloves present elegant silver platters of hot hors d'oeuvres to your guests. Or, guests may go to serving stations stocked with unique ethnic dishes, and perhaps enjoy the stylistic flair of the servers. Sushi bars and Greek-style stations can add depth to your guests' food experience. And serving can become performance art, such as when the waiters light the bananas flambé, sending colorful orange and yellow bursts of flame (safely) into the center of the ballroom. One couple from Indiana requested a hibachi station, complete with a chef who enacted a traditional cutting and carving exhibition, flipping curled pieces of shrimp and catching them expertly on the edge of his knife. Such a performance brings life to your menu, entertains your guests, and incorporates your preferences into the celebration. Presentation is of the essence!

Garnished and Grand

Another word on presentation: Professional and celebrated chefs worldwide specialize in expert presentation—garnishes, creative carvings of radishes and tomatoes, swirls of sauces pooled together and run through with a spoon's edge to create a fine art of blended color and flavor, sprinkles of spice and dusts of sugar over dishes to create extra detail—and color is the order of the day. Whatever food choices you select, inquire about and inspect the method of presentation, the flair of the food designer and presentation experts. How will each dish be displayed on a station or buffet table? What will be the architecture of the display? Towers of skewered beef?

Food Specializations

Start with your own experience with food to determine your choices, and take it upon yourself to learn and speak up! Personalize the bill of fare by asking for changes to the standard menu. Ask for flair in the presentation. Request specialty dishes for your guests with religious or health considerations (such as avoiding all dishes with nuts in them due to potential guest allergies), stock meatless dishes for your vegetarian friends, and offer appropriate dishes for vegan friends. Please your "imported" guests by giving them a taste of here *and* a taste of home, something their palates are accustomed to.

Play to your guests' tastes, and choose dishes that remind you of special moments in your lives—perhaps a five-star chef's interpretation of your favorite home-cooked meal; items from the dinner you enjoyed the night you were engaged; or those medallions of beef, chicken baked with tomato and goat cheese covered with melted Swiss cheese, and fondue that remind you of your first date at a French restaurant. A meal that says something about you is a very special ingredient for your own wedding meal.

Your Cake

Wedding cake is a symbol of your unity, where wishes are made and silent dreams logged for life. That explains the fuss made over all that whipped butter, flour, and sugar.

Today, cakes are so beautiful and creative that guests often think cutting them would be a shame! Ah, but it must be cut and eaten to be fully enjoyed.

You've probably seen beautiful designs from Sylvia Weinstock and Ron Ben-Israel on the covers and in the pages of *Martha Stewart Weddings* and bridal issues of magazines such as *In Style*. You've seen the delicate lace-design piping, the

Q&A Bridal

We're going with the "More Is Better" approach for our reception menu, and we know from attending past weddings that there are likely to be a LOT of leftovers. My father will want to take some of it home, but we'd also like to do something more socially correct. Can we request that our leftovers be brought to a shelter for the homeless or for abused women and children?

By all means, yes! Many established reception halls handle this request often. If they haven't, then you can arrange to have a volunteer pick up and deliver your leftovers to charity establishments that have been informed of your donation well in advance. More popular establishments on the "serving list" include retirement homes, shelters for abused women and children, hospital wards, veterans' homes and hospitals, hospitals in general, firehouses, and police departments. Be sure you get permission from the reception hall, as some do not allow such acts of charity to carry through. In this age of lawsuits, some companies have a rule not to extend their charity.

ornate towers, the unique shapes and designs from daisy themes to smooth fondant workings that make the cake look like a wrapped gift, a Cinderella carriage, or a castle. Wedding cakes are works of art, created by your imagination and the visions and efforts of a gifted cake designer.

In decades past, couples popped into their local bakeries and flipped through a photo book of similarly frosted three-layer wedding cakes and chose from a list of half a dozen fillings and half a dozen cake flavors. Not so anymore! You can now commission cake designers to create a unique, edible masterpiece for you! You can work your cake into your wedding's theme, using sugar-paste flowers in bright or pastel colors. Your cake designer can even copy the pattern of the lace of your gown to unify your wedding look and formality!

"Today's bride is older, more sophisticated. She's dined in fine restaurants and perhaps traveled the world, so she has a finely developed palate, and wants to move away from the plain white wedding cake," says renowned cake designer extraordinaire Sylvia Weinstock. "Now, wedding cakes are more daring, reflecting the couples' own feeling about the wedding. They're going with color to reflect the season of the wedding—from bolds in summer and fall, to winter whites in winter. They're using not only round cakes, but squares, ovals, octagons, more exciting graphic shapes. Right now, we're doing a wedding cake in the shape of the Eiffel Tower for a bride and groom who got engaged atop the Eiffel Tower in Paris. We do basket-shaped cakes, vases, anything of quality. And for cake accents, we do lace designs, beading, and can use real 24-karat leaf and silver leaf edible accents on the cake."

The world of wedding cakes knows no boundaries!

Ahhh, but there can be a limit. Sharon spoke to Ron Ben-Israel, the owner of Ron Ben-Israel Cakes in New York City (www.weddingcakes.com) for his defining line of how far into the ethers of creativity 21st-century wedding cakes can go. Ron maintains that when couples come in to request a truly unique cake (and some come up with wild ideas!), Ron still encourages them to *keep a traditional wedding cake silhou-ette.* Yes, you can personalize your cake, but keep in mind that the cake does not stand alone! The cake, too, needs to work into the tapestry of the wedding's style, formality, colors, theme, and design. Here Ron Ben-Israel comments on how he guides couples through the design-ing of their wedding cake:

- Brides want something different—not just different from their mother's wedding, but from their girlfriends' weddings! There's a whole psychology to the bride's idea of the perfect wedding cake.

- When weddings are held in unique locations with unique visual elements, brides generally want a truly unique cake as well.

- When I sit down with a bride and groom, I ask them about their wedding's style and try to get a feel for who this couple is. But I don't stop there. I also look at a picture of the bride's dress, since it says so much about who the bride is. I note the lines of the dress—whether classical in an empire, princess, or sheath style, and the fabric—how it falls, whether it's silk, satin, or vel-vet, and I look at the movement of the dress. All these elements go into visualizing what the cake should look like.

- I also look at the location of the wedding. For instance, is it art deco like the Rainbow Room, or an expansive room with high ceilings and hanging chandeliers? The shape and style of the room also gives me clues to what kind of cake it should be.

- I look at the flower choices and how they will be arranged. Will the room be filled with elements of nature that can be incorpo-rated into the cake design as well?

These few examples should give you a clear picture. The 21st-century wedding is not planned piecemeal, with each decision an in-dependent one. Because all wedding elements should work *together,* your wedding experts will want to know what others are doing, ask you questions, and look at pictures so all can work as a team to create the wholeness of your wedding day design. Your touches of flair, then, come from this team effort.

Speaking of teams, many cake bakers work with a team of professionals from bakers and chefs to the sugar-paste artisans—those well-practiced culinary artists who painstakingly create each sugared calla lily, rose, and leaf *by hand.* The chefs are also the ones who design your cake's taste, which applies not only to its appearance (and we all know how gorgeous today's wedding cakes are!), but also to the delicious wedding cake confection! From fillings to icings, the 21st-century wedding cake is a treat to the palate! Goodbye white cake with strawberry filling! So long to the ho-hum standard list your *mother* chose from when she planned her wedding years ago. When Sharon talked with Ron Ben-Israel, she spoke also with his chef Tad Weliczko about the most popular flavors and fillings of the day. Get ready to salivate . . .

- Coconut cake with passionfruit and lime buttercream frosting (Tad says this complements Asian food)

- Cinnamon cake with honey butter cream (reminiscent of the homey tastes of pancakes and waffles)

- Chocolate and chocolate ganache cake with chunky peanut buttercream

- Very fruity cakes, such as really lemony cake with a raspberry or orange buttercream

- Chocolate cake with a Key lime buttercream (Tad says the couple who order this one hailed from the Florida Keys, where Key lime cheesecakes are all the rage.)

If you had to guess the top taste trends for the 21st-century wedding cake, what would you say? Decadence? Well, you're close. Today's couple defines decadence as a *taste of childhood* or a *taste of home.* That means using childhood favorites, such as crunched-up cookies or peanut butter cups, in wedding cakes. The food stylings of Ben and Jerry's also get a thumbs-up from today's couples and their cake creators, believe it or not. (We not only believe it—we love it!) Tad adds some examples of these homey, comforting, and equally delectable and decadent cakes:

- Pie tastes, like apple and pumpkin.

- Ice cream tastes.

- Ben and Jerry's tastes, such as chocolate chip cookie dough combination with brown sugar, buttercream, and chocolate chips or a banana buttercream with a hazelnut crunch

- Starbucks-inspired tastes such as white or peppermint-flavored mocha, cappuccino, and espresso flavors.

- And, of course, some couples' taste is for liqueur—such as Baileys Irish Cream buttercream, or the rum-soaked layers of a traditional European torte.

> ### sylvia's selection
>
> Sylvia Weinstock also provided a list of popular cake filling flavors that she often sees on wedding couples' wish lists: "We're doing cakes with passionfruit, key lime, blood orange, lemon curds, and berries. Some couples shy away from fillings and cakes that include nuts since a guest might be allergic to nuts of any kind, and we're also not using liquor in cakes so much at this time."

Both Tad and Ron say they can do pretty much anything you ask, and they encourage you to venture beyond white cake with traditional filling to add flair and personality to your cake. It's the last taste of the evening for your guests, so let their last morsels be the icing on the cake of your dream wedding. Send your guests home dreaming about your wedding cake . . . and wishing they had more for a midnight snack.

Groom's Cakes

In many regions, the custom of providing a groom's cake, a separate cake from the official wedding cake, is going strong. Sylvia Weinstock had this to say about today's groom's cakes: "The groom's cake is all about the groom, to honor him and his personality. When you see it, you'd definitely know it personifies *him*. For instance, if he's a runner, we might do a fun cake in the shape of a sneaker. If he's a doctor, we might design the cake as a doctor's bag."

Another option besides the groom's cake is the handing out of individual boxed groom's cakes. Sylvia Weinstock explains this as a "trinket of a cake," individually made and packaged in a 3-by-3-inch box, that's handed out to each guest at the end of the event. Folklore says that a guest who places groom's cake under her pillow that night will dream of his or her true love. Whether true or not, it's a token of good wishes.

Taste Test

When you work with your chosen cake baker, be sure you not only look at their available designs and flavors and request custom flavors, but ask for a tasting. You can't judge a cake by a picture in a photo album! Also, tour the baker's design studio if possible. Ron Ben-Israel takes prospective clients right into his kitchens and perhaps opens the refrigerator door to show them a cake in progress! You too should get a close-up look at the final product and, as Ron puts it, "try the cakes on for size."

Determine the size of cake you'll need, its "personality," cost, delivery instructions, and, of course, get a detailed contract with your selected cake baker. Leave nothing to chance.

Drinks

Again, the choice is yours. Most 21st-century wedding couples have been exposed to good wines and cham-

---

frozen delight

You've probably heard of the tradition that has you saving and freezing the top layer of your wedding cake, so that you and your groom can defrost and eat it on your first wedding anniversary. Sylvia Weinstock says:

This tradition started many years ago back in old England, when wedding cakes were made from fruitcake and would last practically forever. Now, with cakes made with butter and cream, special care has to be taken to preserve them. Wrap the top of the cake carefully in Saran Wrap and seal it inside an airtight plastic bag. Freeze it for the year, then defrost it the night before your anniversary. Then, as a couple, have a champagne toast and share your wedding cake again, one year after your big day.

pagnes, and have definite favorite vintages. Your catering manager can help you work out your own menu of drinks, as well as suggest "must-have" selections. Go for the best quality you can afford, balancing taste with price. Your guests will know when you have cut too many corners. Also, make sure you have specially created non-alcoholic drinks and cocktails. This can be quite embarrassing when overlooked.

Avoid the sometimes troubling taste dilemma ahead of time by hosting a tasting party at your home! If you need a second, third, or fourth opinion, invite your maids and men over for some wine, cheese, and hors d'oeuvres or desserts, and have them help you select some fine wines for your day.

Another option suggested by Robert DeMaria at the Hotel InterContinental is to have your site manager (particularly if your reception will be held in a hotel or restaurant) bring you into the site's wine cellar to pick out potential vintages for a special tasting. "Always ask about upgrading wines and at what price," says DeMaria. "Plus, most hotels have 'dead stock' or plentiful supplies of high quality, but slightly out of trend, wines that they would love to move."

The champagne toast is a must at nearly all weddings, and we encourage you to get the best quality champagne your budget allows. But as we deliciously experienced at Bridgewaters in New York City at the South Street Seaport, you can "dress up" champagne with a dash of extra taste and a blast of extra color. Here's how:

- Add pomegranate juice and a sprinkling of freshly plucked pomegranate seeds in the bottom of the glass.

- Add strawberry juice and/or a small, ripe strawberry (or raspberry) that will sit at the bottom of the glass like a red jewel.

safety first!

Sylvia Weinstock wanted us to remind you to *always* be sure that any cake shop or design studio you're considering is approved by the Board of Health and has food insurance, for your own safety. "When you go to the shop," says Sylvia, "be sure that it's clean, ask to see the inspection certificate, and make sure that the shop and its owners have a great track record. We've been in business for 25 years, for example, so you want to be sure that the expert you trust with your cake is going to be completely reliable."

from ron ben-israel

Whatever portion of your wedding you're planning, never accept a wedding professional's claim of "that's the way we always do it" when you question what they're doing or ask for something specific. If an expert waves you off with "Don't worry, honey," be very worried.

- Try peach, apricot, or any other fruit nectar to give your fine champagne a beautiful, coordinating hue and an extra dash of taste.

Be sure to consider ethnic drinks, such as warm sake, ouzo, or Metaxa, or imported drinks, as well as espresso, cappuccino, and liqueurs at the end of the evening, so your guests have something wonderful in hand throughout the evening with which to toast your happiness.

Fabulous Fabrics

For the ultimate in stylistic touches and eye-catching color that can unite the look of your room and give it depth and interest, consider the fabrics you use at your reception. From table linens to napkins, fabric swags on everything from your cake and gift tables to the bar itself, fabric has made a grand transition from the runways to your wedding head table. Sharon spoke with Wendy Dodds and Monica Morgan, fabric coordinators and the owners of Indigo Moon in New Rochelle, New York (IndigoMoon01@aol.com). Wendy and Monica specialize in designing fabric and linen touches for weddings and special events, and here is their best advice on using fabric to make a jaw-dropping impression on your big day:

- More and more, we are seeing couples incorporate linens to complete the décor of their event! The old ideas of flowers as their total décor, and white to ivory palettes, are gone. Now, the color palette of fire red, mandarin orange, and magenta is a popular trio. We've done several weddings and cocktail receptions using this palette in silk dupioni with sheer organza overlays. The look is hot and transforms any room into a special event!

- The color red, from tomato to deep scarlet, is very popular for weddings of all seasons. Red creates a luxurious, sexy, sophisticated atmosphere and is usually paired with equally color-drenched flowers to create a monochromatic look.

- The color combo of silver and shades of purple, from amethyst to lilac to plum, helps to create a clean look for today's modern couples. This look usually works well with fitted, boxed pleated cloths for a tailored, modern look.

Wendy and Monica discussed types of fabrics at great length and maintain that silk dupioni is the top rental among brides and grooms today. It has a great texture, is available in hundreds of colors, and offers that great draping quality you're looking for. If you're on a budget, satin is going to be more affordable.

Color and treatment designs adhere to the calls of the seasonal months. For summer, Indigo Moon's experts say that full linen cloths with embroidery in colors such as moss, butter, and slate are ideal for summertime weddings.

For chair covers, which are soaring in popularity, thanks to pictures of celebrity weddings and the summertime outdoor weddings couples attend more and more frequently, Wendy and Monica offer some stylish advice:

We do full chair covers in a variety of colors and fabrics, but truth be told, we don't like them! They look messy when you get up! We recommend the tuxedo chair back cover with a cushion cover. The tuxedo back covers the back of the chair and goes to the floor. It is very graceful and looks great in organzas, linen, organdy, and dupioni. It is also less expensive than a full chair cover. We also love the chair topper and cushion cover combo.

As for the cake table, Wendy and Monica say the cake is much too important to sit on a plain ivory cotton or poly cloth. Instead, they offer the option of an allover pearl appliqué on silk organza, hand-applied silk leaves on green bengaline, and sheared silk organza strips with crystal bead trim.

For napkins, creativity shoots for the stars. Indigo Moon specializes in unique napkin treatments, such as hem-stitched linen napkins dyed to match any color and also in a range of stitch sizes. Bringing the unification quest even deeper into the décor, you might also take Wendy and Monica's advice and use monogrammed napkins and napkin rings, taking your style of monogram directly from the design of your invitation.

As you can tell, we've come a long way from the days when brides and their mothers would visit their reception hall and choose from twenty or so shades of the same standard tablecloths and napkins. Now, great focus goes into the color combinations and coordination of colors and fabrics with your cake, flowers, and even your gown. Stitch it all together to create a flawless photo-ready reception site and a magical blended image for your celebration.

Toasts and Tributes

Nothing makes a reception more personalized and meaningful than a succession of heartfelt toasts to the two of you. Some are sentimental, some side-splittingly funny. Some are poetic and some have an edge. Some are even musical. What your loved ones have to say to you, and you to them, is the crown jewel of your evening, the unmapped, unscripted, and unplanned (by you, at least) joys of your celebration that perhaps make the greatest everlasting memories of all.

At no other time in your life will you be surrounded by all your loved ones, closest friends and colleagues, and longtime favorite people, all gathered for one purpose only: to celebrate your happiness together. The love in the room is palpable. It has color, taste, and scent. Words can express the depth of meaning in this magical moment only so much. Cherish this time, each interruption in the dinner hour, each time the band leader or emcee takes a moment to introduce one of your guests who wishes to "say a few words." Something wonderful is about to happen.

In decades past, the best man was the first and perhaps only guest of honor to propose a toast to you as husband and wife. Then parents started grabbing the microphone. Then the bride and groom as a pair, to thank their parents and guests for coming. Now, not only all of the above may do so, but the number is increasing. Here, then, is a list of those who might step on stage with a tale or good wishes before they clink their glasses and drink in your honor:

- The maid of honor, in addition to or perhaps in tandem with the best man

- The bridal party as a group

- The parents of the bride and groom

- The couple who introduced the two of you

- Your children, if you have them

- Your siblings

And no one said you cannot take the spotlight yourselves! Today's bride and groom take up the microphone separately and at times jointly. In fact, brides and grooms sharing their emotional words of thanks and tribute is a 21st-century wedding trend. So you might stand up to thank your parents for helping to make this day possible, and your most far-flung guests for taking two planes, a ferry, a train, and a cab to get here. You might thank your bridal party for putting up with you, special relatives for their encouragement during the wedding planning stress (we call that cloud two), or your children, your child attendants, your college friends, and your colleagues for being here.

from michelle

Henry was master of ceremonies at my wedding. He added tremendous humor and warmth. We laughed, and yes, the speeches added a tear or two. Some words from our speakers I will never forget!

And, of course, no reception tribute list would be complete without you, the bride and groom as individuals, saying a public "thank you" and "I love you" to one another, after your "ceremony nerves" have subsided. You're back on cloud nine, or perhaps hovering over it, happy as you've ever been. Your toasts may be sentimental, certain to bring tears to one another's eyes, and they will be genuine, something you'll both remember forever and repeat to your children and grandchildren when they ask about the best day of your life.

Toasts and tributes might be words, and they might be words put to music. You might consider having a song played or performed as a melodic way to express your feelings for your groom, a tune that will join your official "first song" in the chambers of your heart and memory. We toast to your happiness in the future as well.

from sharon

How far we've come from wedding ways in decades past! Now, couples mix up the order of special moments, whether it's cutting the cake earlier in the night to holding off the father-daughter dance until later in the revelry when Dad has loosened up a bit and can really twirl around the dance floor! You might choose to eliminate the bouquet and garter toss, or introduce original toasts, tributes, or fun elements. One baseball-player groom had his bride "toss out the first pitch" as a symbol of their fun new life together, and then the bridal party signed the ball. Originality takes over now, and amen to that!

Entertainment

Toasts and special tributes might be quite enough entertainment for your guests, but the true test of a successful wedding is this: How much fun is our crowd having? Led by a talented band or deejay, your guests can dance the night away to music that keeps the floor filled and smiles glowing. We encourage you to seek out quality musical professionals, from your cocktail hour pianist to the full band or jazz ensemble for your reception. Audition them, and hear them live in concert and see how they interact with their audience. These party leaders will create the soundtrack for your celebration and fill the hours with great moves, slow grooves, and spotlight twirls around the dance floor.

One fun option that's growing in popularity in wedding entertainment is providing special performances—perhaps a trumpet soloist who steps in to perform a few numbers, or professional singers who serenade you. Whatever entertainment you choose to surprise your guests, make yours the party of the century!

Another hot trend is having your band *change* halfway through the evening. They might change outfits—switching from formal tuxedos and glittering cocktail dresses for the dinner-dance hours of the event to a completely different look for when the music gets hotter and the performance really kicks up. At one reception, the buttoned-up band changed into snazzy zoot suits, the female singers wore shorter skirts and changed their hairstyles, and during the performance the band members threw their horns into the air and did splits. It was a real performance for the crowd. The level of entertainment today is much more specialized, and many couples bring in separate performers as an added treat for their guests. Now, your guests get a show, and not just five hours of the same dance-along music and ho-hum group dances. And for after the wedding, entertainment eases into more of a lounge feel, with bands or DJs spinning smoother jazz and wind-down music that's the perfect finishing note for your event.

from henry

As a part-time deejay, music selection is of vital importance to me. Classic tunes of the '40s, '50s, and '60s can be very hip for today's wedding guests from ages seven to seventy. Keep the volume at talking level. Fluid conversations should not be drowned out by a zealous deejay. Set the volume level in advance.

saying "cheese" with ease

Photography and videography provide lifelong records of your day. Your pictures and videos will remain with you for years and generations, perhaps displayed in your home, perhaps pulled out on anniversaries so you can relive the magic of your big day. Any wedding

© Artists and Associates

Tiffany's Story

W HEN TIFFANY HOSEY, a 32-year-old attorney from Washington, D.C. (and a Michelle Roth bride), married 38-year-old Avery Brown, also an attorney, it was a *party!* As Tiffany described her reception, the entertainment came first, and food second. They featured a live jazz band, including Debbie Kirkland, a jazz artist well known in that area. Plus, a friend sang three songs with Debbie Kirkland as his wedding gift to Tiffany and Avery. Now *that's* entertainment.

expert worth his or her salt will advise you to invest a significant portion of your wedding budget in photography because visual records of your day only get more valuable over time. Your day is not the time to ask a friend to point and click in place of a professional (although guests' candid photos can add great depth to your wedding day photo collection).

Research professional photographers and videographers well, ask friends for referrals, and go to the experts' studios to look at their newest portfolios and samples of their work. A firsthand view is the best-hand view.

Portrait or Candid: Capturing Your Moments for Life

When dealing with photo artistes, it's helpful to understand the psychology and philosophy of what they do. Photographers and videographers capture precious moments in time, but they have different ways of doing it. Some are photo-journalists who approach your wedding day as a story in itself, hunting down the back story and taking pictures that tell the tale of your life. Some are completely visual, using color and light in each frame to intensify their passion for your pictures. Some value candids more than posed photos; some won't do posed photos at all. So ask your picture experts what school of photography they subscribe to, what you can expect in their final products.

from michelle

My photos were a mixture of formal portraiture and artistic photo-shoot-style shots. Memories were caught spontaneously. I am so glad I commissioned my photographer to focus on both styles.

Assess photography package details on the basis of the number of pictures you'll receive and hours of footage they'll take, number of rolls of film they'll shoot to details on the technology and cameras they'll be using. Step into the photographer's world, learn about their trade, and ask detailed questions. This is a valuable investment, so go into it with your eyes wide open.

And as always, once you set your preferences, negotiate for what you want, get answers to your questions, then insist on a detailed contract and be sure you read and understand all the fine print. You don't want to end up in court fighting over who owns the rights to your wedding pictures, or trying to get prints from a photographer who claims you never paid a deposit!

Envision the details you want captured in your images by trying to think like a photographer. Does your reception site have an elaborate gate entrance? Perhaps plan ahead to have your photographer snap a picture of you kissing under its arch. Will your reception hall feature a field of tulips in the distance? Consider arranging a group shot with that as your backdrop. Let your picture experts know what *you* want, what you think looks most romantic in his or her portfolio, and what once-in-a-lifetime shots you absolutely must have.

from sharon

Formal, posed portraits that look like lineups are slowly disappearing in favor of more relaxed group photos, perhaps the lot of you sitting or standing on a marble staircase in stances of your own choosing. Be sure to put the nix on cheesy, out-of-fashion pictures. I don't know one bride who adores the photo of the groomsmen lifting her up sideways as though rescuing her from a burning building.

One trend in photographic flair is getting at least a portion of your photographs printed in either black-and-white or classic sepia tones (like old-time pictures). Such images are timeless and elegant, classic and priceless, so offer yourselves this option. You never know whether you might one day change your home décor and those framed black-and-whites would make a great wall display. Having both color and black-and-white pictures gives you the best of both worlds.

Candid Moments

Your official picture experts might capture you two in wonderful spontaneous moments, but sometimes those throwaway and personally owned cameras capture the best pictures. Your in-the-know guests can spot Kodak moments like no one else, so stock your recep-

Q&A *Bridal*

At my sister's wedding, the photographer spent so much time taking posed pictures right after the ceremony that the bridal party missed the entire cocktail hour! How can I keep that from happening at my wedding?

The crazed photographer strikes again! The lengthy photo session, a common phenomenon at weddings, might not be purely the photographer's fault. Photo experts we spoke with said that gathering excited and wandering bridal party members and getting them to focus on the camera and smile, getting child attendants to cooperate, and adding long pauses to regroup between shots can take (seemingly) forever!

We recommend you gather all bridal party members, parents, and darling but attention-challenged children together and put it firmly: "If you pay attention and pose as instructed, we can get this picture-taking done in less than twenty minutes. Otherwise, you're going to miss the cocktail hour." More than one bride has raised her voice to get everyone to take the process seriously. Offer the alternatives, and your group should focus well. If it *is* the photographer who's dawdling, notify him or her that she has a half hour before you pile into the cars to head for the reception. You can pose whatever shots you missed later in the night.

tion with one-time-use cameras. For a twist, you might even provide a basket of throwaway cameras at the ceremony for an unbelievable array of shots as you walk down the aisle. Your professional photographer is just one person, after all, and might miss the wink you give your grandmother as you approach the altar.

After the wedding, be gracious and share beautiful albums of your wedding pictures with your parents and grandparents, and even with the people who introduced you and your groom. Send or e-mail your portraits to guests who were unable to attend the wedding, and enclose one in each thank-you note you send to your hired wedding professionals. Let them see how happy they helped make you!

the grand entrance: arriving in style

Your guests know that the bride is expected to arrive fashionably late to her own wedding (best to keep him waiting for such a good thing), and they all anticipate their first glimpse of you. In fact, seeing the look on your groom's face when he first sees you may be the priceless moment you're most looking forward to! Your grand entrance is indeed a pivotal moment. And as you take your first steps toward your groom, you're likely to pass guests who have tears in their eyes.

To experience the priceless moment of your grand entrance, you first have to get to the wedding site!

Your wedding day transportation—which not only gets you and your maids in position for the ceremony, but also to the reception and back home—is of the utmost importance. This reliable ride should be taken in grand style. You might dream about a stretch white limousine or a shiny Rolls-Royce, a romantic horse and carriage ride, or an adventurous arrival in a stretch Humvee. Some brides even arrive on horseback and others on the back of a Harley. "Get me to the church [or synagogue or grassy field] on time" becomes your mantra, one with a glossy image to fulfill.

from sharon

Few moments are as exciting for everyone as the second you come into view. All eyes are on you, so be sure you're smiling, breathing, and noticing your admirers' expressions. This is a golden moment you're unlikely to experience again.

Whatever you choose for transport, whatever its flair or image, be sure it's 100 percent reliable! That means researching rental car and classic car agencies well, getting referrals from recently married friends and family, and *always* going to the rental lot to inspect the cars in person. If you're not auto-knowledgeable, bring along a car-smart friend to help you ask the right questions about the car's age; backup scenarios in case of flat tires, mechanical breakdown, or accidents; and the company's policies on cleaning and waxing cars for a gleaming finish to start your day.

Work with the car rental agent to devise a solid and organized itinerary (and directions!) for transporting you, your men, maids, parents, and other family members to and from the ceremony and reception sites. Also, don't forget about your guests' safe rides! Some couples book party buses or hotels' airport shuttle buses to give their guests a reliable, safe ride to and from the celebration, and we think that's a splendid idea.

If you'll use your own car or convertible for the ride in personal style, be sure it's well-serviced and cleaned. If you are a traditionalist, decorate your chariot with perhaps floral pieces and a great big "Just Married" sign. If you're a traditionalist who believes in good-luck customs, your bridesmaids and ushers (or your groom) might attach streamers with tin cans or shoes to the back of the car. And request that whatever car you hire have a bottle of water in the back for two. After taking those vows and kissing everyone in the receiving line, you'll need a cool, refreshing drink. Or, skip the H_2O in favor of an awaiting bottle of bubbly, but only if you're a limousine passenger, for whom it's legal to drink on the road.

Another fun trend we're hearing about is the bride or groom stashing a special gift in the getaway car for making their first (and only) complete private moments as husband and wife even more special and unforgettable. Tucked in the back seat of your limousine or classic car, you can really give your sweetheart the kiss of his lifetime . . . not that proper, polished, for-public-viewing kiss with which you sealed your vows. Grab your quiet alone time now as you wheel off to the party of your lives.

favors and gifts

You've received so much from your family and friends that it's always a gracious gesture to give a little something in return. The notion of wedding favors has always been custom, but favors have moved into a higher level of creativity and charm in recent years. You still might find tulle-wrapped sugared almonds in pastel colors, a European favorite for its symbolism of the sweetness of married life ahead. You'll also see more sophisticated favors and gifts—candles, books of poetry, silver frames, crystal vases.

You cannot go wrong with those little gold ballotins of Godiva chocolate. The box alone carries the same impressive image as the little light blue Tiffany box. Also consider the gold standard in candles, which are always a great favor idea in color- and theme-coordinated looks, at www.illuminations.com.

Favors and gifts might work into your wedding's theme—stylish designer sunglasses for a beach wedding, or a framed family coat of arms for a Renaissance wedding. Whether you go brand-name and top-style, or home-made and priceless with meaning, be sure your favors and gifts say something about who you are as a couple and reward your most helpful and loving guests and family members with a little something to remember this day.

As with your food, presentation can be what makes your favors special! When you display your favors at the reception, be creative and ornamental. Use pedestals and trays to give your favors that department-store-window look, or group them in the centers of your table, or set one at each place setting. Sometimes, the presentation can make even the most modest gratitude gifts look priceless and impressive.

a stylish backdrop

We've saved the most impressive stylistic flair for last. The backdrop and ambience of the wedding location itself may be so awesome, so overwhelmingly beautiful and historical, so filled with natural and intrinsic beauty, that there is little improvement to be made. Perhaps you've reserved a historic estate with magnificently attended gardens,

© Warwick-Weddings.com

Jodi's Story

JODI DELLA FEMINA used the natural beauty of her father's beach estate in the Hamptons as a living, breathing accent for her day. At the place Jodi and her family called home, stylistic flair had already taken up residence—in the form of hydrangea trees in the front of the house (which led to hydrangeas becoming a part of their reception décor) to the floral and greenery-lined walkway to the beach, to the poolside terrace and beach stretching before them for the ceremony. A dazzling sunrise over the ocean was the backdrop for one of Jodi's most memorable moments: "Our wedding lasted throughout the night, and by the time my husband and I gathered on the beach with a few remaining guests, we were all just relaxing on the sand—I was still in my gown—and we watched the sun rise," says Jodi. "I'll never forget how perfect it was."

and you simply cannot improve upon the "decorating" of Mother Nature and a team of highly trained horticulturists. Inside the mansion, treasures such as a library, detailed architecture, mysterious secret staircases, and classic romantic balconies provide your flair and flawless touches.

Your wedding might take place at a reception hall with a garden of flowers near a serene lake or waterfall. Or yours may be a winter wedding where a recent snowfall left the landscape a lovely white and gave the surrounding tree branches the appearance of lengths of crystal sparkling in the sun. Use the most beautiful natural elements around you to emphasize the natural beauty of *you* and your shared love and commitment.

Or, if your idea of natural beauty has less to do with fields of wildflower and more to do with winding staircases and stained glass windows, choose a notable historic site with magnificent architecture and elegant accents. Vanderbilt Hall in New York City's Grand Central Station, for instance, is a breathtaking and unforgettable location for a wedding, with its expansive ballroom and first-class style. Plus, you'd get to boast that your wedding locale has been featured in movies! For just these reasons, more and more couples are using unique choices of location as the setting for their day, impressing their guests with style and views that could not be more of a departure from the standard hotel ballroom, however beautifully decorated.

Final Style

We say that whatever your theme, whatever your dreams, and however creative you are, don't be overambitious. Enjoy your day without creating so many complicated touches that will distract you from the reason you are there: to celebrate your love.

chapter 10

To Have and to Hold: Making Your Ceremony Meaningful

Your ceremony is the focus of your wedding day—the moments steeped in tradition, faith, and beauty that transform you into husband and wife. Your vows are your forever promises, the exchanging of rings an outward symbol of your inner commitment to one another, and any religious elements you choose to incorporate may unite you as one under the law and eyes of your faith. So what changes have the 21st century brought to the wedding ceremony? The answer is . . . many or none (and, yes, we will explain!).

just the way it always was

The 21st-century wedding couple can be as creative with their ceremonies as with their reception plans and wedding day wardrobe. However, despite all the freedom, some couples might need to stay within the bounds of tradition when it comes to their ceremony. You

From a planning perspective, your ceremony arrangements truly tie in with your reception plans. Without a set date and place, most arrangements are in a holding pattern. So think deeply, tread delicately, consult with others, and determine what works for you and what you can make work for you.

might find it easier to sidestep the white puffy ball-gown dress and the Eiffel Tower wedding cake than touch the age-old sanctimony of certain wedding ceremonies.

For instance, your church or synagogue might not allow changes. Some houses of worship administer strict rules of tradition, with little or no "wiggle room" for personalized touches. Some couples wouldn't have it any other way; they want the same centuries-old wedding ceremony as their parents and ancestors, right down to the symbolic rituals and readings. A 100 percent traditional ceremony is *them,* and their families expect nothing different.

Of all the potentially explosive areas, the ceremony is where couples face the most resistance; some families expect traditions to remain wholly intact. You will know if your ceremony is non-negotiable, and can use it as leverage for other wedding day wishes. If you say, "Okay, Dad, we will get married at the Greek Orthodox church in La Jolla," you can go on to say, "But the invitations *will* be silver and mauve." (See more on family politics regarding ceremonies in chapter 11.)

Our Way

Other wedding couples go to the other extreme. They might forgo all religious sentiment and tradition, holding a fully secular and independent ceremony that reflects their level of religious beliefs. This might mean marrying in a judge's chambers to make it legal, or in an outdoor setting with a mayor serving as officiant, or at a restaurant with a licensed nondenominational officiant announcing your commitment. No house of worship is involved so the expression of the couple's shared faith and values can be completely personalized.

Personalizing Tradition

Most common, however, is the religious wedding of whatever faith, held either in a house of worship or led by a religious leader in a location other than a church or synagogue. Today's couples frequently take the "script" of the traditional wedding ceremony and personalize it to some degree. Houses of worship are bending more and more to the wishes of marrying couples, allowing certain freedom in the selection of readings and music, special rituals such as taking a separate set of vows with new step-children, and tributes to departed loved ones. What freedom you'll have depends on your ceremony location and the flexibility of your officiants. Some allow more freedom, while others rule by The Book. It's up to you to undertake this personal journey with your officiant to create the ceremony of your dreams.

from sharon

A wonderful thing about the 21st-century ceremony is that it can be so filled with personalized elements. Great weddings include fun and sentimental unscripted moments, the couples' history woven into the day, family marriage tributes, heritage, and humor. A wedding without personalization is hollow . . . pretty on the outside but lifeless within. Yes, ceremonies are solemn, but with the right choices they will not be somber.

designing your ceremony

Before you begin designing your ceremony, sit down with your groom and answer these questions:

1. What kind of ceremony do we want?
2. What kind of ceremony is important to our parents and families?

3. If #1 and #2 differ, what do we plan to do to have the ceremony we want, while still satisfying our family's need for tradition?
4. Which religious rituals are most important to us?
5. Which additional elements do we wish to add to our ceremony?
6. Which ceremony elements are we sure we don't want?

As this chapter progresses, we'll explore these questions in more depth. For now we want to get you thinking about your deepest wishes for the type and depth of ceremony *you* want and how you will balance family pressures.

You've Got to Have Faith

Some big-ticket issues may be raised while you navigate ceremony arrangements. Before you can complete your ceremony arrangements, book the site, and hire your officiant, take care of the following essential tasks:

- *Paperwork:* In the event of a previous marriage, you may need to present your annulment or divorce papers, or even the death certificate of a previous spouse.

- *Lessons of Learning:* Your church might require you to sign up for premarital courses or counseling led by your officiant. If you live at a distance from your wedding location, you may need to fit those courses and the travel time into your schedule. Will you have to fly in for three weekends in a row, as have some of our brides and grooms, or can you take the classes in a church near you, bringing your "diplomas" along for the officiant's stamp of approval? The logistics can get pretty tricky, but meeting the requirements is extremely important, so handle arrangements with the utmost care and organization. Leave no question unanswered.

- *Fathoming Faiths:* Of course, faith is a highly personal and at times contentious issue. We believe wedding planning brings to the

---

Q&A *Bridal*

We're not affiliated with any church since we're not regular service-goers. How do we find a church and officiant for our wedding?

Even people who do attend religious services on a non-regular basis sometimes have trouble finding a house of worship and officiant who will perform their weddings! Some houses of worship only perform wedding ceremonies for regular parishioners or synagogue members, especially during peak wedding season. You may have to invest a good amount of time and energy making appointments and meeting with prospective officiants in their houses of worship to discuss everything from their availability and fees to any paperwork you might need to fill out before you'll be granted their services.

If houses of worship do not work for your style of wedding, you can go to your town hall or county courthouse to request a list of state-accepted officiants, such as mayors, judges, or township committee members. We recommend you go right to the source to find prospective officiants you can interview and meet with. And do this as far in advance as possible, as some mayors and judges have "busy times" when they cannot perform ceremonies.

What about the Yellow Pages and officiants who hold certificates of ordainment from the Internet? Research well and interview carefully to be sure these "experts" are indeed professional and legal. With so many Internet scams out there, we'd hate to see your beautiful ceremony not lead to a legal marriage!

---

fore concerns and ideology that you must deal with in an upfront manner to bring your future paths together. As you discuss the religious elements of your ceremony, the issue of shared or differing faiths can grow and deepen. As you look ahead to your future marriage and family, religion might become an important talking point. If you have questions now about your differing viewpoints regarding religious practices and what they will mean to your future, now is the time to get the answers or seek counsel from a member of the clergy. As you plan your ceremony, you might just wisely answer those key questions that marrying couples face—sooner, rather than later.

Although chapter 11 will discuss interfaith weddings in detail, we want to share the story of one groom who converted to his bride's religion before the wedding.

Sharing the Faith

"Before our wedding, Christopher decided to convert to Judaism," says bride Danielle Dobin (see her feature on page 104). "He learned about my faith from me, since we were best friends long before we became engaged, and he loved how the practice of Judaism brought my family together. Once we began dating, Christopher signaled to me that he was open to exploring the possibility of conversion. He came to synagogue with me, learned more and more about it, and just gravitated toward becoming Jewish on his own. His family had a rich spiritual life and they were very supportive. His mother even came to his conversion ceremony."

Danielle and Christopher's story exemplifies the importance of faith and family to many couples, and we offer it here as something you might explore as you look into the religious elements for your wedding. If one or both of you feels a spiritual call to convert, get answers to your questions now by researching and seeking advice. Explore the details of all religious elements of your ceremony, by speaking to your religious advisor, talking to friends, checking out books or articles, or visiting websites for in-depth information. A good wedding coordinator can also be a trusted advisor.

Who Will Walk You Down the Aisle?

Let's begin with your first image of your ceremony. Who do you wish to have walk you down the aisle? Some faiths have rules, such as having both parents walk you down the aisle, so that question is already answered. In many weddings of old, the father of the bride was expected to escort his daughter down the aisle and present her to the groom. Slowly, this tradition is changing, as more and more brides choose to have both their father and mother "give them away," or select a present and loving step-father for the honor in place of an errant biological father.

There are, of course, other reasons for a father not walking his daughter down the aisle. He may have passed on, or there may be simmering undercurrents in a blended family landscape. Should this issue be an emotional minefield for you, here are some suggestions that may help you determine your most comfortable option:

- *Grandfather:* Have a grandfather walk you down the aisle.

- *Mother:* Walk down the aisle with just your mother.

- *Brother:* Have a brother walk you down the aisle.

- *Father and step-father:* Invite your step-father to walk you halfway down the aisle, and your biological father walk you the rest of the way.

- *Parents by love:* Have an adoptive parent or parents walk you down the aisle.

- *Family first:* Have your child or children escort you down the aisle and "give you away."

- *Him:* Walk down the aisle with your groom, sharing the stroll together.

- *Me:* Show your independence by walking down the aisle alone and giving yourself away.

Brides who are in the precarious position of not having or wanting their fathers to join them have many acceptable possibilities. The 21st century offers brides the flexibility to deal with personal sensitivities, provided your house of worship allows for such a break in tradition.

Karri-Leigh Paolella will have her brother walk her down the aisle. "My father died when I was eighteen," says Karri-Leigh. "By the time I was planning my wedding, I'd known for ten years that I would have my brother be the one to walk me down the aisle."

Eccentric Entries

As you can well imagine, we have either seen or heard about most ceremony rituals. We've seen super-personalized weddings, including one at which the bride skydived to the site from an airplane. In settings ranging from mountaintops to the sugar cane fields of Louisiana, brides can now decide to walk, run, ski, or saunter down the aisle. Even the sky is no limit when it comes to personal wishes for tradition vs. personalized creativity. Put your personal "signature" on your wedding, and we are sure to read about it!

Selecting Readings and Music

The readings and musical selections for your wedding ceremony speak of who you are and what *you* wish to express about your love and commitment to one another. Again, you may include the most customary choices, such as your church's standard vows and selections from their "menu" of acceptable music, or you may enjoy choosing your own.

Readings might be anything from your favorite verses in Scripture (such as Corinthians 13: ". . . and the greatest of these is love") to works of poetry or passages from an inspirational book you both embrace ("You are my North, my South, my East, my West"). They might be personalized readings written by you two and read by an honored family member, or even the lyrics of a favorite, heartfelt song read as a poem. Readings can put your personalized stamp on your ceremony, bringing your deepest sentiments into your ceremony along with your vows.

Musical choices set the tone for your wedding's ambience (as we discuss in chapter 12), as well as provide a melodious way of expressing additional sentiment. Some ceremonies include as part of their repertoire a musical selection by a choir, pianist, organist, guitarist, or flautist. Some invite the congregation to sing along to printed words of a selected song. Friends of the bride and groom might stand to give a heartfelt rendition filled with emotion and joy. Such personal touches to the ceremony are (to quote Nat King Cole) "unforgettable." Music during the ceremony may be solemn or secular, ethnic and spirited, or even popular and personal. So will it be Beethoven or the Beatles? Schubert or Sting? The choices are yours.

For a wonderful collection of traditional and classical song ideas for your prelude, processional, or recessional, check out the articles on these topics at www.theknot.com.

from michelle

We had this magnificently spirited bride who decided to go down the aisle in Rollerblades, bridesmaids and all. She explained to us that she met her fiancé while they were out Rollerblading! I took a step back then thought, "Why not?" After all, if we encourage today's bride to include significance, symbols, and meaning, then she should let it glide! Of course, the Boston Globe *printed her picture and story.*

from henry

I will never forget a moving wedding I attended at St. Mary's Cathedral in Sydney, Australia, several years ago. The church bells were pealing as we arrived and the doors opened to a grade-school choir singing sweetly, their voices resonating skyward. There was not a dry eye to be seen, mine included.

VOWS

I take you to be my lawfully wedded husband, to have and to hold . . .

So goes the traditional recitation, by which you promise to be true to one another in good times and in bad, in sickness and in health, and forsaking all others for as long as you both shall live. Traditionalists repeat these vows in millions of ceremonies all over the country, and around the world in many languages. They might eliminate "obey" from their list of promises, as do many brides and grooms of this century, but otherwise they stick to the script.

Vows That Wow

For the nontraditionalist, and for those who will marry in secular locations or houses of worship that do not have a prescribed set of vows, here is the point where the sentiment and emotion can rise! We've heard beautifully personalized vows written by brides and grooms who express the deepest feelings of their hearts. *From the first time I met you, I knew you were The One,* they have said. Or *My heart, my tears, my joy is yours. Our lives together will follow one course.* Some *promise to make each day better than the last,* to *always hold true to their friendship* and to *value one another above all else.* They acknowledge that *the path of life ahead is unknown,* but vow to *walk it hand-in-hand, wherever the path may lead.*

They promise to be true to one another, loyal, and hold each other's confidences, to support one another's dreams and goals, and to love each other's family as their own. In situations where families are blending, they promise to love one another's children as their own, and to create a happy, warm, and unconditionally supporting family.

The beauty of 21st-century wedding vows is that they can be perfectly personalized, stylishly succinct, and drenched with emotion and tears of joy. These are the words you have been waiting to hear from one another, that announce the sanctity of your commitment. No more important words will ever pass between you.

Vowing Style Tips

Take plenty of time to write and revise your vows, searching your hearts for just the right expressions. These are not something to be scribbled out on a cocktail napkin two hours before the ceremony, or written on the train going to work. Make creating your vows a ritual. Light some candles, sit down with a glass of wine, a cup of coffee, or your favorite meal, and let your pen do its magic. You can either share what you've written with your groom (and he share his with you), or save it until the big day. We offer these tips for writing wonderful vows:

- Keep them short and sweet. You may have a lot in your heart, but writing a novel then giving a drawn-out speech can ruin the effect.

- Give it the Tear Test. If tears form in your eyes when you practice reading your vows aloud, you're onto something great.

- Be true to your heart. Avoid cliché and speak what you feel.

- Don't wing it! Some people do speak well off the cuff, but many freeze in the spotlight and stammer awkwardly. Prepare ahead of time.

- Put your vows in writing. Write them out on cards, and either hold them yourselves as you read, or have the officiant read them for you to repeat.

- Practice your lines! If you memorize your vows, as many couples do, practice, practice, practice! (And we recommend you give your officiant a copy, just in case you forget a line.)

- Don't be afraid to be funny! If your humor is one reason he loves you, let your quick wit shine.

- Think of it as just the two of you. The fear of public speaking ranks #1 on most experts' top phobia lists, so you might well feel weak in the knees when speaking in front of so many guests. When the moment comes for you to speak your vows, take a deep breath, unlock your knees and relax as much as possible, look into your beloved's eyes, and share this moment as if you're the only two in the room.

special touches

Ceremonies can feature special touches, from the highly symbolic lighting of the unity candle to special prayers and moments of silence offered to departed family members. For your ceremony, you might wish to offer a special prayer for or play the favorite song of a departed parent, sibling, or grandparent.

On a more celebratory note, you might wish to include any of the following:

- *Mother magic:* Present special bouquets or single-stemmed flowers to your mothers.

- *Love connection:* Present special bouquet or single-stemmed flowers to the couple who introduced you.

- *Amazing grace:* Present a small nosegay of flowers before a religious icon or statue, as per your faith's customs.

- *Family matters:* In place of a unity candle, create a symbolic family bouquet. One by one, your closest family members would bring up a single-stemmed blush-colored rose and place it in a vase, with the mixed flowers creating a beautiful collection of coordinating colors. Then, the two of you would each place a single-stemmed white rose at the center of this collection, surrounded by your family's flowers.

- *Join us:* Offer a special tribute to all the married couples among your guests, such as the officiant asking married guests to re-seal their own vows with a kiss.

- *We are one:* Make additional family vows with children and step-children in a blended marriage. You and your groom might present the kids with diamond pendants, birthstone rings, or family medallions to symbolize your devotion to them.

- *Peace and love:* Coordinate the release of doves or butterflies after your ceremony.

- *Peal it to the world:* Arrange to have the church bells or carillon play in celebration as you exit the church.

- *Write it in the sky:* Signal for fireworks to go off in celebration if you're marrying at night, or timing it perfectly for a view of nearby Fourth of July celebrations.

The traditions of your ceremony can have a major stylistic influence on the rest of your wedding. Will you need to have sleeves on your wedding dress or will you wear a flowing chiffon strapless dress by the sea? Will your invitations carry two languages and contain many blessings, or be customized to reflect you? Will you have customary pre-wedding celebrations that can last up to a week prior to the wedding then walk down the aisle in traditional ceremonial wear (as in Ethiopian ceremonies), or have a civil ceremony and a restaurant affair? You and the level of your ceremonial vestiges will decide.

Of course, all your ceremony elements depend upon your personal wishes, your connection with your faith, and your family customs. Coming up next in chapter 11, we'll touch on the wonderful blends of faith and cultures in many of today's weddings.

Saving Grace:
Interfaith Weddings and
Multicultural Matrimony

Marriage itself blends the lives and personalities of two people, and those planning an interfaith or multicultural wedding must blend the faiths, cultures, and traditions of the couple and their families. Such a union should embrace your most important values and beliefs, represent a merging of your families, and bring a new depth of reality to each of you. But when it doesn't go smoothly, the result can be more like "When Two Worlds Collide." We hope yours is of the first variety, but give you fair warning of the pitfalls and perils of the task called Wedding Blending. We also bring forward ways to negotiate, balance, and avoid various faith obstacles so love emerges the winner.

In many instances, couples face harsh criticism from family members who want *their* faith or culture represented fully, not in a watered-down version. Family clashes and battles can erupt, so family diplomacy is essential. Sharon spoke with Lois Pearce, wedding coordinator and owner of Beautiful Occasions in Hamden, Connecticut (www.BeautifulOccasions.com), who lectures often as an expert on multicultural and multifaith weddings. According to Lois, the beginning stages of planning a blended wedding of any kind can be fraught with anxieties and clashes. "Very often, it's not the parents of the bride and groom who have issues with wedding elements of one faith or the other culture; it's the elder relatives who have the strict views of what *should* be done."

Before they even get to the actual planning stage, the bride and groom might have their hands full worrying about potential family flare-ups. "The reality is that the engagement period equals real life," says Lois Pearce. "This is how it's going to be. When you're an interfaith or multicultural couple, some people are going to have opinions about that, and that's just the reality of it. Some couples unfortunately don't make it past this point. If their families are too one-sided, and they can't agree as a couple on the blending of their faiths or cultures, then they just don't make it any further along."

gaining faith and support from families

We recommend various practical approaches to help you gain the support and love you both so want from your families. First, you need to be extra sensitive to the traditions and beliefs of both families. Marching in and demanding your wants will more than likely cause alienation and bitterness.

Lois Pearce reflects the hard truth about this issue, and it is a very intense one for many couples. To avoid a meltdown, you both need to know yourselves. You need to know who you are, what you believe in, what you wish to create for your blended *marriage,* not just your blended wedding. It's absolutely accurate that the engagement period reflects the issues you'll face down the road. It is real life, and you know that. Undoubtedly you've already experienced the realities of being a blended couple; your engagement, however, might intensify the issue.

---

remember the meaning of marriage

We asked Annie Block, an Integrative Therapist practicing Process Acupressure, Energy Medicine, and Systemic Family Constellation (annieblock@aol.com) work, for her top tips for keeping interfaith and intercultural wedding plans on track. Here are her top three:

1. Marriage is the energy of life that ensures that we will endure.

2. When, inevitably, conflict arises, decisions should not be made based upon loyalty to the past, but necessarily predicated upon the support of the marriage union, the children of this union, and the future generations.

3. Respect for those who preceded us is *essential*. The degree of respect and regard we hold for those who gave us life will determine the security, grounding, and vitality of love in our future relationships.

For more info, e-mail annieblock@aol.com.

Only when issues are brought to light can they be addressed. Once these issues are revealed, a healing resolution is possible.

Family Conferences

Your best path to a solution, according to Lois Pearce, is for the groom to smooth out his side of the family, and for the bride to smooth out her side of the family with regard to how you plan to blend your faiths and cultures for the wedding and beyond. Sit down and have a serious discussion with them. Give them their chance to express their feelings, and really listen to their concerns. They will appreciate your inviting their input, but they also need to hear your boundaries and get a clear message that you are working to include all you can of what *you* believe. Everyone involved, all members of your family, need to grow up and accept that while they have a right to their opinions, they need to be adults and accept that not everything will be exactly what they want.

Officiant Support

"I've seen situations where the officiant needed to step in and counsel the entire group to bring everyone together, encourage them to accept

pre-marriage counseling

Some couples need all the professional advice and information they can get. On behalf of *Your Day, Your Way*, Henry Roth asked therapist Annie Block the hard questions on when couples should quit. What if the couple has no support from either family? What if the families either disown them or declare they have no intention of coming to the wedding?

Annie provided us with tremendous insight: "Therapists can only help the couple determine what is most important to them. Couples should be asking each other some very insightful questions, such as these: Does this union really satisfy your souls or are you marrying out of spite or for the benefit of the families?

Are you able to keep your hearts open to your families even when they are not supportive? Can you be forgiving? Are you capable and willing to move ahead despite your families' objections and without family support? Are you prepared to have children without extended familial connections?" These are important questions that only the couple can answer for themselves.

What a therapist can do is help you to find answers for yourselves. In this way, you move in concert with your own souls, to determine the stability and strength of your relationship. We are talking major soul-searching here, so be prepared for several conversations on the topic.

the bride and groom's decisions, and keep everyone from fighting," says Lois Pearce. This may seem an extreme step, but you'd be surprised how often the issue of family acceptance causes enormous problems for the bride and groom.

Bridal Planners

Wedding coordinators such as Lois Pearce are often hired to step in as ambassadors and peacekeeping envoys, to help the couple create wedding plans that honor their own religious and ethnic beliefs without offending the family elders. Sometimes it's best to hire someone with a lot of experience in this arena. "I recently did a wedding where the groom was African-American and Jewish, and the bride was Arabic (a Muslim), Greek, Irish, and other ethnicities I can't recall right now," says Lois Pearce. "But they brought me in to help decide in the most diplomatic way how to incorporate all their desired cultural elements in the wedding when the wedding practices of each culture were so different."

Bridal planners may be a source of help, courage, and clarity. Corinne Soikin Strauss (www.hamptonweddings.com), a bridal planner with much interfaith and intercultural experience, shares how bridal planners can help integrate interfaith wedding plans. Michelle has heard Corinne's thoughts through some of her own clients. According to Corinne, "There is a need to make sure that both bride and groom assure the families that they are not 'losing them.' I encourage the couple to have the wedding in a neutral location if they are from different faiths and the parents refuse to come to either a church or a synagogue." The couple needs to continue honoring their respective cultures and backgrounds. We understand that communicating through bridal planners during various meetings can take the unknown factor away from both families, making the union seem less intrusive and foreign.

will you marry us?

As if the threat of family battle isn't enough, the issue of finding a wedding officiant to perform your wedding can also be a challenge. Once you start looking, you might find that certain rabbis won't agree to come to a cathedral or church to perform a wedding, and a priest won't perform a wedding anywhere but in his house of worship. This is a brick wall that many interfaith couples face. Catholic churches might have strict rules for many wedding elements. Orthodox rabbis will not marry a couple unless the non-Jewish partner goes through a rigorous and time-consuming conversion process. Muslim houses of worship might allow an interfaith wedding only when the groom is a Muslim, and the bride is either Jewish or Catholic. You may face any number of considerations, depending on the faiths involved.

Can't we just look in the Yellow Pages and hire someone who does interfaith weddings?

Be very careful about hiring "non-denominational" or "certified interfaith" officiants who advertise in the Yellow Pages, in magazines, on websites, and in the bridal sections of the newspaper. We won't say they aren't legitimate, as they may very well be licensed to perform marriage rites. But most experts agree that many are essentially vendors who marry people for the money. Be especially cautious when officiants say they're ordained in several faiths because you might be led by someone who is not a true practitioner in either of your faiths.

Sometimes the officiant's fee or convenience of location is not worth the money or time you might save. Follow your own heart about this, but we do advise you to seek an officiant who is a true leader in his or her faith, someone who values religion (and leads you deeper into yours) more than the fee you pay.

The process of finding an officiant who will allow or perform interfaith weddings can require some detailed research, and we encourage you to use all resources possible. Contact your church and ask whether they have a listing of interfaith officiants they recognize. With the demand for interfaith weddings rising, the church staff may already have a list ready to hand out! Or, to find a rabbi who performs or participates in interfaith weddings, check with the Rabbinic Center for Research and Counseling at www.rcronline.org to get a list of nearby rabbis and their requirements. *Note:* the Rabbinic Center website can also point you toward classes and pre-wedding counseling sites for your interfaith wedding, which might help you answer all those big questions!

According to many couples we spoke to on this topic, the Unitarian church (see the Unitarian Universalist Organization at www.uua.org) is most often mentioned as being open to performing interfaith weddings. Again we caution you that such decisions are made by those in charge of the particular church, so we can't give you a magic formula. You'll need to find the answers on your own.

We do encourage you to ask couples you know held interfaith weddings for recommendations on where you might go. Or, hire a wedding coordinator to handle the search for or with you. Many couples say they solved the dilemma by opting for a neutral or alternative location, such as a home or outdoor setting, a country club or beach, and then sought officiants willing to perform the ceremony there.

"This is often the best solution for several reasons," says Lois Pearce. "When you find an officiant who will come to your site, such as a Reform rabbi rather than the Orthodox rabbi who might be unwilling to come, or (more likely) a cantor who might have fewer restrictions than a rabbi yet is still licensed to perform marriage rites, then you can open your minds to whatever is out there. You're not limited by the bounds of a church or synagogue, knowing that there's the aisle, and the bride's side is over there, the groom's side is over there, and it's all set.

"Now, you can open your minds and look at the opportunities to personalize your ceremony site, whether it's in the mountains, on the beach, by the lake, in the woods." For many couples who choose to express individuality over traditionalism, this is the ideal solution.

Once you clear these two hurdles, you'll be free to explore options for your interfaith wedding, plus any multicultural elements you wish to include. Before we get into multicultural ideas, let's focus on the ceremony and religious elements.

> ### signing the papers
>
> As always, the main concept is *permission*. Talk with potential wedding officiants to learn how to master their sometimes tricky and detailed permissions process, paperwork jungle, and list of rules. You're likely to find so many differing regulations and conditions out there, because individual faiths often differ greatly from one another, that you might have to agree to certain "terms" in order to marry. While signing on the dotted line with one or two officiants may seem more complicated than buying a house, you'll find your legwork worth your effort.

designing your interfaith ceremony

Whatever your religion and whichever Higher Power you believe in, the universal rule is that ceremonies reflect the beliefs of the couple marrying. Period. The ceremony has to be *them.* So your first step in designing your ideal ceremony is to know what you believe and what your fiancé believes. Immerse yourselves in each other's faiths. If you're like most couples, you've been doing that during the time you've been together. Perhaps you've attended mass or special services, gone to his family's house for a Shabbat dinner, or done some reading on each other's faiths and practices. Perhaps talking about your faiths was an important part of your courtship, when you opened up to one another and shared your values and beliefs. Or both of you might be neutral on religion right now, but wish to reconnect with your spiritual foundations and community. In this era, more and more couples are considering the depth of spirituality they wish to bring into their marriages, so that may be an important topic for you to tackle now.

In short, it's time for soul-searching. Whether you are of different faiths or culturally diverse, or come from similar backgrounds, make sure that you and your fiancé are on the same page. Sit down and educate yourselves about your respective religious practices and beliefs, and how those beliefs take form in who you are. Talk about what is important to include in your ceremony, and where you're willing to make concessions. This might be the deepest conversation you have throughout the wedding-planning process!

As you build your ceremony, include your officiants in the process, as they're likely to have performed other interfaith weddings and can explain how they tailor the process, how they weave even very different religious traditions into one unified ceremony, and how they might make traditional liturgy more group-friendly by changing certain wording and passages to reflect a more blended crowd.

Elements You Share

Start with the basics—ceremony elements your faiths have in common, such as the reading of scripture or prayers. Look at the wedding ceremonies of both faiths to see whether you can use, for instance, the traditional Jewish procession, the Catholic exchange of greetings between guests, the circling of the altar, wearing the traditional crowns of marriage, what have you. Your officiants, again, can guide you. Design a ceremony including your readings, your music, your vows, and any additional religious rituals, according to your wishes.

Inclusive Love

Once you have designed your ceremony, consider printing up a wedding program that explains these rituals to your guests. They will appreciate being included, understanding the deep and sentimental symbolism of each element of your ceremony, and being enlightened about your beautiful blending of faiths. Tell them what those marriage crowns represent. Tell them who those people were who presented the platter of offerings. In many faiths and cultures, a "sponsor" couple is chosen to serve as the bride and groom's marriage mentors. For instance, Lois Pearce reports, in Mexican weddings this sponsor couple is called the "Padrina" and the "Madrina." Whatever the specifics, sharing such details with your guests adds to their level of understanding and sense of involvement.

blended love: multicultural weddings

As you've just read, multifaith weddings can take on a multicultural flavor. For many couples, heritage includes expressions and rituals of the faith in which they grew up. So a "multicultural wedding" can have many levels of expression through the ceremony and the reception, depending on your values, family experiences, and most treasured rituals.

When you consider including elements of your cultural background in your day, keep an open mind. If you're blending very dissimilar ethnic heritages, a dose of creativity and some guidance can help you measure up the perfect blend. For example, Lois Pearce spoke of a Korean/Mexican wedding she recently helped coordinate. The ceremony featured traditional Korean dress, the entrance of the geese as symbols of marriage, and the presentation of symbolic gifts to the grandparents and each set of parents. The reception, on the other hand, was a full-fledged Mexican fiesta. In this case, the bride and groom chose the most important elements from both their backgrounds, appeased both sets of families, and found the perfect way to customize their wedding day with full honor to both cultures.

Designing Your Multicultural Elements

You might need to brush up on your traditions to ensure that your customs are appropriately represented. Your first step is to research the wedding customs and traditions of your individual backgrounds. Start by talking to elders within your family about traditional wedding customs in their native lands. (They'll feel honored that you're asking!) Further investigate your chosen ethnic traditions either on the Internet, in books and magazine articles, or at cultural clubs and heritage centers. Many heritage clubs exist throughout the country, so consider stopping in to spend some time, attend events, talk to club leaders, and perhaps get some great contacts, such as the club's dance troupe, musicians, or ethnic specialty cooks you can hire for your wedding's most important moments.

Keep an open mind as you do your research, and work as a team. You might just receive another "wedding gift" at this time in the form of reconnection to your cultural community and the opportunity to "plug in" to your extended families, both of which can enrich your future together.

from michelle

I will never forget a wedding Henry and I attended three years ago when our alterations coordinator, Evangelia, who is from a proudly traditional Greek family, married an equally proud Italian man. We were absolutely enthralled with how the couple intertwined their heritage, creating a wonderful synergy of cultures. At the reception (following the wedding in a Greek Orthodox church), the mixture of classic Italian and Greek folklore songs was masterful. Dancing was both in Greek and Italian music. Speeches were in Greek, English, and Italian. The food was a culinary delight, a combination of Greek and Italian. Of course, when Henry got up and sang "Amore," the guests loved that cultural touch. The most important benefit of blending cultures is that it involves all your guests.

Wedding Coordinators, We Need You!

Great wedding coordinators can help you define and blend your multicultural wishes with ease, as they have had a great deal of experience. Some even have printouts of deeply embedded cultural traditions to give you, pictures of former clients' weddings to show you so you can see the decorative and inclusive results, and perhaps lists of ethnic specialty wedding vendors to share with you, or lists of websites that provide a great deal of information. Your wedding coordinator can be a priceless resource, as well as a diplomatic mediator for those overly interested relatives of yours!

Corinne Soikin Strauss, bridal planner, shares a memorable experience she had with a couple's intercultural arrangements. She helped coordinate an Asian-Irish wedding several years ago. The bride wanted to forgo all her wonderful family traditions to avoid causing disharmony with the groom's family. She was ready to totally obliterate her background and be married in a completely Western ceremony. Corinne went where "angels fear to tread" and forcefully suggested the bride was making a mistake she would regret for the rest of her life. With help and encouragement, the bride had a Chinese banquet the night before her wedding and a beautiful Tea Ceremony on the wedding day. Not only did the groom's family participate, but the bride's grandmother was so touched that she came to the reception dressed in the finery she brought from China forty-five years ago. It was her first venture out of Chinatown in all those years!

from sharon

Today's busy and coast-crossing couples may face a different challenge than couples of decades past. We often move for our jobs and relationships and often venture far from our families of origin. Those who don't live close enough to attend family socials and parties miss much of the regular immersion into family background and traditions. Instead of living the cultural life, you may visit it from time to time or even find it necessary to research family customs and culture. Today's couples often choose to honor their cultures within their weddings as a way to reconnect with who we are and where we come from.

Multicultural Menus and Music

By far, the most common ways that couples incorporate their cultural backgrounds in their receptions is through the food and entertainment. According to the wedding planners with whom we spoke, the menu is the number one point of focus for multicultural "flavor."

---

from michelle

We coordinate our brides' requirements, however special, to make sure that we take into account all cultural elements the couple want. Recently, we designed and coordinated the wedding of a Western bride marrying a Japanese groom. Our bride wanted to walk down the aisle in traditional Japanese slippers so we adjusted her hem accordingly. I encouraged the blend because it was so thoughtful and inclusive.

Talk to your caterer and bar managers about your wishes for Italian, German, Korean, Mexican, or Japanese food. Include French or Australian wines, international coffees, or mixed drinks that relate to your culture. Research traditional wedding fare in your culture's cookbook, and again talk to family elders about must-have menu options. Food is where you can be all-inclusive. Please your guests, get creative, unique, and spicy, and still pull together a world-class reception menu. Your caterer knows just how to blend the tastes of the world for the perfectly assembled buffet, meals, and desserts. He or she might even surprise you with delectable ideas you hadn't considered.

Multicultural Music

After the food, the next most popular point of multicultural inclusion is in your selection of music and entertainment. Today's professional wedding musicians are ready and waiting with a full repertoire of international music styles, since most weddings—even non-blended ones—include smooth jazz, hot Latin salsa music, and other ethnic favorites. Lois Pearce pipes in on this growing trend in music for receptions: "It used to be that the Jewish reception started off with the hora as the main ethnic piece, but now more couples with Jewish backgrounds are incorporating more Klezmer music [traditional Jewish Eastern European music] into their cocktail hours and throughout the reception."

Couples want to honor their heritage in song, so we spoke with professional cellist and owner of the special event music agency Music in the Air (www.musicinthe air.com), Daniele Doctorow: "We are seeing so much more cultural inclusion in musical choices for ceremonies and receptions," says Daniele. "Weddings are a family event, so naturally brides and grooms want to honor their backgrounds, and also have music to honor parents and grandparents who may or may not be in attendance. Playing cultural music is a way to have those who have passed on there in spirit."

Daniele recently worked with a wedding couple in which the groom was of Native American descent. To honor his heritage, she located a Native American musician who played the traditional American Indian love flute. Growing in popularity are bagpipe musicians for weddings with Irish or Scottish flair, as well as mariachi ensembles for Latin events.

Clearly, ethnic music is enjoying a special spotlight at receptions across the country, as more couples wish their entertainment to reflect them and their backgrounds, rather than what's hot on the radio these days.

> ## go global with musical choices
>
> Daniele Doctorow's Music in the Air shows the broad range of multicultural wedding music opportunities. You might choose a jazz ensemble, Caribbean steel drums, Chinese string or wind music, African percussion, dulcimers, sitars, or Brazilian musicians. When researching your reception musicians, check with professional musicians' associations, contact companies that specialize in locating ethnic entertainment, or ask individual professional musicians for ideas.

The Best of Both Worlds

In short, the bland cookie-cutter wedding is out. And without personalized elements in both your ceremony and reception, without some bow to your heritage and faiths, you're apt to have a cookie-cutter wedding. We encourage you to make your day a true family affair, to honor your backgrounds and beliefs, to put your stamp on the day to make it rich and deep and a stylish reflection of the beliefs and values you hold most dear. You'll create a "Best of Both Worlds" wedding,

Q&A Bridal

Where can we find out more about the wedding customs of our heritage? We looked at some ethnic websites, but we didn't find much.

Check out books written specifically about multicultural weddings. Look in your library, bookstore, on amazon.com or bn.com, and at cultural centers. For good primers on some customs in African-American, Muslim, Russian, Eastern European, Irish, and many other cultural weddings, check through the online articles at www.theknot.com, www.bridalguide.com, www.modernbride.com, www.brides.com, www.weddingchannel.com, and www.marthastewart.com. All have comprehensive lists of popular ethnic traditions for weddings, plus ideas on how to put a modern, 21st-century spin on some of the oldest and most symbolic traditions.

blending your lives through one incredible and sentimental celebration of your deep and lasting unconditional love, the cornerstone of all religions and cultures.

Final Faith

Not all couples walking down the interfaith and/or intercultural path are compelled to undertake intense soul-searching. However, many of the issues raised above apply to all couples making permanent commitments. Remember to celebrate your differences, but ensure that your fundamentals are in sync.

part four

on the wedding day

chapter 12

Breaking the Ice

You have many opportunities before and during your wedding to create the impression of a lifetime.

On your wedding day, your many months of wedding planning will come together to create a wedding wonderland, and your guests will step into your themed vision. As the finishing touches are made to your makeup and your headpiece is placed "just so" for your grand entrance, your guests will arrive at your wedding site, marveling at your exquisite taste, and buzzing with the celebration ahead. Dressed in their finest, dressed to impress, dressed to celebrate, they arrive for your Big Day.

The ceremony is about to begin!

Today's brides know this moment isn't just about them and how they'll look gliding down the aisle, but is a moment to be shared with family and guests. Your responsibility is to make your family and guests feel welcome, comfortable, and eager to witness your nuptials. It's about warmly inviting your guests up onto your cloud nine, greeting them with your extended arms and sharing your feelings of joy.

231

Be appreciative of the effort your guests have invested to participate in your wedding, coming from near and far, from within the country and overseas. As diverse as the family, friends, strangers, and new friends may be, all have something in common: the desire to be there for you on your wedding day. Welcome them all in fine style and encourage them to mingle, to bond in celebration of your marriage. Dispel those social jitters by making everyone feel at ease from the start.

when your guests arrive

We feel the success of the wedding day depends so much on guests feeling welcome and free to interact that we offer the following tips for infusing warmth and love into your event.

Right This Way!

Decorate the outside of the ceremony site. Décor such as floral garlands wrapped around railings announces "Right this way!" If your event is by the beach, perhaps lit lanterns will herald your guests to join you. If you are at a magnificent loft, candles will add glow and romance. Use decorations that are appropriate and meaningful to your own signature theme.

Establish a Welcoming Committee

Appoint one or two family members to stand as a welcoming committee at the entrance to the ceremony site. Several ushers may do this, or—if they're busy seating your guests—parents or close family members might be the ones to smile broadly, shake hands, hug arriving guests, and welcome them to the celebration. Your welcoming committee is there to put your guests at ease. They might direct your guests to the coat check, to gift placement, restroom facilities, the guest book, directions to the nearest parking area, the daycare center in the ceremony site's annex, whatever is needed upon the guests' arrival. Make sure that if they cannot help your guests, they should seek out someone else who can. Brief your committee to never leave a guest's question and requirements unattended.

Converse and Smile

Make sure that you brief the welcoming committee to open conversation. Give your ushers and groomsmen some tips on making small talk with guests, welcoming them, never walking in silence. "How was your journey in?" "We are so delighted to welcome you." "I am the groom's college friend." The welcoming committee should always be responsible for introducing guests formally to each other. They should never assume that people know each other, even if they are from the same side of the family. This also gives your guests a way out from the embarrassing moment when they recognize but forget a person's name. A lot of ice is created right at the start of a ceremony when people stare in recognition, but become frozen from name memory loss. It happens to all of us and you must stop that from happening at your own celebration.

Pass Out Programs

The welcoming committee might be the ones to hand out your elegant wedding programs, or appoint two honor attendants for that task. Wedding programs act as a sort of bonding tool. It is kind of a members-only key card. So make sure your welcoming committee presents your wedding programs with a flourish and care, served as a fine wine.

Herald the Celebration with Music

Be sure that beautiful music is playing during the guests' arrival. Nothing sets a tone of joy more than deep classical piano or flute music

the rehearsal dinner

The rehearsal dinner has become an important aspect of weddings. Taking place during the week before your wedding, the rehearsal dinner gathers your family and major players to a sit-down meal at a restaurant or home. This breaks the ice between members of the wedding first and foremost, providing them with a common experience. With your main players acquainted, the stage is set for unifying all who will attend your big day.

playing in the expansive ceremony building, or your favorite theme song raising its notes to the skies above. We cannot emphasize enough the importance of music as the guests arrive; it breaks the awkward silences and fills the atmosphere with celebration and love. This is the time to pull those heartstrings. Spend time in advance to select this pre-ceremony music specifically, so that you know the tone will be expectant and joyful. The music spotlights the importance of what is to come shortly.

Brief Your Ambassadors

Your men are the first point of contact for the day, the first representatives of your bridal party the guests will see and speak to. They have quite a responsibility to set a tone of joy and welcome . . . and appropriate behavior. The groom's "chosen few" are your wedding ambassadors! At the rehearsal, take your ushers and groomsmen aside and talk to them about the process of escorting guests to their seats. Explain and demonstrate how they should offer their arm to a lady, how the lady's male partner should walk a few paces behind, and which special guests are seated where in the first few rows. Tell them about family diplomacy rules and that assigned seating is imperative! Include ushers from both sides of the family so that guests are recognized by someone "in the know." Instruct them to ask "Bride's side or groom's side?" when first offering an arm in escort to the guest, and then seat accordingly.

The Groom: Relaxed and Ready

Assure that the groom is kept at ease in his waiting chambers. He may be joined by his best man, or several of his closest men, and those nerves can build up as the clock strikes closer and closer to his achieving "married man" status! Instruct one of his men to stand on "tie alert," watching to make sure the groom's tie and boutonniere are in place, and that he's ready to go when he's called to the moment.

The Bride: On Time

Brides tend to either be ready way ahead of time or running a little behind to hopelessly behind time. Entrust one of your bridesmaids to discreetly keep you in touch with the real world and your actual time zone. If you are ultra-prepared and ready as the clock strikes your hour, it is still advisable to add a ten-minute wait before starting the proceedings. It adds a sense of anticipation, a greater crowd-warmer. However, being over twenty minutes late is not considered fashionable anymore, and is not a crowd pleaser.

The Show Must Go On!

If the elements are not exactly what you planned for, never let anything rain on your parade. Of course, you should always prepare to avoid foreseeable glitches. Send a "scout" in advance to be sure the ceremony site is air-conditioned or heated well (depending upon your wedding season) so your guests notice only the beauty before them, not oppressive heat or bone-chilling cold! Yet whatever unfolds, never allow any flaw to mar the joy of your moment. It will certainly not help with the celebration at hand if you exude disappointment.

walking up the aisle with style

The moment you have dreamt of has arrived. You are about to walk down the aisle. Whatever your emotions, let them show. If tears come, let them flow. If laughter and huge smiles overtake you, then beam. Your walk down the aisle is the time to truly connect with your feelings . . . and with your guests. Whether you make eye contact or look straight ahead is your decision; however, we are certain of this: Take it slow, very slow, and savor every second. Let every step forward be a beautiful one. Give your groom, parents, in-laws, family members, and friends plenty of time to absorb the scene. Sweep everyone in the room into the poignancy of your moment as you radiate pure joy.

immediately after the ceremony

You've taken your walk back down the aisle together, arm in arm, now husband and wife! Make sure you connect well with all your guests as you walk down the aisle. As you kiss and hug your bridal party and parents, the first ones to follow you to the site entrance and embrace you, really *listen* to their congratulations. Whisper something special to them and hug them close to make this a golden, precious moment for all. Here then are some thoughtful suggestions to keep the atmosphere festive and inclusive:

- *Just for You.* Guests may be given confetti/birdseed/rose petals/ bubbles to throw at you when you dash for the car. Be sure to attach a little welcome note from the two of you to each packet or bottle of your chosen "toss-it" for an added touch and a first "thank you" for sharing in the moment.

- *Directions.* An efficient and welcoming touch is to have an honor attendant at the exit door hand out printed directions to the re-ception site. Some guests may have forgotten to bring along the map or directions included in their invitation packet. This simple and considerate step could keep your guests from traffic and parking hassles, especially in the case of unforeseen detours or construction delays, thus keep them in their happy mood all the way to the party.

the receiving line

The receiving line is an excellent way to commence personal contact with guests at your wedding. This can take place immediately after the ceremony, but is usually conducted at the cocktail hour. Whenever you receive, keep the following in mind:

- *Give individual greetings.* Line up in receiving line formation and greet each guest warmly and personally! Watch out for the lipstick kisses from your great-aunts and affectionate grandmothers, and be prepared to dip and protect your gown and veil. This is also the point where you might want to bustle your train so it doesn't trip you up.

- *Be meaningful and real.* Really listen to the congratulations of your loved ones, and share a personal sentiment with each. Release your emotions. Don't just say, "Thank you, thank you, thank you," to each and every guest, or you'll sound like an unimaginative broken record! Rather, personalize each greeting and say what is in your heart. Very often, spoken words from bride and groom, their private conversations with the stars of the day, are what stay with wedding guests. So share a quick thought, ask how their trip was, and tell those you noticed their little wave, wink, or the tear in their eye as you walked down the aisle.

from michelle

Approach your wedding day the same way you would approach a huge house party. Being aloof and inaccessible is not appropriate.

- *Bring all your guests into the fold.* If a guest hasn't yet met one of you, the other should take a second to make introductions. Say who the person is, and how you know them.

- *Introduce guests to one another.* As guests go down the line, start the introductions among them! Introduce your single male cousin to the bridesmaid you hope he'll dance with later.

- *It's a Listerine moment.* Have breath spray or mints handy for the receiving line. You'll be up close and personal with your guests, and nervous breath isn't the first impression you want to make . . . or remember! Try the breath slides that come in a tiny packet and pack a punch.

at the start of the reception

Lose no momentum between the end of the ceremony and the commencement of the reception. Today, ceremony and reception can be either adjacent or several miles apart, requiring transportation. Whether you schedule no break or an hour interval, make sure you pick up where you left off. Don't let the celebration fall flat at any time. These tips will help you maintain a festive, melodious atmosphere:

- *Music maestro.* From the moment your first guests come into the cocktail hour room or ballroom, be sure the ambience is set with lovely music playing.

- *Let the champagne flow!* Be sure champagne and drinks are available from moment one, as you don't want parched guests wandering around looking for the bar! Have your reception manager be sure all is ready to go when the first guest arrives, or is prepared to lead early-arriving guests to a comfortable lounge area with great service and atmosphere. Guests having to wait for the bar to be "ready" or for servers to pour the champagne puts a wrinkle in your seamless plans for the reception, so have this arranged and call ahead or send your "scout" to give the reception site staff fair warning that the guests are on their way. Make sure you have non-alcoholic alternatives available for abstaining adults and overcurious kids.

- *Food for talk.* If possible, be sure the cocktail or celebration hour is ready for service at moment one as well, and the servers are prepared with their stocked silver platters of delicious hors d'oeuvres. Immediate service leads to happily mingling wedding guests.

- *Parent and family unit power.* The reception is where the parents and family members are in their glory. With their bright smiles and emotions, they'll greet their oldest friends and lead the introductions. Instruct your parents and top bridal party attendants to make the rounds, introduce guests who may not know one another yet, and help direct guests to their appointed tables. The first moments at a wedding reception are often awkward for guests. They don't know where or with whom they're sitting and wonder who they'll have to talk to. Those party jitters will evaporate following a wonderful round of introductions and once all guests have a drink or treat in hand.

- *Strategy synergy.* If time permits, introduction mavens can go further to establish points of common interest to ensure that tablemates and other guests have much to talk about.

- *Combine and include.* Combine your guest tables for a more intimate party atmosphere. Don't separate sides of family as if the Great Wall runs through your reception area. Now that you're married, there's no more "her side" and "his side"; you're all one big happy family. So blend those tables and get those guests mingling!

table and guest dynamics

Brides and grooms often spend hours with table diagrams trying to seat all their guests appropriately. This task can require days and much agonizing. However, on the wedding day, you will thank your lucky stars ten times over. The effort is not only worthwhile, but it will help your celebration take off naturally. Keep these tips in mind when you determine seating arrangements:

- *Wedding backgammon.* The best way to lay out your seating plans is to get a big sheet of paper and create a layout diagram. Put every guest's name on a small strip of paper and start placing names on each shape that represents a table. This process helps you visualize the result and make changes easily.

- *Number by design.* To do your table-assignments task well, seat interesting guests together. Protocol normally requires the closest family members and friends to sit together and nearest to the bride and groom, and the rest of the guests at the remaining tables. Choose people who will have a common point of interest, such as a graphic designer and an advertising executive, to share a table. Bank clerk with financial salesperson—perfect interest rate connection! Your high school girlfriend with your groom's ex-roommate—Cupid's arrow! Chemistry is what is needed to get the laughter and sparkling conversation flowing among those at table 4 and table 24.

- *Don't go too far!* Avoid overexperimenting. Now is not the time to put a far-fetched friend theory into practice.

- *Seat assignment free.* We have attended weddings that had no seating assignments other than a few reserved main tables. This can create a far more informal and relaxed atmosphere, but you will become more responsible than ever for encouraging your guests to intermingle. Depending on what tone and theme you have set, open seating can work like a charm.

- *You sat me where?* Yes, seating does go down in bridal folklore as a touchy area. Know now that you may not delight all your guests and that you can do nothing to prevent that. Be prepared to smooth over any issue with grace.

- *Buffets and standing affairs.* Some brides and grooms choose a standing affair for their wedding style. They may include an array of chairs and bistro tables placed intermittently around the room. You might implement this technique because it's your preference or because you wish to avert wedding acrimony. When divorce produces strain or interfaith marriages cause dissent, this informal arrangement might do wonders for your guest placement. Make sure that, regardless of the style you choose, you put seating aside for your elder guests and family members.

- *Mingle, smile, kiss, and shake hands.* Throughout the night, the two of you should mingle, both as a couple and individually, sharing personal time with each guest. (If you have 400 or so guests, just do your best!) Your loved ones, especially those who came from a great distance, will remember the personal moments most.

- *Camera bonding.* To get your guests table-hopping and talking to one another, provide a throwaway camera or two for each table, and attach a note encouraging guests to take pictures of the group at their table and other guests interacting throughout the reception. We experienced another great photo idea during the Shaquille O'Neal wedding. A photography station was set up just outside the reception site. Throughout the night, guests had their shots taken and immediately printed to take home as personal keepsakes. It worked wonders.

- *Menu bonding.* The cocktail hour buffet table and exotic-food stations will certainly keep your guests mingling and sharing their admiration for the chef's supreme work and your supreme taste in menu selection!

let the music play

Music is the key to get the celebration in motion! Here are suggestions for selecting music that will please your guests:

- *Assess your crowd.* Your band or DJ will certainly assess your crowd and play just the right first few songs to get the dance floor packed. If you prefer, meet with your musical director ahead of time to create your chosen play list. Work through your ideas both creatively and methodically.

- *Set the stage for special performances.* If you have some live performers or if your friends can be coaxed to sing, then coordinate with your music director so that any changes or additions are integrated smoothly.

- *Mix your music up.* Here is where you can be most creative, if you know your guests' musical preferences. After all, you know better than anyone whether classic Motown music, Top 40, or country music will get your guests on their feet. Intertwine your traditions with music: Latin American merengue and salsa, Hebrew folk songs, Indian bang rah music, hip hop. All is good when played tastefully, and some can also serve to pay homage to your family's culture. (Look back to chapter 9 for more on entertainment and music during the reception.)

- *Couple's Top 10.* Designate some special songs, such as a group dance with just the ladies, or a fun kids' song to get the little ones in on the action (and provide material for great pictures!).

- *Agree on your musical score.* Talk to the entertainers ahead of time to have your say on their ideas of what will get your guests danc-

from henry

Being a designer and a part-time DJ makes me extra sensitive to music. You can't plan too much when it comes to music for your wedding. Music is the soul of joy and provides a pool of happiness guests can dive into. It is also the perfect ice breaker. Music that's appropriate for the crowd is a must. Definitely include some classics, as Top 20 music of today doesn't always go over well. Your theme will help direct you to the right music. Remember that the wedding party and guests are generally dressed more for slow dancing than getting wild on the dance floor. Nothing looks worse than a bride "all shook up" in her ball gown, or a groom perspiring in his three-piece formal tux. Breaking the ice with music does not need to result in bridal meltdown!

ing. Perhaps the DJ thinks the world of Elvis, disco balls, or conga lines, but that's definitely *not* your style. Don't leave room for surprises when it comes to entertainer-guest interaction.

If you do it right, your guests will be laughing, smiling, dancing, and enjoying the shared company—all of which makes for a truly successful wedding reception!

master of ceremonies

You have the opportunity to personalize and add character to your wedding, break the ice right from the start of your celebration, and unite your entire group of wedding guests by choosing the right emcee. The master of ceremonies is much like a head attendant on your celebration flight. Choose your emcee carefully, making sure he or she knows you both as well as possible and is a natural with people. No single person can influence the tone of your reception as much as your emcee.

Ladies and Gentlemen . . . Introducing

When you make your grand entrance as a couple, all eyes will be on you. This is a unifying experience for all your guests and a signal that the party has truly begun. Make the most of the moment, greet your guests as you come in, and let your emotions flow. When the time comes for your first dance, be sure you have bustled your train so you can move with ease and grace.

Your Opening Remarks

As bride and groom, you should be seen *and* heard. And the ice will break when you end your first dance to kick off the reception, grab the microphone, and speak a few words straight from your hearts. As Henry says, "To me, a brilliant, well-thought-out speech by both the bride and groom is priceless—whatever your style wedding. It serves as a record for the rest of your lives as well." After your impromptu speech, then the toast-making by the best man, maid of honor, parents, and friends can begin. Who says the best man always gets the first word? It's the 21st century, and you're free to welcome your guests first if you choose.

from michelle

My brother Henry was the emcee at my wedding. It was a natural choice. Henry is gregarious, warm, and friendly, and he executed the job with love and humor. Of course, I held my breath when he introduced himself as the EC (which he proceeded to define as "The Emotions Coordinator") and invited all our family and guests to join him on an emotional rollercoaster as he spoke of Peter and me. He did it with originality and flair, and we loved it.

Some brides love to invite speeches from the traditional speech givers, but when you give one of your own, it adds a new dimension to your event. Whether there are to be several speeches or only one, wit and brevity are the spirit you want and need. Set time limits and remain firm about your guidelines. (See chapter 9 for more on toasts and tributes.)

We encourage speeches. An amazing speech not only adds a personal touch but can be wonderful entertainment. While we're on the subject of speeches, the traditional lambasting of the groom by the best man is out of place these days; humor and clever repartee are in!

cast those icebergs into the sea

We want to leave you with some uplifting thoughts as you and your loved ones prepare for your wedding. We live in a world of stimulus—Web sites, Internet interaction, television and cable channels, DVDs, cell phones, digital cameras, and . . . you name it! Even the moon and the stars are no longer the limit. That is why it's so important that weddings today be planned with human interaction in mind. What we took for granted just a few decades ago has evaporated before our eyes. We now need to work far harder to make magic happen at weddings. Be under no illusion; your responsibility as a couple is to take charge and make sure all your guests are welcomed, entertained, visually excited, gastronomically delighted, and leave with tremendous feeling in their hearts.

Love conquers all. Taking initiative from the moment you are engaged to the last dance is crucial, as we have pointed out. Creating positive energy around you without the angst is primary. From the first moments of planning your wedding to the commencement of the first chapters of your lives, keep the big picture in mind. Nothing can be more profound.

chapter 13

Looking Luminous on Your Wedding Day . . . and Forever After

With all those eyes on you, you may be concerned about how you will look, feel, and be on the actual wedding day—and rightfully so. Of course, everyone will be taking second glances at you, kissing you, hugging you, crying and rejoicing with you. A secret ingredient every bride has on her big day is a complimentary dose of adrenaline that shoots through her system at great speed. Adrenaline helps create your "bridal glow."

We believe that confidence makes you look beautiful—no matter your age, size, coloring, or style—and that knowing what works for you is the key to your confidence. And we also firmly believe that true beauty comes from being your natural, healthy self. So welcome to our beauty and health bar, where we will help you highlight your natural beauty, make the most of your features, and—most important—*care for yourself* throughout the wedding planning process so you are centered, balanced, and pampered in mind, body, and spirit.

First, let's get to the heart of the matter . . . your wedding day look.

your beauty assessment

Getting professional advice is the best way to create your wedding day look, therefore an initial beauty assessment is Step One to your wedding day beauty and glamour. This is also the ideal time to assess your current beauty and health regimen and set a positive one for your lifetime.

On behalf of *Your Day, Your Way,* Sharon Naylor spoke with Edward Tricomi, owner and partner of the Warren Tricomi Salon in New York City (212-262-8899) for his advice on what today's bride should do to kick off the countdown to her wedding-day beauty look:

> SHARON NAYLOR: Edward, what should a bride-to-be do first in order to plan for her hair, makeup, and overall beauty look on her wedding day?
>
> EDWARD TRICOMI: We suggest that each of our brides come in for a two-hour consultation with our hair and makeup artists, bringing along a picture of her gown and headpiece so we can assess her style plus the features of her face and body. We then go through several different hairstyles with her—up, down, curly, straight—to help her discover the look that suits her best. We photograph each possibility so the bride has a record of the effect of each look. Trying out different looks is so important to give the bride an expert run-through of what her possibilities are for the wedding day.
>
> SN: Is there a certain bridal look that's "in," that every bride seems to be after these days?
>
> ET: Each bride is different, with different tastes, so no one look dominates. Ultimately, the bride wants to look great, but some want to feel comfortable and some want to be really dramatic and put on a show. So the looks range from just a polishing of

their natural look to very dramatic face and hair. Brides want to make the most of their personal style, and they also are asking to make their look work with the theme of their weddings. For instance, we are getting a lot of brides who want a look that works with an 18th-century gown style or a 1920s look, whatever their theme is.

SN: How far in advance should brides come in for their beauty assessment and look try-ons?

ET: At least one month before the wedding, if not more.

SN: Is there anything else today's brides need to keep in mind as they start exploring their wedding day look?

ET: Yes, do not let your mother or anyone else try to influence your style for the wedding day. It should be up to you.

Going It Alone

While many brides do hire professional makeup artists to create their wedding-day look, either by going to the salon or having the makeup artists come to their home or hotel room on the day of the wedding, some brides choose not to have an expert's help either because of budget restrictions or—in the case of a destination wedding—because a makeup artist cannot come to the site. If you plan to "go it alone," we recommend you follow this advice of makeup artist Laura Geller:

> If you choose not to have a makeup artist create your look on your day, it's a good idea to attend a private makeup application lesson with a professional makeup artist for guidance ahead of time. For example, we provide a one-hour private consultation for brides with one of our top makeup artists, at which the bride is shown exactly how to apply the ideal shades on her wedding day. She then walks away with a full diagram of colors and the order in which to apply each product, a full step-by-step guideline to help her re-create the look.

Don't Overdo It

It's a misconception that a bride should apply her makeup with a heavier hand and in brighter shades on her wedding day so that she "shows up" in her pictures. As Laura Geller states, "You want to look as beautiful to your guests as you do to the photographer's eye." In other words, your in-person beauty is what matters most, and your in-person beauty depends on a slightly enhanced natural look that's a lovely version of *you*. Do not overdo it. Don't try to look different because it is your wedding day. Laura Geller applied natural makeup that worked wonders for the lunchtime wedding of Michelle Roth, who recalls: "I felt so majestic, without feeling like I was on stage in a Broadway musical. It was light and natural."

Invest some time and thought into what you want your wedding-day look to be, practice with the help of experts, and approach your big day with confidence that your look will be perfect, both live and in print.

Aisle Style

Your focus will be on looking great for your wedding day *and* in your pictures. Regarding makeup for your best look, the solution is not just avoiding overly pigmented shades, but *avoiding shine*. Laura Geller says, "Any oiliness or shine on your skin reflects off the camera lens and makes you appear to have an extra light on your face. So be sure to eliminate shine by using loose powder to give your face a more matte appearance. You can still have a creamy complexion without going *too* matte, but keep your skin shine-free." When asked whether brides should then avoid the shine of lip gloss, Geller clarified that the shine factor applies *only* to the face. A little shine on lips and perhaps on eyelids is just fine.

Avoid the Radical

Every hair and makeup expert we spoke to said that the bride of today wants to look like her best self, a glamorous and beautiful version of "Me," rather than a color-treated, totally transformed beauty queen who no one recognizes as she comes down the aisle! This is not the time to try out radical changes in hair color, laser peels, or heavily applied makeup if that is not your personal style. Avoid going too far in the name of beauty, but do empower yourself by taking healthy, smart steps to care for yourself and bring out your best throughout the process.

If you wish to experiment with self-tanners and the like, do so *far, far, far* before the wedding, getting in some practice and perfecting your methods. Consult with experts in beauty, fitness, and nutrition, and invest in your own well-being by getting a massage once in a while to keep wedding-planning stress from showing up in your face, your hair, and your posture. The stressed-out bride isn't her most beautiful self, so take a deep breath and relax, cast those magnified beauty worries aside, and read on for some pointers on how to bring out the best that is already *you*.

a primer on wedding day beauty

We can point you in the right direction for the specifics of hair care, skincare, makeup, and the like for your best wedding day look, but we leave it to you to consult with experts who can customize your beauty rituals. You'll find plenty of magazines and beauty Web sites to check out, as well as beauty books by celebrity makeup luminaries such as Bobbi Brown. So read on for pointers and perhaps identify specific issues you'll want to address with your chosen beauty professionals . . .

Hair

Healthy hair is essential to every wedding day style, so have your hair-stylist lop off those split and dead ends, shape your hair to make the most of your facial contour and best features, and find the right shade of color and highlights for you. Face it: The wrong hair color is eye-catching but in a negative way. Stay away from dramatic changes in color for your makeover (or "make*under*"), and experiment with ideal hairstyles before the big day.

Edward Tricomi of Warren Tricomi Salon has these hair tips for you:

- Start growing your hair out as early as possible if your wedding day look includes upswept hair.

- Get a trim at least two weeks before the wedding so that your hair is in manageable condition.

- Wear your hair off your face so you are not hidden behind curls. Your face should show.

Yesterday, today, and tomorrow. Updos are chic, sophisticated, and have always been and always will be great for bridal coiffure. Today's hairstylists can create dramatic upswept styles like Audrey Hepburn, or smooth, straightened styles to match your ideal vision.

Hair jewelry and tiaras love height, so plan to work with your stylist early to create your ultimate look. If you plan to wear a hair addition or extra hairpiece and extensions to make your hair fuller or longer, consult with your stylist to find a hairstyle that glamorizes you and suits your headpiece.

As always, the health and shine of your hair can make any style beautiful, so ask your stylist to recommend the ideal shampoos, conditioners, hair packs, styling gels, and frizz fighters for your 'do. Many brides come away from pre-bridal beauty assessment appointments learning something new about hair care and hairstyling, lessons they use in their daily beauty routine even after the wedding.

Michelle Roth asked beauty expert Laura Geller for her top advice on wedding day hair. Laura agrees that healthy hair is beautiful hair, so she recommends working pre-wedding to pamper your hair. "Getting a half-hour conditioning treatment at a salon gets your hair in shape and brings out its natural luster," she says. Get your hair colored or cut at least two weeks before the wedding so that the shape is nice, crisp, and fresh, and if you'll wear your hair *up* on your wedding day, know that most hairstylists find it easier to work with "day-old hair" (hair that was washed *the night before* the wedding). Day-old hair also keeps its style much longer.

If you've had long-term hair issues, your wedding may serve as the perfect catalyst for you to seek professional advice that you may use for a lifetime.

Skin Care

Healthy, radiant, smooth skin is essential to a beautiful wedding day look, and that applies not just to your face but to the skin all over your body—those arms and shoulders your strapless gown will put on display, the back revealed by your dress's plunging backline, and the rest of you during the honeymoon! Good skin care is a top priority for the healthy and radiant bride, so as far in advance as possible, put the creation of a healthy skincare regimen for face and body at the top of your list!

Consult a skincare specialist to assess your face and body needs, and schedule a facial several months before your wedding. (*Warning:* If you've never had a facial, do not schedule one the week before your wedding, as facial irritation and breakouts can result!) Talk with the expert about your skin needs, including the best cleansers and treatments for your skin type. Also get advice on safe tanning practices.

Glowing skin and healthy hair come from within, so drink plenty of water, get plenty of sleep, eat well, and take your vitamins. A healthy lifestyle shows in your glow. And remember that the skin you're in stays with you for life, so find the best exfoliating and moisturizing products for your face, body, hands, and feet.

We'd like to add a word about tanning or using self-tanning lotions to achieve a bronzed, sun-kissed look. Think not only about the healthy skincare vs. sun damage tradeoff in your tanned look, but this worthy side point that Laura Geller brings up: "Be careful about tanning too much since you don't want to look dehydrated on the wedding day, and you don't want your too-tan skin to not match your groom's skin tone in your wedding day photos." As with all things, moderation and healthy practices are the real way to look your best.

from sharon

It might be a smart idea to visit a dermatologist for an all-over look at your skin and assessment of moles and birthmarks. Dermatologists can prescribe fading creams and eye creams to get rid of inherited dark circles beneath your eyes, medications for stubborn blemish or acne problems, skin treatments for dry skin and dandruff, or laser hair removal options. Sometimes a professional medical assessment of your skin is just what the doctor ordered!

Makeup

Well-applied makeup that's smooth and flawless is a must for your wedding day look, so again we encourage you to seek the guidance of a makeup expert. Brides who insist on doing this part of their beauty rituals without the benefit of expert advice run the risk of using the wrong shades that make them look washed-out in their wedding pictures. Leave your wedding-day makeup to the experts to determine which hues work best for your face and skin color to achieve the look you're after; they know how to bring out your best features for bright daylight or nighttime, dim candlelight, and yes, in those wedding pictures.

For extra top-level advice on makeup shades, application, tools, and trends for outdoor, low-light, dramatic, and natural looks, visit our favorite makeup mavens' websites:

Bobbi Brown: www.bobbibrown.com

Laura Geller: www.laurageller.com

Laura Mercier: www.lauramercier.com

Each of the sites listed provides detailed makeup application do's and don'ts, point-and-click purchasing, illustrations of makeup effects, and even specific bridal beauty pointers to help educate you.

It goes without saying that with mascara, go waterproof! Tears of joy will flow throughout your big day, so waterproof mascara is a must . . . for you, for your mother, and for all the ladies of your day.

Keeping Your Face On

Maintaining your makeup look throughout the hours of your ceremony and reception is essential, so bring along your makeup kit and stash it where you can access your pressed powder to get rid of shine, your lipstick and gloss for subtle lips, and eye color and liner pencils to redefine your eyes. Enlist a helpful bridesmaid to "give you the signal" when to retreat for a quick touch-up. And while you're in the ladies' room reapplying your face, also adjust your veil (if you're still wearing one) and your neckline.

Nails

The French manicure has long been a sign of a bride's hand, and the tradition continues. Now, though, brides are using color on their nails to coordinate with their bridal looks, matching the tones of pink and plum and red to the flowers they and their maids will carry. As always, invest in having a professional manicurist do both your finger- and toenails, giving you the perfect, polished look for your day.

Outdoor-wedding brides whose toes will be on display, be sure to choose a pedicure polish that coordinates with your look—perhaps red to match your fingernails or a French manicure.

Beauty Extras

Consider these additional beauty treatments to bring out your best and brightest look on your best and brightest day:

- *Plucking and waxing.* Hair removal treatments run the gamut from bleaching to tweezing to waxing to laser and sugaring removal processes. Don't experiment on your own, especially not too close to the wedding day. Have a hair removal specialist de-fuzz you in time for your wedding weekend, and consider lasting treatments like waxing to keep you stubble-free throughout your honeymoon. (And it's not just the ladies who are lining up for waxings! Salons across the country report a growing number of male clients signing up for waxings and eyebrow shapings.)

- *Eyebrow shaping.* Beauty experts say that having well-groomed and perfectly shaped eyebrows are a top way to make your eyes (and your entire face) look well-framed and beautiful. This process alone can open your eyes and give an all-around fresher look to your face.

- *Teeth bleaching.* Your smile says it all, but you won't want to say anything if your teeth are an unsightly shade of yellow. Everything from red wine to tea to cigarettes to certain foods can stain your teeth, so look into all the options. Teeth-bleaching treatments at the dentist can be pricey but effective, and bleaching trays and strips used at home can be less expensive but require an investment of time and effort. Whatever your chosen strategy, work now to get your teeth pearly white.

the well-rested bride

A good night's sleep is essential for your health, not just your looks as mentioned earlier. Studies show that the average 21st-century person does not get enough sleep to function well, and we all know that sleep deprivation can make us mentally foggy and unable to handle stress or make sound decisions. Planning a wedding can be stressful, especially when added to your work, home, family, and social responsibilities, so the best way to stay on your feet and remain mentally sharp is to make time for adequate sleep. It should be among your highest self-care priorities. Barbara Heller, renowned "Sleep Maven" and author of *How to Sleep Soundly Tonight: 250 Simple and Natural Ways to Prevent Sleeplessness* and *365 Ways to Relax Mind, Body and Soul*, has this to say about getting more and better sleep at a time when you need it most:

> It may get difficult to settle down for the night when you're thinking about settling down for life. But brides-to-be need their sleep—maybe even more than they did before the wedding plans. Sleep loss weakens our immune systems, leaving us more susceptible to major illness, accidents, weight gain, and even the common cold. Lack of sleep decreases our concentration, productivity, and effectiveness, and nights of tossing and turning can fuel those common pre-wedding emotional highs and lows. So, brides-to-be, to stay sharp, sexy, and sane, get some sleep!

be kind to yourself

It seems we all run on adrenaline these days, stressed out and snappy, running on empty half the time. When asked what your blood type is for the marriage license, do you answer "Starbucks"? With caffeine and cortisol running through your system, you (like many brides) are

the "sleep maven" speaks

1. *Allocate enough time for a full night's sleep.* Adequate rest and relaxation need to be priority items on your long to-do list. Depending on your past patterns, try for seven to nine hours nightly. On the weekend before the wedding, sleep in at least one day without an alarm.

2. *Channel any of your excess energy.* An afternoon walk is one of the best natural sedatives. If you're feeling anxious, squeeze in a fitness class (for better sleep, aerobics or yoga are good choices) before dinner.

3. *Create a soporific (sleep-inducing) evening ritual.* Take a moonlight stroll, wind down in a warm bath, and listen to a soothing song. One study found that a majority of people with insomnia fell asleep more quickly and stayed asleep after listening to new age or classical music.

4. *Use sedative scents in the bath and the bedroom.* Try relaxing scented bath salts. Slip a small lavender sachet between your pillow and pillowcase. Enjoy a cup of calming chamomile tea in the evening.

5. *Prepare for married sleep.* You've made your bed, so now lie in it! Spouses sleep better when they discuss their sleep expectations with one another. Do you agree about bedtimes, the bedroom environment including mattress type and size, temperature control, and whether television, computers, or pets are allowed? For some people, sex is a sleep aid, but for others it is a sleep thief. And if you or your partner snore, early intervention, including a medical evaluation, can help.

6. *If you haven't been sleeping well for a couple of weeks, check in with your health practitioner.* The short-term use of an over-the-counter sleep aid or a prescription medicine can help you break the cycle of sleeplessness. Obviously, don't take a sleeping pill for the first time on the eve before the wedding!

To enjoy the big day, relax into your night. Sweet dreams.

Barbara L Heller, MSW, psychotherapist and author of *How to Sleep Soundly Tonight: 250 Simple and Natural Ways to Prevent Sleeplessness*

Printed with permission of Barbara Heller, copyright 2003

on hyper-alert. We see stress get to so many brides in the form of extreme mood swings and personality changes, meltdowns, and flare-ups. Planning a wedding with endless outside "requests" and assorted family and vendor dilemmas can definitely push you to your limits.

Right here is time for you to seek shelter from the storm, calm down and center yourself, and breathe. Look at how you've been "de-stressing" so far in the process: Are you faithful to your yoga practice or to eating frozen yogurt? Are you jogging on the treadmill or juggling a bag of chips, a candy bar, and a soda in front of the television set? We all handle stress differently, often without thinking about how effective and healthy our stress-relief measures are. Discipline your reactions to stress and release any negativity by taking action. Stress release is not just a cerebral exercise; it is a physical activity as well.

The following stress-relief ideas will get you started on the path to calm:

- *Lotus your stress.* Try yoga. Whether at a class at the gym, using a videotape or DVD, or just breathing and moving along with a *Yoga Zone* program on television, give this effective routine a chance to slow you down and center yourself.

- *Express yourself.* Write in a journal: "Dear Bride . . ." Vent those emotions and feelings in a safe place. Then write about the positives of your wedding planning experience since focusing only on the negative is likely to stress you out even more.

- *Exercise!* Walk, jog, cycle, lift weights, play with your dog, play basketball with your fiancé. Exercise is not only great for your heart and body, but it releases calming chemicals in your brain and induces more relaxation and better sleep.

- *Eat well.* Eat for your health, not for your emotions. A balanced diet will also keep you calm, especially if you limit stimulants such as sugary foods and drinks, baked items, alcohol, caffeine, and cigarettes, which have other addictive properties as well. Cut out the bad habits and stop revving your engines.

- *Soak on it.* Take a warm bubble bath, light candles, enjoy a good book and some soothing music, or invite your fiancé to join you in the tub.

- *Get toxic free.* Limit your exposure to toxic people. Stand clear of the chronic complainer, the pushy parent, the jealous sibling, the bottomless pit of a drama queen friend. These people can suck the life out of you and add to your stress. Keep more company with positive, upbeat people to absorb some of their lightness of being.

- *Communicate.* Nothing causes more stress and tension than bottled-up emotions. Use your best conflict resolution and assertiveness skills with everyone from your coworkers to your mother to your fiancé so you don't flip out over finding an expired carton of milk in your refrigerator. Such irrational outbursts are far more likely when you don't communicate. So set up a time to talk calmly and diplomatically, and don't let resentments simmer and fester.

- *Get out in nature.* Find a peaceful park or scenic walk, a quaint neighborhood, or a beachside path, and then spend time in the great outdoors, surrounded by nature. It's calming and recharging to do so. If you're landlocked and can't get to a beach or forest, then listen to a tape of ocean sounds or thunderstorm sounds . . . the music of nature can then lull you into relaxation.

- *Play more.* Laughter is a big stress-reliever, so spend time playing with children, playing with pets, or just playing board games in a group. Laugh along with a comedy on television, or read something that tickles your funny bone. Smiling is a stress-buster, so find things to smile about.

Make stress relief a priority in your life. You might have an existing regimen that works for you: knitting, painting, dancing, doing crossword puzzles, sniffing fragrant aromatherapy oils. Whether you keep doing what you know works or experiment with something new, make sure you're always working on your own calm and centeredness.

Distract, release, and relieve your feelings of stress and don't forget that the world is still revolving!

Remember to *breathe deeply and keep all in perspective.*

the bride's best body

Of course you'll want to be in the best shape possible for your wedding day, to have great arms, slim hips, flat abs that make you look incredible in your wedding dress. Strive to be fit and healthy . . . and that's the key word: healthy.

We asked fitness guru Radu, from Radu Physical Culture in New York City (212-581-1995) for his top tips targeted to the healthy 21st-century bride. Radu offers the following insights for those desiring to achieve their best bridal body:

- The biggest mistakes brides-to-be make when attempting to get in shape for their wedding days are starting way too late and wanting to have results yesterday. In extreme cases, brides starve themselves . . . which is the biggest mistake possible.

- If a bride doesn't already have an established health and fitness plan, she should see a doctor first for a health evaluation, and then consult with a trained and licensed fitness expert for guidance.

What you do should depend on the history of your body shape and whether you need a maintenance or actual weight-loss program. Moderation and slow steady progress are the way to go; crash programs are not. Look at this as a long-term rather than a wedding-specific solution.

Arm-Aware Brides

The most popular wedding gown styles show off the arms and shoulders. If you wear a dress with illusion net sleeves or a strapless gown,

---

radu on couples who play together . . .

From the moment we met Radu, we knew he was a man with a mission. One of his philosophies is that couples who make fitness a shared activity and high priority experience extra perks in their partnerships. We asked Radu to suggest some activities that bride and groom can enjoy together as they both get in shape for the wedding day. Radu suggests "jogging together, biking, Rollerblading, tennis, golf, hiking, dancing (including ballroom dancing), volleyball, or basketball." Any activity you both have an affinity for is a great bonding activity, a great stress-reliever, and a great way to shape up for the big day.

---

you will want to tone up your arms so they look great in your dress. Although spot-training is never the total answer and all-over diet and cardio will improve the look of the whole body, Radu offers these suggestions for arm-specific training to get those great biceps, triceps, and shoulders in shape: "The best choices for arms are a range of pushups, modified pull-ups, and chin-ups, boxing, hitting the heavy bag, and also exercises with dumbbells, medicine balls, and calisthenics for area enhancement."

Luckily, today's women have absorbed healthier messages about the best body look, and realize that the fit body outranks the hunger-strike look in attractiveness. So knowing that you are likely to begin a diet and exercise regimen to get in shape for your walk down the aisle, we join the chorus to remind you to keep yourself healthy and be smart. Seek the assistance and advice of professional nutritionists and personal trainers, give yourself the gift of a membership to the gym, or adopt a more fit and active lifestyle with your fiancé to improve *both* your health levels as well as enhance your relationship. The couple that plays together stays together, and making a pact to get healthier together is a terrific way to start your future.

Strength in Numbers or Solo

Every bride knows what fitness system and plan works best for her individual style, schedule, and budget. Perhaps you're a personality type that works best with group support, so joining a group system such as Weight Watchers is ideal for you. Or, if you like doing things on your own, you might check into www.shape.com for its diet and fitness plans, as well as interactive tools to help you figure out your body mass index and count calories. At that same site, you can sign up, for a fee, to receive customized menus and advice from a personal trainer—a whole plan set up just for you and your goals. And check out the message boards for additional inspiration and a sense of community.

Research the various nutrition plans out there once you've made your decision to eat more healthfully, drink more water, eat five small meals a day rather than skipping breakfast and snacking at night. There's no better time than your wedding time to commit to your health, and the earlier you start, the greater chance you'll have of achieving your fitness and body shape goals for your wedding day look.

Remember, despite what you see advertised, there are no magic pills and shortcuts, and extreme measures are best left untouched. So lace up those sneakers, and take your first steps toward a healthier lifestyle that will last not just for your wedding day, but will keep you in top form for the rest of your life.

the day-of salon visit

After months of self-care and primping practice to find your best look for the big day, it's finally time!

We recommend you start your big day off in plush and pampered style with a visit to a salon or day spa where beauty specialists will transform you from head to toe into Beautiful Bride. Now's the time to follow your established pre-plan and perhaps look at Polaroid shots

turning healthy into fun

Michelle and Henry asked their sister Lilian, a health enthusiast, to list cutting-edge health programs brides will love. Here are Lilian's suggestions:

- *Exercise videos.* Choose from an extensive selection of aerobic, muscle toning, stretch, yoga, Pilates, and tai chi videotapes for beginner, intermediate, and advanced levels with varying lengths to suit exercise schedules. You can also purchase workout accessories by visiting Web sites such as www.collagevideo.com (or call 800-433-6769).

- *Super Slow Weight Training.* The Slow Weight Training Method is touted as the ultimate toning in only twenty minutes a week. You'll need a certified personal trainer. Visit the Super Slow Exercise Guild at www.superslow.com.

- *Pilates Mat Classes.* Pilates classes are very effective for toning. You can use videos or go to a class.

- *Home gyms.* For information on setting up a complete home gym, from purchasing minimal equipment such as hand weights, rubber balls, and elastic rubber bands, visit www.homegym.com.

- *Low-carb products.* If you are on a modified Atkins plan, you can order low-carb products from www.atkinscenter.com, 800-6-ATKINS.

- *A sensible eating style.* I recommend the following books by nutritionist Pam Smith:

- *The Diet Trap* and *The Smart Weigh: The Simple Plan for Losing Weight Forever Without Losing Your Soul.* (For more information, visit www.pamsmith.com.)

- *E-diets.* Visit Ediet.com, where you can weigh yourself in and get over-the-Web support. This program is great for a bride who needs assistance 24/7.

or digital images of your look as a reference. (*Note:* Some brides arrange to have their hair and makeup done where they are preparing for their day. Yes, it's a luxury, but we recommend you do it this way if you can. It will help you center on the rest of your day.)

Salon stylists can set and style your hair, sculpt a gorgeous upsweep, insert your accent pins, secure your headpiece and veil, apply finishing spray, and hand you off to the next specialist to put on your final touches. All the while, you're transforming with a smile,

Happily Ever After

Michelle Marks of New York City (see her feature on page 269) started off her special day with an on-site visit from her hair and makeup artists, who came to her suite at the Hyatt to create her wedding-day beauty look. Earlier that day, Michelle and her best friend started their beauty ritual with a short visit to the tanning beds.

soothed by the results you see. You'll walk in as Nervous Bride-to-Be and walk out as Radiant Bride.

Your mom and maids might also join you to get their hair, makeup, and nails done. A bridal party caravan to the beauty palace is a wonderful ritual in your transformation. You and your favorite ladies can be primped and primed, relaxed and ready for the excitement to come.

So many beauty salons and day spas offer Day-of-Wedding packages for brides and their maids, and the offerings range from the standard hair-makeup-nails treatment to The Works. With the purchase of a more grandiose pampering package, you might be on the receiving end of a champagne breakfast, a massage, a luncheon, or even first-class transportation in a limousine—all part of the wedding day spa package for brides. Investigate the offerings carefully, and consider indulging yourself by starting your day in celebrity style.

You Are Beautiful to Me

We have seen a dramatic shift in the attitude of brides during their months—even years—of preparing for their wedding day. Rather than focusing on their wedding and a bit beyond, today's brides have a healthier, broader, and more realistic outlook on the wedding day as just the beginning of a long life together.

chapter 14

The Distance Factor
and Destination Weddings

The world is wide open to today's brides and grooms. Couples born in far-flung parts of the world fall in love in their newly adopted cities. Matches are made through the Internet, old-custom matchmaking services, networking, vacationing, all of which tend to make distance a major factor in bridal planning. Add the adventurous trend for destination weddings, and we're talking far-flung excitement (and perhaps, far-flung stress.)

Today, the bride and groom may bring a small group of their closest friends and family to a remote island resort or international city for an intimate wedding experience. Exchanging vows on a Hawaiian beach, by a waterfall, in a 14th-century castle is the ultimate escape. Not only do couples and their guests enjoy a once-in-a-lifetime getaway celebration, but the destination wedding is *the* way to avoid having the same wedding your mother, sister, and all your friends had.

The destination wedding is hot, hot, hot, and we're sure this trend will continue to grow. After all, who wouldn't love the adventure of

a second wedding on the sand

We spoke with Beth Reed Ramirez, editor-in-chief of www.brideagain.com, a website for brides marrying for the second, third, tenth, or twentieth time in their lives, about the trend in destination weddings for brides who have already been down the aisle. Beth says, "Destination weddings especially lend themselves to the encore bride. Her wedding is generally smaller, more intimate than that of a first-time bride, and often reflects her own sense of style rather than her mother's. Most likely, her first wedding was in a church with all the trimmings. This time she feels comfortable setting aside tradition and doing things her way. A destination wedding can be just the ticket. She simply selects a beautiful and romantic locale, finds her perfect wedding dress, and then leaves all the planning chores and details to the on-site wedding coordinator to handle. All she and her groom have to do is show up, she looking beautiful, he looking handsome. They are worry free, stress free, and able to truly enjoy their special day."

flying halfway around the world to an exotic locale and marrying in a truly sun-kissed and naturally gorgeous environment, surrounded by tropical flowers? Stretch your dreams to the Alps of Switzerland or a tiny piazza in Venice, Italy. . . . You can wake up now!

As more and more couples buy their houses before the wedding, the financial break of planning a wedding with just twenty or so guests on a vacation getaway (where you have perhaps arranged discount travel and lodging prices for *them* to pay!) can be a welcome alternative to footing the bill for 200+ guests at an elegant and expensive reception hall. Most priceless of all . . . is that you'll have a unique wedding and your guests will have one of the most decadent trips of their lifetimes planned for them. And did we mention that your photos will be gorgeous in those tropical or stately city backgrounds?

© Frank Ammaccapane

Michelle's Story

WHEN MICHELLE MARKS married Erez Tal, they counted among their guests family and friends from around the world. Their loved ones came from Israel, England, Wales, the West Coast, and the East Coast to attend the celebration, which reflects a growing trend in global invitations and international guest lists. Michelle and Erez, after all, met through friends, so it was only fitting that their far-flung loved ones be in attendance. Plus, the couple "went global" again with their honeymoon, waiting one month after the wedding for a joint trip with another recently married couple for a two-and-a-half-week vacation in Thailand.

Every couple we speak with who plans a destination wedding positively beams in anticipation of having their fantasy wedding on a Bali beach or in their favorite European city with their closest loved ones in attendance.

To some, a destination wedding doesn't mean flying off to the islands or a Scottish castle. It might be Topeka, Chicago, Las Vegas, or even your hometown, which may be far from where your busy work and social life transplanted you. Ah, planning from a geographical distance is also a trend for 21st-century brides and grooms, so mobile and global is their lifestyle. They hop from city to city for jobs and for love, meet and date and marry people on opposite coasts, from other countries and cultures.

Distance is no barrier to love, but it is a factor when you're planning a wedding. That's why we're handling the Distance Factor now. Whether you're planning your wedding in a city or hometown a hundred miles away or on an island a thousand miles away, you're here and the wedding is *there*. Distance makes the planning a bit more complicated.

---

from sharon

Keep in mind that a destination wedding doesn't always mean flying to an island or jetting off to an international city. I spoke with wedding coordinator and distance wedding specialist Sarah Stitham of Charmed Places (www.charmedplaces.com), and she spoke of a growing trend in more nearby destinations.

According to Sarah, couples often plan their weddings in resort towns that are closer to home. They might want, say, to take their wedding out of the city or out of their hometown and into the mountains just a few hours' drive away. This is a great idea for those who want the getaway wedding, but don't wish to impose on their guests' budgets or willingness to fly or otherwise travel great distances. For instance, Sarah's New York City clientele will book up the grand and ornate resorts and cozy inns in the Catskills, the Berkshires, and the Adirondacks for a woodsy vacation with all the outdoor wedding weekend activities you could want. So here's another option: Look closer to home!

---

planning at a distance

We'll start with the most common situation first. Let's say you've moved to Seattle for your job. Your wedding will be back in your hometown of Atlanta where your family and almost all your friends still reside. You wouldn't dream of having everyone pick up and come all the way out to you, and you really do want to be married back home, perhaps in the same church where your parents married. Such situations are a common challenge for the 21st-century bride and groom. How do you plan for a wedding in a different city, in a different time zone? The answer is, the same way you do business—through communication, organization, delegation, and by "being there."

Yes, by being there. We don't advise that you plan your entire wedding over the phone, handing off all the work to a wedding coordinator or your mother. You need to factor in a few in-person visits, packing those weekends with trips to reception sites, bakers, caterers, florists, and photographers. Face-to-face meetings and doing as much as possible in person is the best method. Yes, you can easily do much of your research and planning over the Internet, via e-mail, and through fax and FedEx. (Even brides who marry in their own towns

Happily Ever After

Bride Danielle Dobin (see her feature on page 104) lived in New York City when she planned her wedding to be held at The Breakers in Florida. "It was a challenge to plan from that distance, so we flew down there a lot to work with the wedding coordinators and the very talented floral designer at the hotel," Danielle says. "That meant we needed to find the time and take on the expense to fly down there for a few weekends, and do a lot of the planning in clumps on those available weekends.

"But we did it; it was just a challenge we took on to have the wedding we wanted, where we wanted it. My parents live down in Florida, and my husband, Christopher, and I met in Miami. So it was only natural that we'd have the wedding there. Half of our guests were coming down from New York City for the wedding, so we wanted to make sure the entire trip was a great getaway for all of them."

do much of their legwork through these communication channels!) With three-quarters of your work done this way, that remaining quarter still demands your presence. So reserve those plane tickets and get there when you can, as early in the process as possible.

Here are some tips to keep you on target while you plan your dream wedding from two or three (or six!) time zones away:

- *Get wired.* Be sure you're accessible by e-mail, cell phone, pager, fax, and a reliable address, whether it's from work or home. All of your distant wedding professionals will need to get in touch with you consistently, and you won't want to miss important calls and e-mails because you're not a regular message-checker. Consider your communications channels to be your umbilical cord to your wedding plans. Be reachable.

- *Get their digits.* Similarly, you'll also need to have reliable contact information for all of your wedding experts and locations. That means getting the e-mail address, cell phone and pager numbers of your wedding coordinators, family assistants, and out-of-town bridal party members in order to send and receive those important messages and updates.

- *Be organized.* This is the Queen of all wedding-planning rules. You'll need to be extra vigilant about every note, every phone appointment, every deposit made, every phone call connected, every plan set in stone, every contract signed. Especially from a distance, good records are a must so you know what's where and what's happening when. Organization is the golden key to a successful wedding planned via remote access.

- *Follow through.* Call or e-mail and confirm receipt of all sent files, pictures, samples, and messages. Ask that your wedding experts show you the same courtesy. While this is part of the organization rule, we want to remind you that communicating over e-mail or phone adds intricacy. E-mails can disappear into the

ethers of the cyberspace, never received and sometimes misdi-
rected. Confirm, follow through, and ask *extra* questions.

- *Hand it off.* Distance planning is a time to delegate—to ask your
mother, mother-in-law, father, and any other special family
member or friend who's local to the wedding region to handle
some of the planning details. At first, you might resist giving up
some control over your plans, but you'll find that simply adjusting and sharing the joy will make the process easier for all
of you. Your mom can pick up samples from the photographer.
Your dad can comparison-shop at nurseries or wine stores.
They can save you legwork and long-distance phone calls, plus
such a group effort may unite your family as much as the wedding day itself. Just employ smart rules of delegation, reminding your assigned helpers that they're relaying the information
to *you,* and you require good and efficient communication on
their part. Delegate tasks only to the responsible and reliable.
They'll be happy to help.

- *Allow plenty of time.* Planning from a distance can mean that you
have only a few weekends for traveling and making plans in
person, or that making all those planning phone calls must be
done outside work hours.

- *Go 3-D.* Don't forget that many wedding professionals have interactive websites. You might be able to boost your initial research process by viewing 3-D pictures of ballrooms and
ceremony sites, wineries, mansions, hotel rooms, and the like.
Today's technology can help you get a better vision from clear
across the globe. One great site to go to for 3-D interactive views
of destination wedding sites is www.getawayweddings.com.

Planning from a distance is a different kind of adventure in the
wedding world. As planet bride goes global, fortunately she's usually
wired for sound and sight. So take advantage of the same technology

Karri-Leigh Paolella (see her feature on page 107) lives and works in California, with her wedding to Joseph Mastrangelo planned to take place in Boston (both she and her husband are originally from New England states). "On top of the limited number of weekends we were able to fly in to make our plans, I was also dealing with my ability to call during work hours in a different time zone," says Karri-Leigh. "So we did lots of e-mailing, and we had a lot of extra stress trying to work our schedules so we could fly in to meet with the priest the required number of times before the ceremony. It also meant more responsibility for my mother, and it was tough for us not to share a lot of the planning with my bridesmaids and his ushers. But since we had a long engagement and gave ourselves plenty of time to do all this planning at a distance, the stress was way less than it might have been."

Happily Ever After

and efficiency mindset that helps you do your job from a distance, and work it to plan your wedding as well. With help from gadgets and online sites, you're the CEO of your wedding-making decisions from afar. Distance, again, is no barrier.

the destination wedding

Imagine marrying in paradise: As the sun sets over the ocean, the surf laps against the shore in a hypnotic rhythm, colorful hibiscus flowers line the walk to your ceremony altar, a rainbow arches over volcanic outlines and the deep blue sea in the distance; the air smells of a recent rain, and clean, and warm tropical breezes carry the faint scent of hibiscus flowers. Instead of organ music, steel drums play your processional music, and your officiant wears a lei around her neck. Your guests are

Q&A *Bridal*

We've done the Internet search and sent for brochures from various resorts and reception halls, and now we have a ton of information that all looks so good! I think we've made more work for ourselves! How can we tell which places are right for us, without spending every weekend visiting all of them?

We spoke to Sarah Stitham of Charmed Places (www.charmedplaces.com) for this one, and she suggests (and we agree!) that it's a wise move to talk to a wedding coordinator in a two-hour consultation on the specifics of the getaway wedding sites you have in mind, plus her recommendations on additional sites that fit your wedding's style. (*Note:* Today's wedding coordinators also offer piecemeal services such as just helping you narrow down your potential wedding locations, without hiring them to do the whole wedding!)

A good coordinator who's local to the area you're scouting will know all the best places to consider because she's likely to have done weddings there before. She'll tell you all about the resorts and what they have to offer your guests for their wedding weekend activities, which historic manors have recently been completely restored and redecorated (and perhaps featured in travel magazines!), which perfect inns have great outdoor sites on lakes or with mountain backgrounds.

You'll never find all this firsthand information and personal referral just through a brochure, and Internet site pictures might not be current! Plus, you can find out what these destinations have to offer in different seasons. For instance, Stitham said that a lot of the resorts where she plans weddings offer colorful fall foliage scenery in the autumn months, and in winter they offer beautiful crowd-pleasing fireplaces, sleigh rides, cross-country skiing, and ice skating. Even better, since these resorts are not "wedding factories," you may get more reasonable prices and more elements and activities than you would in a standard wedding package at another resort! A wedding professional can help you with your choices of getaway locations without the risk, and even recommend the best wedding professionals in the area for the rest of your planning.

tan, barefoot, and relaxed as you approach in your gown with a flower tucked behind your ear. . . . The island getaway wedding is a dream come true for more and more 21st-century brides and grooms.

By far the most important question you'll ask is "Which destination is *us?*" Before you take step one in planning your destination wedding, sit down together and decide which type of location best suits your style as a couple and the style of wedding you'd like. Are you tropical island all the way, or do you dream of a winter wonderland for your wedding? Have you fantasized going to St. Lucia, or flying back to Switzerland, where the two of you met during a European backpacking trek? What's in your history, and what's in your future when it comes to the *where* for your plans? When traveling for your wedding, also look at peak seasons and weather patterns in distant lands, and do a bit of research to come up with your shared Top Dream Destinations list before you make your final decision.

How Difficult Will This Be?

Is it easier or harder to plan a destination wedding? That depends on the level of involvement you choose. Many well-established resorts in exotic locations offer all-inclusive use of their own wedding planning departments and coordinators. With one phone call and a detailed interview with a resort's coordinator, you can set the wheels in motion, choosing everything you'd like right down to the flavor of the cake and the vintage of wine for the reception. The on-site coordinator then takes care of just about everything else. You exchange a few e-mails or faxes, view a few JPEG files e-mailed to you, and read over a contract or two, and voila! All that's left for you is to show up for the wedding in your gown and veil.

Not so fast! For most brides, the interaction is more frequent, the plans more a team effort, and even a weekend flight to the resort is a must so you can personally check out the ceremony location, the guests' rooms, and the honeymoon suite. Some brides smartly call their on-site coordinators often, ask for updates, and request at least slight changes to the plans. It's your day, so do it your way . . . even if you're on the mainland.

Follow the advice mentioned earlier in this chapter on planning from a distance, as the same rules can apply. (And for the travel aspect—such as getting passports and making your flight plans and hotel reservations—we encourage you to get full details, travel and destination Web sites to check, smart travel tips, frequent flier points information, and packing lists in *The New Honeymoon Planner*, written by Sharon Naylor.) Here are further tips for smart planning of a destination wedding:

- *Ask others for recommendations.* Ask your friends, family members, or colleagues if they've held or attended a great destination wedding at an island or international resort, or been to island resorts that took their breath away. Add these places to your research list. Firsthand recommendations are often the best.

- *Ask the experts.* Consult travel agents to get brochures and picture packets from the best-known and highest-rated destination wedding locations.

- *Scan the sites.* Browse through travel websites such as www.travelandleisure.com to view their articles, reviews, and the results of their annual World's Best surveys to find resorts to consider. Watch the Travel Channel when you can to find out about additional destinations, and look at some of the books written specifically on destination wedding sites across the globe. Keep in mind that specific information in them might be a bit outdated, so do fresh research using their contact information.

- *Check the legalities.* Your wedding license and valid marriage count first and foremost, so do your research with the resort's planner, the board of tourism, and your own state of residence to triple-check on necessary documents, waiting periods, medical or blood tests needed, and the paperwork process that will seal your marriage deal.

- *Choose a reputable resort.* Of course, you'll want the best of the best, so stick with a well-rated resort name for your entire destination package. Ratings on travel sites, AAA, the Better Business Bureau, and hotel associations' websites can mean the world to your plans and the quality of your wedding weekend. (For a listing of the top-rated resorts around the world, broken down by categories of best island, foreign and regional locations, spa resorts, and resorts with the best cuisine, look at the World's Best survey results at *Travel and Leisure*'s website: www.travelandleisure.com.)

- *Come in early.* You and the groom, plus a few key helpers and family members, should arrive at the destination a few days early to make last-minute arrangements, check on the progress of your site's preparations, and just get ready for the week ahead. A last-minute rush will stress you out, so try to handle pre-wedding matters before other guests start arriving.

- *Package your honeymoon.* Decide whether you'll spend your honeymoon at the same resort (many couples enjoy further hospitality at their wedding site resort) or will continue on to a different

Happily Ever After

Carrie Marcus Youngberg (see her feature on page 63), a Michelle Roth bride who married David Allen Youngberg Jr. at a destination wedding in Las Vegas, told us she planned a second full "reception" four months after her actual wedding (which was to be attended by immediate family only). In June, Carrie and David had a clambake in Rhode Island at the site of the America's Cup Museum, which is on the beach. It was casual, with 125 guests (including the original seventeen who attended their Vegas wedding), including children . . . lots of family fun in an informal setting that's special to them.

honeymoon destination. Perhaps you'll fly to another island, or simply move to another resort on the same island for guaranteed alone time. The choice is yours.

- *Plan ahead for a full reception back home.* If you want to celebrate in grand style with all your 200+ friends, relatives, and clients, your destination wedding might just be phase one of your wedding experience. Decide now whether there will be a phase two, a reception-only celebration with your full guest list, later down the road.

Your On-Site Wedding Coordinator

Work with the best. Top resorts and resort spas often have established wedding coordinator offices of their own. They might have a team of thirty wedding coordinators and staff, or one planner with a big workload. Since this on-site wedding coordinator is your lifeline, the stand-in for *you* as the wedding plans begin to form, be sure you're hiring the best expert possible. Use every interviewing skill you have. Be sure this person is professional, available, efficient, complete, and patient with your questions. Many island wedding coordinators love their jobs, and it's a deep part of their character and integrity to make the bride and groom happy. You can sense how important it is to them to follow through, answer your questions, set every plan exactly as you've requested, and go the extra mile to make your wedding vision come to life.

Then there are other wedding coordinators you want to avoid, especially once you have committed your arrangements long-distance. The people who are inefficient and fail to respond to your needs or recall your initial requirements will only get worse. Create a few prebooking tests that will help point you in the right direction. If the coordinator cannot e-mail you price revisions on a menu promptly, what can you expect when the wedding date is closer and urgent matters require attention? Put in your research, trust your instincts when

Michelle Roth has this to say about the care and handling of gowns for getaway weddings: "I love the tremendous passion and excitement destination weddings evoke. If theirs is to be an island wedding, I advise my clients to consider fabrics that are flowing, soft, and practical. Chiffon, silk organza, and silk charmeuse are not only perfect for warm climates, but are great fabrics to press and steam. I also advise my brides to carry on their wedding dress when they board the plane. Never check it in with your luggage. Call your airline ahead of time to pave your way with your bride status.

"Dresses packed with a cardboard body form and loads of tissue arrive in remarkably good condition. Whatever your destination, make sure that a wedding dress professional is on standby to refresh and press. We also advise our brides on whether a steam or warm iron is required.

"Always, always keep the iron well away from your veil. It is steam heat all the way for veils!"

speaking with each coordinator you're considering, and remember that word of mouth will generally give you the most accurate information.

We've spoken with couples who came home complaining that their coordinator was out of touch, or that details requested were either different from what they'd asked for or not there at all. Yes, there are bad apples in every profession; but when planning a destination wedding, it's especially important that you choose wisely and not stick with a bad apple. If you can't depend on him or her, say *sayonara!* Choose a different expert to lead you along your wedding way.

This is not the time to be shy or to worry what they'll think about you. Assertiveness is essential; stand up for your right to have your wedding as you wish. A good on-site wedding coordinator dealing with you from a distance will understand that, and will assure you that all is in your control.

an unforgettable weekend

The wedding weekend is not just for couples taking a dozen guests to Hawaii. Now wedding couples welcome their loved ones to their hometowns with a three-day schedule packed with activities, sightseeing, and fun. Out-of-town guests haven't come all this way for just the wedding ceremony and reception. Instead, they're greeted with a full weekend's worth of shared time with family, friends, and loved ones. The bride and groom may or may not attend all the activities (after all, you have a wedding to get ready for!), but the shared weekend requires that you schedule in some downtime for fun activities with your guests!

Create a Website

Wedding websites reign supreme when it comes to wedding weekend activities. Your guests can log on to your site to see what wedding weekend itinerary you've set up for them, and can then look forward to your events, plus make plans with other guests for side trips and private dinners when no official events are planned. Be sure to provide a link to the resort destination so they can also check out the spa packages, activities for kids, plus get details such as whether there's already a hairdryer in their hotel room!

We hope the wedding destination trend continues to grow. We love seeing families come together from scattered locations, friends reunite, and all—even the bride and groom—have more time to spend together on the wedding day itself than is typical. We love seeing college friends finally meet one another's spouses, hold each other's babies, take pictures, play as in the old days, and share the beauty and history of their hometowns. Destination weddings invite guests to share more time together, which makes your wedding an unforgettable event for everyone in a much larger way. It's not just all about you. It's about *all of you*.

Whatever your style of wedding, wherever its location, we offer the following ideas for a full wedding weekend:

- *Welcome aboard!* Schedule a welcome lunch or cocktail party at the hotel where all your guests will settle into their "home base" for the weekend.

- *Let's break bread.* Host a casual dinner at a restaurant or at the home of a family member.

- *Beauty and the beach.* Consider planning a party on the beach, with champagne toasts by the sunset, dinner served in an airy tent, and a bonfire after dark.

- *Come sail away with me!* Plan a lavish dinner cruise with gourmet food, music and dancing, and great views and starry night skies.

- *Take it outside.* Have an afternoon barbecue with games for the kids.

- *We are a team!* Schedule a softball, touch football, or miniature golf or regular golf tournament. To make it even more fun, teams can consist of His Side vs. Her Side or men vs. women. Be sure to have a small trophy or prizes to give the winners.

- *Get moving.* Arrange some great bonding sports activities, such as kayaking, hiking, city sight–walking, or biking trips for those interested.

- *Out for adventure.* If your location offers them, include activities such as climbing ancient ruins, swimming with dolphins, parasailing.

- *Take a look at that view.* Take advantage of what's unique about your location. For example, you might arrange a top-of-the-town viewing at the tallest building or wooded scenic overlook with a distant view of the city.

- *Get some culture.* Arrange local activities such as attending an ethnic street fair or the resort's calypso dinner, tour heritage museums and special spots with great history and mythology.

- *That's entertainment!* Sometimes what will amuse your guests is right at your fingertips. Consider movie theater schedules or theater tickets for those who are interested. Check nearby theaters for their upcoming shows, and give guests the option of reserving their own tickets in advance via a website and phone number.

- *Feel footloose and fancy free.* Attend free outdoor concerts in the round or at a gazebo if your hometown offers such great community cultural events.

- *Wine and dine.* Invite all to join you for dinner and dancing at a restaurant or piano bar known for its romantic slow-dancing atmosphere. Or kick it up at a country-western bar and watch your wedding guests attempt line dances.

- *Bond with your buddies.* Include a night where the girls go out for drinks or dancing, and the men watch a big game at a sports bar or the groom's home.

from sharon

Check the newspapers and your regional magazines to find out about upcoming special events for your wedding weekend. A big-name star might be at your community theater; an ethnic, arts, or music festival may be scheduled; a steeplechase or fair may be planned for your weekend in a town nearby. At a distance, check www.festivals.com to see whether any special affairs (and big crowds) will be present at your site on your wedding weekend.

- *Go stargazing.* Line up some high-powered microscopes, get a great guide to the real stars' "homes" in a book or on the Internet, or go to a planetarium for a true, expert-led stargazing session.

- *Enjoy those winter daze.* In winter, plan a day of ice skating or sledding, tobogganing, sleigh rides, or a good old-fashioned snowball fight or snowman-building contest. Then warm by the fire with mugs of hot chocolate or hot toddies. It's these returns to childhood and homey activities that unite families most and relax everyone completely before the more intense days and nights ahead.

- *Beautify.* Open your spa day for those who are interested, or provide contact information for nearby beauty salons and day spas for your guests' appointment-use.

- *Just for kids.* Don't forget activities for kids, such as supervised childcare, plays, movies, games during outdoor picnics and parties, pony rides, magic shows, trips to the arcade or indoor laser tag centers, batting cages, mini golf, bowling, in-line skating, or a slumber party with great DVDs to watch and lots of pizza and junk food to eat. Add in a make-it-yourself sundae bar, and those kids will call this the best weekend of *their* lives. This may also give parents some downtime or time for romantic afternoon "dates."

- *People movers.* Have shuttle buses available to take guests to the mall, religious services, or somewhere they can spend time on their own during the wedding weekend.

Itineraries for Wedding Weekends

A Word of Caution: Don't overschedule your guests. Plan activities, dinners, and cocktail hours, but give them the freedom to attend or not attend. Your guests might want some quiet time together, a few hours to unwind in the hotel room, or time to get their nails done, get a massage, lie by the pool, or meet with other guests for a private drink (this definitely includes your single-and-available guests!).

Let your guests know what's on the schedule, plus all the pertinent details, including how to dress for each event, by creating a wedding weekend itinerary for the entire weekend. Don't underestimate the importance of letting guests know how to dress! You'd want to know that you'll need more than one dress-up outfit, right? You'd want something casual and good sneakers in your bag for that softball tournament, wouldn't you? Providing your guests with this itinerary *ahead of time* allows them to come prepared and avoid feeling underdressed, overdressed, uncomfortable, or unprepared in any way.

Happily Ever After

Some wedding weekend activities can be more about tradition, religion, and culture than about game-playing and cocktail-drinking. For instance, two of our brides shared their stories of wedding weekend rituals that meant the world to them and their families.

Attorney Danielle Dobin and her attorney husband, Christopher Smith (see page 104), arranged for a Friday night Shabbat dinner at her parents' house the night before the wedding day.

Jodi Della Femina (see page 199) honored her husband-to-be's cultural background by planning customary Korean wedding rituals the night before their planned wedding celebration (the groom's parents were elated to plan this very important cultural ceremony!). Jodi dressed in a full Korean wedding outfit and, with her in-laws' guidance, participated in fascinating and meaningful Korean traditions, such as holding out her skirt to catch thrown figs to symbolize the fruitfulness and fertility of marriage.

Including all-important family rituals during the pre-wedding hours can unite the families, honor each other's heritages and religious beliefs, and build lasting bonds between the couple and their future families.

An Unforgettable Welcome

The gracious bride welcomes her out-of-town guests not just with a stylish cocktail party or a down-home cooked dinner, but with a fully stocked "goodie bag" in each guest's hotel room. Part "comfort of home" and part "pampering indulgence," these goodie bags will delight your guests and make you the hostess with the most gracious welcoming style. Here are some ideas to include in your guest goodie bags, baskets, or silk-lined boxes:

❧ chocolates ❧ packaged snacks ❧ bottles of water, soda, and juice ❧ bottle of wine or champagne and two glasses ❧ a bag filled with name-brand toiletries in sample sizes ❧ a bag filled with

---

not just for the invitations...

For the growing trend in destination weddings, add custom-made print options to your save-the-date cards, your invitations, and your detailed wedding weekend packets. Ellen Weldon has created information packets that give destination wedding guests the complete scoop on airline and hotel reservations, even luggage tags, and an itinerary and dress code for the lunches, cocktail parties, and other events to take place on the big weekend. "Giving them information about dress codes will make your guests more comfortable and more able to enjoy themselves," says Ellen.

"beach needs," such as sunscreen, sunglasses, aloe vera gel, and a trashy paperback novel ✑ slippers ✑ sleeping masks with aromatherapy scent ✑ candles ✑ bubble bath ✑ massage oils ✑ breath mints ✑ music CDs ✑ prepaid phone cards to call home without those big phone charges from hotel rooms ✑ tickets to special events or free coupons for breakfast or brunch ✑ ticket vouchers for movie theaters ✑ magazines ✑ postcards and a pen, plus postage stamps ✑ throwaway cameras ✑ contact phone numbers for you and for other event hosts ✑ a second copy of the weekend's itinerary ✑ and of course a handwritten welcome note from the two of you ✑

Another way to make your guests feel welcome is to have something other than a goodie bag waiting in their hotel rooms or guest suites at family members' homes. Here are a few ideas:

✑ floral arrangements ✑ fruit and cheese platters ✑ midnight snacks ✑ a complimentary bottle of champagne with a bowl of fresh strawberries or chocolate-dipped strawberries ✑ luxurious satin sheets on the bed, sprinkled with rose petals ✑ arrange for bubble baths to be drawn in their rooms by a very attentive room service attendant ✑ arrange for free massages in their hotel room, prepaid by you and scheduled by the guests with the hotel's spa staff ✑ Have a different "treat" brought to your guests' hotel rooms each night: one night could be flowers, another night could be chocolates, another night could be a book on the island's native culture and recipes

You can personalize the welcome for all your arriving guests in many ways. Some couples go all out to welcome their guests, sending transportation to the airport to pick them up and deliver them in style. Upon their arrival, hotel staff will whisk the guests' luggage right up to their rooms without a moment's hassle while the guests themselves are whisked off to the welcome cocktail party. A gesture is all it takes, no matter how grand or small. You can choose to add welcome notes in their hotel rooms and perhaps a bowl of fruit or a vase of flowers that say, "We are so delighted that you have made it here for our wedding."

After the wedding, of course, these guests are sent off in style—perhaps after one final celebration over drinks or brunch before their departure (see chapter 12, "Breaking the Ice," for more on welcomes and send-offs). And of course, always give a gracious hug and thank-you from the two of you. We have no doubt you'll be embraced equally in return, after giving your loved ones such a personalized and special getaway weekend event.

Getaway weekends are planned on all kinds of budgets, from the cash-to-burn set to the low-budget crowd. It doesn't take extravagant wealth to create a homey and welcoming atmosphere for your guests, or a weekend filled with delightful activities. In fact, the best events we've heard about and attended were simple and uncomplicated, some completely spontaneous, and some with no price tag at all. What makes the wedding weekend so special is the love that money can't buy. Shared time buys you plenty of happiness and enough memories to last a lifetime.

With distance weddings now a reality for anyone, weekends planned with all attendees in mind are the ultimate in *Your Day, Your Way* weddings.

a final word
from the authors

Before we leave you all, we want to wish each of you tremendous luck.

The savvy, contemporary advice you have read on how to arrange and plan for your wedding is intended to point you, your groom, your families, and others helping you in the right direction.

Too often wedding advice is based on promises of perfection, on fantasies that can melt away in the real world of weddings. *Your Day, Your Way* has provided you with practical, realistic advice focusing on the meaningful commitment and personalized ceremony that couples strive to achieve in this day and age.

May you and those who interact with you enjoy the new freedom of self-expression in weddings rather than rely on the formulaic protocol of yesteryear. May the invaluable information you have gained provide you with courage to plan *your* day in *your* way.

May you oxygenate your dreams and bring them to the light of day, in a beautiful manner. May you take your walk to the top of the aisle in style and appropriate decorum, however formal or informal your wedding.

And when you or those around you feel frustrated or just plain exhausted, remember this: Wedding planning is an initiation of sorts—to budgeting, family politics, timetable juggling, traditions that will become part of your lives together. What is and what is not important to you will surface during the planning of your wedding. Take comfort in knowing that this opportunity is a *gift* you must embrace.

As the story of your new life together commences, we wish your first line to read: *We grew to love and understand each other more by each and every passing moment.*

Our best wishes for the day of your life and for the life of your days.

✑

For more information or to contact us directly,
visit our websites at www.michelleroth.com,
www.henryroth.com, and
www.sharonnaylor.net

✑

your essential
wedding planning timetable

One Year Before the Wedding

☐ Announce your engagement to friends and family.

☐ Attend engagement parties in your honor.

☐ Discuss as a couple what your shared wishes are for the wedding of your dreams, and record your initial designs.

☐ Discuss your wedding plans with any family members who will participate in planning (or paying for) the wedding.

☐ Begin looking through magazines, books, and Web sites for wedding-day ideas.

☐ Hire a wedding coordinator (if you so choose), *or*

☐ Determine who will be your right-hand assistant (if not wedding coordinator).

☐ Discuss any interfaith/intercultural issues you may need to broach and coordinate your joint approach.

☐ Select and book your ceremony location, *or*

☐ Book a date to visit your destination wedding location.

☐ Choose the wedding date (plus two or three backup dates for booking purposes).

☐ Inform your family and friends of the wedding date.

☐ Determine your wedding budget.

☐ Work with all involved parties to decide who will pay for which elements of the wedding.

☐ Allocate your budget by placing realistic sums and percentages next to all items requiring expenditure, ranking each item (such as gown, reception, and flowers).

☐ Begin online and phone research for dates, prices, and options.

☐ Request brochures, spotlight videotapes, and DVDs for destination wedding sites.

☐ Create organization system for all wedding plans (such as file folders or computer files).

☐ Decide on your desired level of formality.

☐ Make up your own personal guest list.

☐ Request guest lists from parents, fiancé's parents, and siblings.

☐ Create your final guest list and head count.

☐ Select and book your ceremony officiant.

☐ Discuss your ceremony plans with your officiant.

☐ Tour, select, and book your reception site.

☐ Research rental item agencies and schedule appointments, if necessary.

☐ Create rental item needs list and visit with rental agency planner to view and select from their supplies, choose linen colors, china patterns, tent, and so forth.

☐ Choose the members of your bridal party and inform them of their roles and time requirements.

☐ Choose and order your wedding gown and veil.

☐ Collect bridesmaids' size cards and ordering information through e-mail, mail, fax, or phone.

☐ Choose and purchase your bridesmaids' gowns.

☐ Choose a florist and meet with the floral consultant to design your floral theme and additional décor.

☐ Choose and book a caterer.

☐ Choose and book a cake baker.

☐ Choose and book a photographer.

☐ Place engagement photo and announcement in local newspapers.

☐ Choose and book a videographer.

☐ Choose and book your reception entertainment, DJ, or band.

☐ Choose and book a limousine or classic car company.

☐ Look at invitation samples and select your desired design.

☐ Set up your website, register your address, and start constructing your site.

☐ Notify your boss about your upcoming wedding and arrange for time off for the wedding week or weeks.

☐ Assess your current health and beauty regimen. Improve health and appearance without making extreme changes or dieting excessively.

☐ Other items you wish to include

Nine Months Before the Wedding

☐ Continue to negotiate, learn about, and balance cultural and interfaith requirements. See pre-marriage counselor where needed to smooth understanding.

☐ Start promoting your website to the bridal party, family, and friends.

☐ Notify out-of-town guests of the wedding date so that they may make travel plans, and use your Web site to post recommended travel and hotel accommodation packages.

☐ Choose and reserve a block of rooms for your guests at a nearby hotel.

☐ Find out your local marriage license requirements.

☐ Meet with officiant about designing ceremony elements and signing up for pre-wedding classes.

☐ Meet with caterer to discuss menu, presentation requirements, and other details.

☐ Plan beverage requirements and bar setup.

☐ Select packages with photographer and videographer.

☐ Select packages with entertainment.

☐ Meet with florist to design bouquets, corsages, boutonnieres, and floral décor.

☐ Choose and book your honeymoon site.

☐ Meet with travel agent to plan your wedding travel (if necessary) and your honeymoon travel, lodging, and so forth.

☐ Apply for passports and travel visas, if necessary.

☐ Book your honeymoon suite for the wedding night.

☐ Order your invitations packages.

☐ Order your wedding programs, or make plans to create your own.

☐ Order your stationery.

☐ Order wedding rings.

☐ Have wedding rings engraved (if you so choose).

☐ Assess your current health and beauty program and determine an appropriate regimen for your wedding look. Keep fine-tuning your program in a healthy, balanced way to achieve long-lasting results.

Six Months Before the Wedding

☐ Help bride's and groom's parents select their wedding day attire and accessories.

☐ Help select children's wedding day attire.

☐ Order preprinted napkins, matchbooks, other items as desired.

☐ Create maps or directions sheets to ceremony and reception locations for enclosure in the invitations and placement on your Web site.

☐ Begin to plan the rehearsal dinner.

☐ Begin writing vows.

☐ Select ceremony music.

☐ Select ceremony readings.

☐ Audition ceremony music performers.

☐ Book musical performers for ceremony.

☐ Register for wedding gifts.

☐ Send for name-change information, if necessary.

☐ Reserve approximate number of hotel rooms needed for guests, and have your guests book direct at your preferred guest accommodations.

☐ Book wedding-night accommodations for bride and groom and for family members.

☐ Arrange for transportation for guests.

☐ Plan "wedding weekend" activities, such as brunches, sporting events, barbecues, children's events, if necessary. Refresh all Web site information.

☐ Continue your pre-wedding beauty treatments, such as skin care, relaxation, massage, and tanning.

☐ If holding an at-home wedding, hire a landscaper to trim shrubs, add extra plants or flower beds, mulch, and care for your lawn.

Three Months Before the Wedding

☐ Apply for your marriage license, according to your state's current requirements.

☐ Go for blood tests, according to your state's time requirements.

☐ Attend premarital classes, as required by your faith.

☐ Choose and rent men's wedding wardrobe.

☐ Begin gown fittings.

☐ Choose your shoes and accessories for the wedding day.

☐ Begin bridesmaids' fittings.

☐ Consult with your wedding coordinator for updates and confirmations, additional tasks, and outstanding deposits.

☐ Consult with caterer or banquet hall manager for updates.

☐ Complete writing your vows.

☐ Ask relatives and friends to perform readings at the ceremony.

☐ Finalize your selections of ceremony readings and music.

☐ Submit song "wish list" to DJ or band you've hired.

☐ Submit picture "wish list" to photographer.

☐ Submit video "wish list" to videographer.

☐ Arrange for a babysitter to watch guests' kids on the wedding day (*Note:* Have several babysitters if there will be a lot of children) or look into the guests' hotel's babysitting or daycare services.

☐ Finalize and book plans for rehearsal dinner.

Two Months Before the Wedding

☐ Go for fittings of wedding gown.

☐ Start bridesmaids' fittings.

☐ Have attendants' shoes dyed in one dye lot (if shoes are to be dyed).

☐ Choose and purchase your "going away" outfit and honey-moon clothes if you are going the traditional route.

☐ Address invitations to guests.

☐ Assemble invitation packages.

☐ Buy "Love" stamps at the post office.

☐ Mail invitations to guests six to eight weeks prior to the wedding (or nine to twelve weeks prior in the case of a destination wedding).

☐ Order or make wedding programs.

☐ Order, make, and label wedding favors.

☐ Meet with ceremony musician about song list.

☐ Formally ask friends to participate in wedding, such as attending the guest book, transporting wedding gifts from reception to home, and doing other tasks.

☐ Fill out and send all name-change documents, such as your passport, credit cards, and driver's license, if you are changing your last name.

☐ Pose for formal pre-wedding portrait.

☐ Enlarge and frame portrait of the two of you for ceremony entrance.

One Month Before the Wedding

☐ Use de-stressing techniques that you have put into your program.

☐ Arrange your marriage license.

☐ Meet with officiant to get the final information on ceremony elements, rules of the location, and other details.

☐ Invite officiant to rehearsal dinner.

☐ Plan the rehearsal.

☐ Invite bridal party and involved guests to the rehearsal and rehearsal dinner.

☐ Confirm honeymoon plans if you are going away.

☐ Confirm wedding-night hotel reservations.

☐ Finalize plans for wedding day transport of your guests (such as making arrangements for use of the hotel's shuttle bus or scheduling volunteer drivers).

☐ Post up on your Web site transportation options you'll provide for your guests.

☐ Make beauty appointment for wedding day.

☐ Visit your hairstylist to "practice" with hairstyles for the big day.

☐ Get pre-wedding haircut or trim.

☐ Do your final fitting for gown.

☐ Pick up wedding bands.

☐ Attend showers.

☐ Write thank-yous for shower gifts (by hand, no shortcuts!).

☐ Call wedding guests who have not RSVP'd to get the final head count.

☐ Devise your seating chart for reception.

☐ Write up seating place cards and table numbers.

☐ Either pick up honeymoon travel tickets and information books or reconfirm your E-tickets.

☐ Make up welcome gift baskets for guests.

☐ Purchase gifts for each other, parents, bridal party, and honored guests.

☐ Wrap and label gifts.

☐ Arrange for wedding-day transportation for the bridal party if they will not be in limos.

☐ Purchase unity candle.

☐ Purchase garters (get two—one for keeping, one for tossing).

☐ Purchase toasting flutes.

☐ Purchase cake knife.

☐ Purchase guest book.

☐ Purchase post-wedding toss-its (birdseed, flower petals, bubbles, bells, other) and decorate or personalize small containers, if you so choose.

☐ Purchase throwaway wedding cameras.

One Week Before the Wedding

☐ Try to keep this your work-free week.

☐ Confirm all wedding plans with all wedding vendors, *having them tell you what date, time, and place they have on record.* Keep a detailed list of all vendors on a contact sheet with phone numbers, e-mail addresses, and cell phone numbers for easy retrieval.

___ Caterer (give final head count now!)

___ Florist (give delivery instructions now!)

___ Cake baker

___ Photographer

___ Videographer

___ Ceremony musicians

___ Reception entertainers

___ Officiant

___ Ceremony site manager

___ Reception site manager

___ Wedding coordinator

___ Limousine company (give directions now!)

___ Rental company agent

☐ Pay final deposits for all services.

☐ Place tips and fees in marked envelopes for such participants as the officiant, ceremony musicians, coordinator, valets, and others.

☐ If supplying your own beverages, conduct a shopping trip (with plenty of assistants) to the local discount liquor and beverage supply house for a major spree.

☐ Drop off guest welcome baskets at hotel.

☐ Pick up wedding gown.

☐ Have groom, best man, and ushers pick up tuxes, socks, shoes, and accessories.

☐ Pack for honeymoon.

☐ Break in your wedding day shoes.

☐ Remind groom to get new shoes for the wedding day.

☐ Remind groom to get a haircut for the wedding day.

☐ Arrange for house- and pet-sitters.

☐ Notify the local police department of your upcoming absence, so that they can patrol your neighborhood.

☐ Get travelers' checks (if you so choose).

☐ Plan wedding day brunch and invite bridal party and special guests.

☐ Write out your special toasts and tributes.

☐ Submit address change notification to the post office (if you will be moving after the honeymoon).

☐ Ready your wedding announcements to be mailed the day after the wedding, and assign a responsible person to mail them.

☐ Attend bachelor/bachelorette party (consider telling attendants and friends that this week would be good for you, as you do not want to be out the night before your wedding).

The Day Before the Wedding

☐ Meet with your hands-on coordinators or your bridal planner for last-minute checking.

☐ Supervise or have bridal planner arrange delivery of rental items to wedding location.

☐ Supervise or have bridal planner supervise setup of all items at wedding location.

☐ Finish packing suitcases and carry-ons for wedding night and honeymoon.

- ☐ Stock your bag with your car keys, house keys, passports, ID's, marriage license, wedding night and honeymoon hotel confirmations, medications, ATM card, and other necessities.

- ☐ Arrange for someone to leave your car, with your suitcases in the trunk, securely in your wedding night hotel's parking lot for use the next day.

- ☐ If you are not going on your honeymoon immediately after the wedding, but have arranged a decompressing weekend, reconfirm all your arrangements.

- ☐ Lay out all wedding day wardrobe and accessories.

- ☐ Very important: Discuss with your bridal party/attendants a rolling timetable for next-day preparations, including showering, styling hair, and applying makeup.

- ☐ Hand out printed driving directions to all family members and bridal party members (if necessary), plus a wedding-day schedule in half-hour increments (optional).

- ☐ Confirm times and places for all attendants to show up on the wedding day.

- ☐ Arrange for reliable relative to transport wedding gifts to their home for safekeeping.

- ☐ Arrange for honor attendant or reliable relative to be in charge of handing out payment envelopes.

- ☐ Hit ATM to get cash on hand for emergencies, tips, valet, and other incidental expenditures.

- ☐ Assemble emergency bag with extra stockings, lipstick, pressed powder, emery boards, and other items.

- ☐ Put a cell phone in the emergency bag.

☐ Gas up the cars.

☐ Go to the beauty salon to get waxed and tweezed.

☐ Stock up on supplies for wedding-morning breakfast.

☐ Place final call to caterer or coordinator to answer last-minute questions.

☐ Attend rehearsal and rehearsal dinner.

☐ Get a good night's sleep!

On the Wedding Day

☐ Have your wedding coordinator or bridal planner arrange all the last-minute details under your supervision.

☐ Set out favors and place cards at reception site, if manager will not be doing it.

☐ Set out post-wedding toss-its where appropriate at ceremony site.

☐ Set out guest book and pen.

☐ Attend bridal brunch.

☐ Have hair and nails done at beauty salon, and get a massage while there as well.

☐ Have photos taken at home.

☐ Double-check to be sure someone responsible has arranged for your suitcases to go to your hotel room or in the car that will be taking you to the airport.

☐ Double-check that the appropriate people have the wedding rings for transport to the ceremony.

☐ Make sure the bag with your car keys, house keys, ID's, passports, and other necessary items travels with you to the wedding and thus to the wedding night accommodations.

☐ Relax and know that everything will be fine!

☐ Get married!

The Day After the Wedding

(Assign these tasks to a responsible family member or friend if bride and groom already left for their honeymoon.)

☐ Have someone supervise the rental company's cleanup of the site, if necessary.

☐ Get a signed receipt for the return of all rented items.

☐ Have tuxes returned to rental store.

☐ Hold day-after breakfast or brunch for guests and bridal party.

☐ Graciously accept all compliments on the wedding.

☐ Transport guests to airports, train stations, and other facilities for travel home.

wisdom of the elders: wedding advice from michelle and henry's parents

Michelle Roth and Henry Roth spoke to their parents about the recipe of love, life, and top bridal planning tips. Aneta and Joseph Weinreich, who have been married for 49 years, are also bridal designers with 42 years of experience. Their design studio, Henri Josef, is one of the largest bridal houses in Australia. They share this wisdom with you:

Q: What advice can you give a young couple to make sure there is harmony throughout the bridal planning process?

A: Be tolerant of the other party's point of view. Always communicate. Never leave anything between you left unsaid.

Q: A bride today is under a lot of pressure. How can she keep things in perspective so she can enjoy her planning at every stage?

A: Remember that there will be "hiccups" all along the way until you reach the top of your aisle. The bottom line is this: In the context of everything around you, the reason you are getting married and your future together is what's important. Anything that is not 100 percent as you planned it is a small matter in the big picture. You will eventually look back at details that were less than perfect and realize their insignificance; only your happiness is forever.

Q: **Mother, when you were selecting your mother-of-the-bride outfit, what did you take into account?**

A: I wanted my outfit to reflect the importance of the day. It had to be stylish and reflect up-to-the-minute elegance. I wore a charcoal brown suit and hat to Michelle's lunchtime wedding on a snowy January day in New York City. I wanted to complement the deep mahogany interior of the Penn Club, while making sure Michelle would be the one to shine on her day. To be honest, even though I am a designer myself, the most important consideration for me was my daughter's delight and future life with her fiancé, Peter Roth.

Q: **What advice do you have for a bride and groom to make sure that tiny children who attend the wedding have fun—but not at the expense of the grownups?**

A: Keep in mind that children are children, and no matter how much you admonish them or ask them to behave, the general excitement of the occasion may encourage them to get out of control. (We had a lot of experience with Henry on that issue!) Just enjoy their presence and remember that you were also once a child.

Q: **What major changes have you seen between weddings at the time of your marriage and those for which you design and create dresses today?**

A: As bridal designers, we have been carried by the influences of the day. Throughout over 40 years of bridal design experience, we have remained on the cutting edge. That takes an open mind and a love for what is different, new, and forward-looking. Bridal dresses in the past were much more conservative, and the bride's mother had the main say in the decision. Today, wedding dresses have more style, imagination, oomph, and daring—in part because the bride has the main say. Whether the bride is conservative or outrageous, her dress can be a translation of her personality and part of her dream. We love the fact that brides can be far more personal about who they are. The days of the cookie-cutter bride are over, which means that the challenge for us as designers is very much heightened.

Q: You have been married for more than 48 years. What advice can you give brides and grooms as they embark on this new chapter in their lives?

A: Being experts at marriage, we could write volumes! But in a nutshell, for a marriage to succeed you must start on these solid foundations:

- *The power of love.* Love, affection, and, above all, respect for one another are essential.

- *Unity at all costs.* If either of you has an argument with a member of the family or a friend, always take the side of your spouse, even if you think your spouse is wrong. (There is plenty of time to discuss the situation in private.)

- *Wifely support.* Wives, put your spouse on a high pedestal and lift up his spirits. (If you tell your husband that he is a schlemiel, he will finish up a schlemiel!)

- *Your wife the queen.* Husbands, treat your wife with utmost respect. Treat her like a queen. Make sure that everyone around her, especially children and other family members, do the same. Never drop your standards.

- *Time out for you.* Take time off to be together at the exclusion of everybody else, even for a weekend.

- *The nighttime principle.* If you have a little misunderstanding, do not leave it for the next day, but solve it before you retire.

- *You are boss.* You must present a united front vis-à-vis your children. Do not let your child pull you apart. Yes, give them your love and freedom, but it is incumbent on you to guide them in the right direction.

- *Thorns and all.* Marriage is not always a bed of roses. Everybody experiences some difficulties along the away. Therefore, never lose your courage and faith. When you are *determined* to have a happy, harmonious marriage, nothing in the world can stop you; you can overcome any obstacle. We assure you this is the recipe for a healthy and happy marriage.

michelle roth's personal wedding day organizer

The following is the wedding day organizer and day plan for the wedding of Michelle Roth and her husband, Peter Roth. This will give you a complete and detailed example of a wedding day organizer.

Weinreich/Roth Wedding

January 18, 1998

The Penn Club

30 West 44th Street (between 5th and 6th)

Telephone: 212-403-6619

Fax: 212-403-6616

Contact at Penn Club:

   Direct: 212-403-6619

   Sunday: 212-764-3550 (front desk)

Parking available at the Hippodrome on 44th Street, near 6th Avenue.

Can also enter on 43rd Street.

Peter's cell phone: 555-555-1111

Friday, January 16th

- Catering staff begins to kosherize the kitchen.

    Please: If there are any questions during the wedding, please direct them only to the bride's brother and sister, Henry and Lilian. Neither the bride's parents nor the groom's parents are to be disturbed. Thanks.

    Also, please keep your schedule with you at all times. As the wedding is based on three to four floors between the ceremony, reception, and welcoming cocktails, we need to be organized amongst ourselves. Many thanks.

Sunday, January 18th, 7:30 A.M.

- The bride, Michelle Weinreich, arrives at The Penn Club.
- Jewelry is with her.
- Gown to be with the bride. Room has been arranged for the bride; check reception on day of wedding.
- Mother of the bride, Aneta Weinreich's, hair is done by Noreen. Telephone: 555-2222 (home), 555-3333 (work).
- The bride's hair is prepped and styling is started.
- Florist arrives to set up Chuppah on the second floor.
- Contact at florists:

    Tel: 555-4444

    Fax: 555-5555

    Sunday home: 555-6666

    Cell: 555-7777

Sunday, January 18th, 8:00 A.M.

- The bride's hair is completed.
- Mother of the bride's makeup is done by makeup artist (work number: 555-8888).
- Sister of the bride Lilian's hair is done.

Sunday, January 18th, 8:45 to 9:15 A.M.
- Sister of the bride Lilian's makeup is done.
- The bride's hair is done.

Sunday, January 18th, 9:15 A.M.
- Families of the groom, Roth and Mittman, arrive. Please go to Chestnut Room, 4th Floor, Room 402. Coffee will be provided there.

Sunday, January 18th, 9:30 A.M.
- Roth and Mittman families meet for rehearsal. Go directly to Chestnut Room, 4th Floor, Room 402. Please note this rehearsal is vital and, as you will be all dispersed throughout the club, you must be on the fourth floor at 9:30 A.M. sharp.

  Wesley and Jordan (Peter Roth's nephew and niece): Please go to Room 402.

  Stuart and Elizabeth (Peter Roth's brother and sister-in-law): Please go to Room 402.

  Ellyn and Larry (Peter Roth's sister and brother-in-law): Please go to Room 402.

  Lilian and Henry (Michelle Weinreich's sister and brother): Please go to Room 402.

  Groom, mother, and father of the groom: Please go to Room 402.

  Mother and father of the bride: Please go to Room 402.
- Chuppah (florist) will be completed at 9:45 A.M.

Sunday, January 18th, 10:00 to 11:00 A.M.
- Both the Bride and Groom's families are photographed. Location in front of Chuppah on the second floor.
- Florist work to be completed by 10:45 A.M.

Information on photographer:

Owner and assistant

Home Phone: 555-8888

Work Phone: 555-9999

Sunday, January 18th, 11:00 to 11:30 A.M.

- Rabbi Roth arrives at 11:00 A.M.
- Cloakroom attendant on duty (no tips allowed).
- Guests begin to arrive.
- Yarmulkes on silver tray attended in lobby by a person from Penn Club staff who will hand them out.
- Place cards for seating in lobby on round table for guests to pick up.
- Gift receiving area in lobby on the 1st floor; Penn club staff to collect.
- Cake by Sylvia Weinstock arrives.

Rabbi Roth's home phone number: 555-0000

Sunday, January 18th, 11:30 A.M.

- Signing of the Ketuba (Jewish matrimonial document) in the Chestnut on the 4th floor. Simon Lauffer and Rabbi Roth to witness.
- Ketuba will be brought to the wedding by the Bride.
- The Groom will have the marriage license (NYS) and two Jewish documents for Rabbi.
- Guests begin to arrive. Break the ice immediately upon guest arrival.
- Music playing on the first floor (Jewish with clarinet/violin). Check with Ray Cohen on songs.
- Ray Cohen playing on second floor to greet guests (Hebrew music to be determined).
- The Groom to have given wedding bands to Wesley and Stuart.

Sunday, January 18th, 11:55 A.M.

- Private Bedeken (veiling ceremony): All family members invited to the Chestnut Room, 4th floor.

Sunday, January 18th at Noon

- Wedding party gathers on the 4th floor in the Chestnut Room and will be led to the second floor by Mauricio. The Bride and her parents brought separately.
- Processional order:
    Cantor
    Wesley and Jordan
    Stuart and Elizabeth
    Ellyn and Larry
    Sister and brother of the bride; Lilian and Henry
    The groom and his parents
    The bride and her parents
- Violinist joins Ray Cohen upstairs to play Baroque music for Processional and Recessional.

Wedding Begins

Note:
- Wine, table, cup under Chuppah must be set up beforehand (confirmed with Wesson).
- Seat for Frank (father of groom) needs to be kept free on the side (confirmed with Wesson).

Sunday, January 18th, 12:30 to 1:00 P.M.

Recessional.
- The bride and groom go off for seven minutes into Room 402, the Chestnut Room.
- Cocktail hour begins.
- Ray Cohen Jazz Trio plays.
- Band begins setting up upstairs.
- Florist dismantles Chuppah and places columns on floors in designated area.

Sunday, January 18th, 1:30 P.M.
- Guests go upstairs for lunch (will take at least 15 minutes).
- Seating place cards will be downstairs (sister of the bride Lilian has the master list).

Sunday, January 18th, 1:45 to 5:00 P.M.
The Reception.
- Guests seated.
- First dance, might lead to Hora.
- Brother of the bride Henry welcomes the guests.
- Jordan does blessing over the bread (table to be set up in center).
- Appetizer.
- Dancing.
- Salad.
- Brother of the bride Henry introduces father of the bride, Joe/Joe's speech.
- Dancing.
- Main meal.
- Brother of the bride Henry talks about Michelle.
- The groom talks.
- Dancing/Plates cleared by waiters.
- Brother of the bride Henry introduces Joseph/Joseph's speech.
- Cake-cutting ceremony.
- Cake/dessert/coffee.
- Dancing.

Note:
- Confirm music with Ray Cohen (tango, Cole Porter/Gershwin, Hora).
- Microphones and a small podium for speeches will be stationed where band plays.

Sunday, January 18th, 4:15 to 5:00 P.M.

- Music stops at 5:00 P.M.
- Farewells.

Note:

- Gifts to be set aside on the first floor and looked after by The Penn Club.
- Gifts to be taken home by the bride and groom Sunday night (to be confirmed).
- Mother of the bride checks the bride's room at The Penn Club to make sure nothing is left behind.

STYLIST NOTE: THE WEINREICH /ROTH IS A DAYTIME WINTER WEDDING. ALL FAMILIES OF BOTH SIDES SHOULD ENSURE THAT ALL GUESTS ARE WELCOMED AND INTRODUCED TO OTHER GUESTS AS A MATTER OF COURSE. THIS IS WHEN OUR FAMILIES OFFICIALLY BLEND AS ONE! GOOD LUCK, MICHELLE AND PETER.

then and now: a look at modern-day weddings

In Charge of Wedding Planning
Then: Mother knows best.
Now: Mother takes a rest. Brides plan their weddings on their own, with the help of their mothers, grooms, or wedding planners.

The Dress
Then: White billowing dresses, mainly ball-gown style.
Now: Fashion takes over. Red Carpet bride with the aisle as her runway, confident and sexy, she plans it *her* way.

Bridesmaids
Then: Pink polyester and monstrous bow.
Now: Maids are elegant, discerning, and chic. Emphasis on wear-again dressing.

The Rock
Then: Groom proposes and presents the ring.
Now: Groom proposes and often involves the bride in engagement ring shopping.

Ceremony Location

Then: Church ceremony and a beautiful hall.

Now: Location explosion! Celebrants are often willing to marry a couple at exotic locations. Beach and destination weddings are two of many options.

Mother Attire

Then: Conservative and quiet; tonings were generally in brown, navy, or pastels.

Now: Super chic glamorous dressing. Mothers dress fashionably and in keeping with style of the wedding.

Father of the Bride

Then: Dad foots the bill.

Now: Sharing of expenses with groom's side or couple is now the norm.

Formality and Guests

Then: Large parties of 300 or more were the regular expectation.

Now: Intimate to large, from formal to casual and smart.

Bouquets and Flowers

Then: Demure white was used throughout, including bouquets and bows.

Now: Freedom to explode with color and creative add-ons. Fuchsia and other strong colors are no longer avoided. Grapes and berries add stylistic touches to lush arrangements.

Honeymoon

Then: Secret honeymoon destinations, with immediate departure for the trip.

Now: Couples often take a small break and save the honeymoon vacation for later.